Utopia Drive

A ROAD TRIP THROUGH
—— AMERICA'S ——
MOST RADICAL IDEA

Erik Reece

FARRAR, STRAUS AND GIROUX
NEW YORK

CYBELE KNOWLES

Erik Reece
Utopia Drive

Erik Reece is the author of several previous books, including *Lost Mountain* and *An American Gospel*. He is the winner of Columbia University's John B. Oakes Award for Distinguished Environmental Journalism. He teaches writing at the University of Kentucky.

ALSO BY ERIK REECE

Lost Mountain: A Year in the Vanishing Wilderness: Radical Strip Mining and the Devastation of Appalachia

An American Gospel: On Family, History, and the Kingdom of God

The Embattled Wilderness: The Natural and Human History of Robinson Forest and the Fight for Its Future (with James J. Krupa)

A Balance of Quinces: The Paintings and Drawings of Guy Davenport

A Short History of the Present

Animals at Full Moon

Utopia Drive

Farrar, Straus and Giroux
18 West 18th Street, New York 10011

Printed in the United States of America
Published in 2016 by Farrar, Straus and Giroux
First paperback edition, 2017

The Library of Congress has cataloged the hardcover edition as follows:
Names: Reece, Erik, author.
Title: Utopia drive : a road trip through America's most radical idea / Erik Reece.
Description: First Edition. | New York, NY : Farrar, Straus and Giroux, 2016.
Identifiers: LCCN 2015041553 | ISBN 9780374106577 (hardback) |
ISBN 9780374710750 (e-book)
Subjects: LCSH: Utopian socialism—United States—History. | Utopias—United
States—History. | Communitarianism—United States—History. | BISAC:
HISTORY / United States / General. | HISTORY / United States / 19th Century.
Classification: LCC HX653 .R44 2016 | DDC 335/.020973—dc23
LC record available at http://lccn.loc.gov/2015041553

Paperback ISBN: 978-0-374-53701-2

Designed by Abby Kagan

Our books may be purchased in bulk for promotional, educational, or business
use. Please contact your local bookseller or the Macmillan Corporate and
Premium Sales Department at 1-800-221-7945, extension 5442, or by e-mail
at MacmillanSpecialMarkets@macmillan.com.

www.fsgbooks.com
www.twitter.com/fsgbooks • www.facebook.com/fsgbooks

P1

Frontispiece: Melting snow, Utopia, Ohio; photograph by Arthur Rothstein;
courtesy of the Library of Congress

FOR MELISSA

A map of the world that does not include Utopia
is not worth even glancing at.
—OSCAR WILDE

. . . se hace camino al andar.
—ANTONIO MACHADO

Contents

Utopia Drive

Nonesuch

The corner of Fifth and Elm Streets in Cincinnati, Ohio, has held a certain significance for me since the day I stood there with my parents, as an eight-year-old in 1976, and watched the Cincinnati Reds return to the city after their seven-game victory over the Boston Red Sox in what was, as my father told me then and as I still believe, the greatest World Series ever. I made note of the cross streets where we stood because I felt sure that catching a glimpse of Pete Rose, Joe Morgan, and Johnny Bench would be the most important thing that had happened up to that point in my life, and might well be for some time to come.

Ten years later I was scanning the "radical thought" section of a used bookstore in the town where I had just arrived for college. My eyes fixed on the faded purple spine of a book by George B. Lockwood called *The New Harmony Movement*. It is a history of this country's first secular utopian experiment, undertaken in 1825 by the Scottish industrialist Robert Owen in a small Indiana town called New Harmony. The copy I pulled from the shelf was a first edition published in 1905; its cloth cover had been worn smooth, and the gilt lettering on the spine had almost disappeared.

Still, there seemed to me something talismanic about the book; it held, after all, a secret—the secret of society. I slowly flipped through its pages until I hit upon this passage: "On the 18th of May, 1827, there was unpretentiously opened at the corner of Fifth and Elm streets in Cincinnati a small country store, conducted on a plan new to commerce. It was the first Equity store, designed to illustrate and enact the cost principle, the germ of the cooperative movement of the future." And 149 years later, I would stand at that same corner, the crossroads of utopia, as it turned out, to watch a ticker tape parade for the world champion Reds.

I can point to that afternoon in 1986 when I bought *The New Harmony Movement* for a few dollars as the first day of my fascination with a strange coterie of nineteenth-century world menders— men and women such as Robert Owen, "Mother" Ann Lee, John Humphrey Noyes, Josiah Warren, and others—who plotted paradise across the eastern United States. From 1820 to 1850, close to two hundred utopian communities sprang to life. In 1840, Ralph Waldo Emerson wrote to his British friend Thomas Carlyle, "We are all a little wild with numberless projects of social reform. Not a reading man but has a draft of a new community in his waistcoat pocket." Commercial employment had grown "selfish to the borders of theft," said Emerson, so there was nothing for the virtuous American to do but "begin the world anew." It was, after all, a very young country. Such things seemed possible. What's more, the religious revivals that stirred unexpected foment at the beginning of the nineteenth century convinced many men and women that Christ's Second Coming was imminent and they had better start preparing an earthly kingdom. Many secular utopias were a response to the economic Panic of 1837, when, much as in 2008, reckless speculation sank banks and plunged the country into a prolonged depression. As a result, a number of Americans fled urban life and went looking for more just and compassionate ways to organize human affairs. Others simply saw communal living and sharing as a means to better realize the country's founding principles; in the United States of the early 1800s, the newly coined word *socialism* carried none of the heretical freight it does today. What these communities all took up, in one form or another, was an experiment in radical idealism.

Two decades later, the Civil War brought most of those experiments to an end. But contrary to the common perception, the majority did not fail because their founding principles proved naïve, or overly optimistic, or contradictory to the inalterable selfishness of human nature. In fact, many were great successes, and their stories have been obscured only by the larger American story of a union preserved, slavery abolished, and the rise of an industrial economy. That economy also helped to crush the utopian movement in this country, and it ultimately created an American consumer culture so unsustainable and so devoid of idealism that we now stand on the verge of both environmental calamity and an intractable federal plutocracy—a government given over to the rich by a bewildered, defeatist populace. Americans live in a world we are too ready to accept. We acquiesce too easily to the *inevitability* of the way things are. Indeed, many of us think of our consumer culture as its own version of utopia, where we are absolved of the responsibility to question where our food, our clothes, our cellular devices, our energy come from. Of course an astonishing amount of cruelty and violence makes this utopia possible—a violence done to the land, a violence done to human and nonhuman life.

To resist, or at least escape for a while that air of inevitability, I began to conceive in my mind a road trip through this country's alternate economic and social history—its utopian past. For twenty-five years, I had been casually reading and collecting materials about those nineteenth-century visionaries. Last October, I finally felt ready to go. With a map of the eastern United States spread out across my kitchen table, I plotted my prospective route with a green marker. It would start right down the road from me, at the site of a Shaker community called Pleasant Hill, and it would end in Oneida, New York, where the perfectionists, led by John Humphrey Noyes, invented a free-love philosophy called Bible communism, which was at once the opposite and the apotheosis of the chaste Shakers. My plan was to pick through the ruins and the reconstructions of those utopian dreams in the hope of piecing that story back together. I wanted to examine those remains to find what images and ideas might be exhumed and perhaps breathed back to life. The economist Milton Friedman, who was wrong about a great many things, was right, I think, when he said, "Only a crisis—actual or perceived—produces real change. When that crisis occurs, the actions that are taken depend on the ideas that are lying around. That, I believe, is our basic function: to develop alternatives to existing policies, to keep them alive and available until the politically impossible becomes politically inevitable." Because I believe our country is in the midst of great political, economic, social, and environmental crises, I decided to set out in search of those alternatives that now seem impossible but might soon prove inevitable.

I will not, of course, visit every utopian community that ever took shape in this country, and the account that follows is in no way meant to present a comprehensive history of the American utopian movement. I'm not a social scientist; I'm a guy with a truck, a gas card, and a few boxes of old books shifting around in the cab. In fact, I made a deliberate decision to limit my peregrinations to the eastern states. That leaves out communities and movements such as the Mormons of Utah, the Icarians of Iowa, Colorado's Drop City, and Paolo Soleri's "ecotopia," Arcosanti, in the Arizona desert. Among others. This, unfortunately, could not be helped. I am afflicted by a bizarre mental illness whereby the analytical portion of my brain stops functioning whenever I cross the Mississippi River. While it's all fascinating out there, out west, I've spent my whole life in the eastern United States, and as a result, I don't trust my instincts to read the western geographical and cultural landscapes with any real sense of understanding or acuity. But more than that, of the two hundred or so utopian communities that formed between 1820 and 1850, almost all of them took root in the eastern half of this young country. It was here in the East that preachers, publishers, and backwoods prophets began the hard mental and physical work of conceiving paradise on earth. Many of those visionaries eventually wandered or were

forced westward, but the elemental intellectual history of the utopian movement still lies, or is buried, on Long Island, in upstate
New York, or on the banks of the Wabash River in Indiana. Beginning near the latter and roving east toward the former, I suspect
there will be plenty to see.

Road trips are usually fueled by restlessness and discontent, a
deeply personal reason to get away from one place and go look
for another. In his classic travelogue *Blue Highways*, William
Least Heat-Moon lamented, "Daniel Boone moved on at the
sight of smoke from a new neighbor's chimney; I was moving
from the sight of my own." That's not quite the case with me. It
isn't some sense of personal disaffection that sends me off on my
solitary way. Last year I married my ex–best friend's ex-wife and
we bought a house far from town, on a forested hillside that overlooks a beautiful body of moving water called Clear Creek. If that
sounds like a country song with a happy ending, maybe it is.
The point being: I like my woodstove and my chimney just fine.
In fact, the closest town to our house is a little hamlet about five
miles up the road called Nonesuch. And if you think about one of
the Greek roots of the word *utopia*, *outopia*, "no place," then Nonesuch itself suggests something of that original meaning. According to the *Kentucky Atlas & Gazetteer*, "The origin of the name is
obscure," but it would be easy to see how an extremely fertile farmland overlooking the Kentucky River might have looked rather
inspiring, perhaps even utopian, to an early settler such as Boone.
And here it's worth remembering that the *other* Greek root of the
word, the one most people forget or ignore, is *eutopia*—not "no
place," but rather "good place." Often one hears political com-
mentators reject some idea or proposal because it seems too "utopian." What they are saying, of course, is that they find the idea
too implausible, too unrealistic, too naïve. Yet given the grim state
of our nation, why *not* engage in a little utopian thinking? Given
that our current political and economic systems bear only the
slightest resemblance to anything called democracy, why not

7

consider the alternative—especially the radical alternative? Even as a parlor game, a thought experiment, why not consider where that future might take us? As Anatole France once said, "Without the Utopians of other times, men would still live in caves, miserable and naked." Then he added, "Out of generous dreams come beneficial realities." The argument for utopian thinking is not that it represents some fantasy of escape, some "No Place," but rather that it holds out the specter of a more beneficent reality, something substantially better than what we have: a Good Place. As I set off from Nonesuch, that is what compels me to go.

Yet besides the vague phrase "good place," what exactly do I mean by the term *utopia*? Perhaps I should establish at least a working definition before going anywhere. It is of course subject to change, but at least it will get this show on the road. To wit: *a utopia represents a community's deliberate separation from the larger society so as to enact a new form of organization that offers both a critique and a corrective to the values of the dominant society.* Let that stand for now as a way of designating a collective of social radicals, which all utopianists are, from, say, eight liberal vegans living in a group house.

There are, at least to my thinking, four different versions of utopia, and as I venture forth, these will act as the four points of my mental compass. Along the north–south continuum lie what the great social critic Lewis Mumford has termed "utopias of escape" and "utopias of reconstruction." The former are largely works of fiction—Plato's *Republic*, Thomas More's *Utopia*, Samuel Butler's *Erewhon* (*nowhere* spelled, almost, backward)—while the latter tries to set up what Mumford called "a condition for our release into the future." The utopia of escape takes place on floating islands and in imaginary pasts, while the utopia of reconstruction conceives of a near future that offers a vital corrective to the present. Along the east–west axis lie what I call the utopias of solitude and the utopias of solidarity. In Albert Camus's short story "The Artist at Work," a poor painter named Jonas retreats to his attic garret to work for months on one painting. He hardly comes down for meals or to speak with friends. When he does finally appear, he announces that his painting is done, then promptly faints from fatigue. His friends and family climb up to have a look, but all they can discern is one tiny word painted in the center of the canvas, and no one is quite sure if the word is *solitude* or *solidarity*. Both words, however, suggest a utopian impulse, even if Camus intentionally leaves it ambivalent as to which path the artist, or anyone, should follow. Nathaniel Hawthorne went off to the famous Boston commune Brook Farm, at least briefly, to join George Ripley's experiment in solidarity; Henry David Thoreau adjourned to the solitude of Walden Pond so he could, as William Ellery Channing said, devour himself alive. No doubt this compass will point in several directions at once—Thoreau walked the ten miles east to visit his friends at Brook Farm—and sometimes all four. While each of these utopias sits at a separate end of its continuum, none is necessarily exclusive.

I think a book like this, the story of a road trip, needs some kind of *daimon*, some patron saint or guardian angel. For mine, I choose the Angel of History, as conceived by the German critic Walter Benjamin, and I imagine its image dangling from my rearview mirror like one of those cardboard air fresheners. Benjamin invented this daimon based on the Paul Klee painting *Angelus Novus*. Looking like no other ethereal visage in the history of art, Klee's wide-eyed angel floats against an orange background, its wings raised, its gaze fixed on something that appears to be happening over our shoulders. In one of the more enduring fables of our time, Benjamin imagined a violent storm sweeping the Angel of History farther and farther into the future. The angel's wings are spread open, and its gaze is fixed regretfully upon the past. "Where we perceive a chain of events," Benjamin writes, "he sees one single catastrophe which keeps piling wreckage upon wreckage and hurls it in front of his feet." The angel would like to go back and awaken the dead, fix what has been smashed. But the storm fills its wings, propelling it farther into the future. And like all great storms, this one has a name: Progress.

Today the storm of progress goes by other names: growth, capitalism, technology, genetic modification, bioengineering. In a way, I will be driving against all these headwinds in an attempt to retrieve this country's utopian past, along with the possibility of a fundamentally different future. To some degree, as I've said, all of us as Americans imagine ourselves being swept into the future by forces we believe are beyond our control, too powerful to be stopped. Yet for the first time in human history, they may be sweeping us into a future that has no future—a future of catastrophic climate change, diminishing natural resources coupled with a world population of nine billion by 2050, and ecosystems that are no longer sustainable because of human overuse and abuse. I say this not as someone trying to win an argument, but as a writer whose work is motivated largely by a fear of what the future holds, a fear of what we have brought upon ourselves. However, that fear, at least for me, is somewhat leavened by the lingering utopian impulse that imagines a course different from the trajectory we are now following. In other words, it is not too late for the Angel of History. It can't go back and fix the past, but it might salvage those ruins and build something new out of that wreckage.

Walter Benjamin believed that certain revolutionary moments can break the trance of history's forward march and release us onto a new path. It is as if a trapdoor lurked within history's linear narrative, and through that door we might escape into the future dreamed of by the Angel of History—the future that isn't scarred by catastrophe. Utopia, by definition, is a product of the imagination, and therein lies its power: it *imagines* something better, then calls on us to enact that vision.

Sometime around the middle of the nineteenth century, a Scotsman named A. J. Macdonald made it his life's work to visit every utopian community in America and document what he found there. John Humphrey Noyes, the founder of the Oneida perfectionists, remembered him as small in stature, with dark hair and sad eyes. "We imagine that the sad scenes he had encountered while looking after the stories of so many short-lived Communities had given him a tinge of melancholy," Noyes later wrote. Macdonald amassed a great deal of material for his book, but he died of cholera in 1854, before he could bring his project to completion. Noyes, wanting to write his own history of what he called "American Socialisms," tracked down Macdonald's brother-in-law, who had Macdonald's whole cache of documents boxed up in an attic. He was happy to be shed of them, and Noyes was more than happy to take possession of what turned out to be 747 pages of materials, including pencil sketches and watercolor paintings of various communities, along with wood engravings of the men and women who had called the communities into being. Macdonald had also written a preface to the book that would never be published. "I performed the task of collecting the materials which form this volume," he wrote, "because I thought I was doing good." And though his archive would surely have buttressed the anti-utopian argument—there were, after all, many cases of failure—Macdonald hoped his volume would "increase the charity" of readers when they realized that "it was for Humanity, in nearly all instances, that these things were done."

It remained, Macdonald said, for a "future historian" to continue the work he had begun: to prove that "it is possible yet, in the progress of things, that man will endeavor to cure his social diseases" by learning from both the successes and the failures of the American utopian movement. I am far from a historian, but I take his challenge seriously enough to set out as he did, to retrace parts of his sojourn in that same spirit and with the same desire: to discover a radical idealism that might deliver us from our social diseases, and unto a humanity more worthy of the name.

The New Creation

I live with my wife, Melissa, and our dogs, on top of a wave of limestone that rose up half a billion years ago and swelled across the eastern United States from Alabama to Lake Erie. Known as the Cincinnati Arch, it crested here in the Inner Bluegrass region of Kentucky, where the landscape rolls like a smaller series of waves along the top of that sedimentary landmass. The first white settlers who followed Daniel Boone through the Cumberland Gap inevitably described the Inner Bluegrass in prelapsarian terms, at least until they ran into the Shawnee, who had a hard time understanding European notions of enclosure and property rights. But five million years before all that, the Kentucky River began the slow work of cutting a deep, meandering trench across the original wave of limestone. The result is a gorge of gray-and-white cliffs called palisades, and on those walls one can read the river's ancient autobiography.

Our property is mostly wooded, and it slopes down to Clear Creek. If I were to paddle from its mouth up the Kentucky River, I would soon reach two tall "chimney rocks," columns of limestone that rise up like stalagmites from the cliffs where the surrounding rock has fallen away. Beside those formations, a narrow creek called Shawnee Run finds its confluence with the Kentucky. If I were to disembark here and walk upstream, I would come to the spot where, about two hundred years ago, a group of unlikely visionaries started one of this country's first utopian experiments. They called themselves the United Society of Believers in Christ's Second Appearing, but the world called them Shakers.

What most people know, or think they know, about the Shakers is that they forbid sexual relations and died out because of it, that they worked from morning to night, and that they produced some of this country's finest, most minimalist furniture. The Shakers, we think, were "simple," as the famous Aaron Copland song has it. But in fact, the Shakers invented a theology and a way of life that was as complex as it was profound. And there's no better place to understand that than here on the banks of the Kentucky River.

The Kentucky Shakers soon proceeded upstream from those modest beginnings at Shawnee Run to the place they would come to call Pleasant Hill. They set the cornerstone of their utopia's first permanent structure in 1809. It's a limestone dwelling that still stands, with a second-story room where I plan to spend my first night away from home. But I don't intend to spend it alone. When Melissa gets off work, she's planning to meet me at Pleasant Hill for dinner and our last conjugal night together—spent in the birthplace, as it were, of the deeply unconjugal Shakers.

My own route today follows the road, not the river, to Pleasant Hill, and it is a short, winding drive. I gas up at the Nonesuch Grocery and Hardware, the only business in town, really—it dresses down as a karaoke bar on Saturday nights and dresses up as a small church on Sunday mornings. Then I head out past, not the tony horse farms that made the Bluegrass famous, but some patchy operations with leaning barns and geldings that certainly never saw the money end of a stakes race. The farms stop as abruptly as does Route 33 where it runs up against a monolith of limestone. I take an abrupt right and wind down through a narrow gorge, across the Kentucky River and into Mercer County, where a community of weather-beaten homes stands on stilts along the riverbank. Sunlight washes across the gray-and-white palisades that rise two hundred feet above the green water on the opposite bank. A rim road clings to the rock wall on this side of the river as the road slowly winds back to the top of the Cincinnati Arch. I reach a curve in the road where the sedimentary rock seems to have eroded away. But as I will learn later, this is where the Shakers cut one of their first quarries, and perhaps cut the stones for my primary destination, the first Centre Family Dwelling. Soon I emerge from deep shade and am again driving past farms with vaguely utopian names such as Canaan Land and Mount Zion. After a few miles, the black plank fences turn to much older stone walls that corral a few drowsing shorthorn steers. In front of one of the walls stands a wooden sign that reads PLEASANT HILL: WE KINDLY MAKE YOU WELCOME. After only sixteen miles and twenty-five minutes, I'm sitting in the parking lot, gazing out at the stone, brick, and clapboard buildings that constitute the most well-preserved Shaker community in the country.

For the Shakers, the path to Pleasant Hill was far more arduous. In his classic study *The Communistic Societies of the United States* (later leavened to *American Utopias*), Charles Nordhoff called Shakerism the country's first "communistic" utopian movement. However, what we call communism (the joint ownership of property) the Shakers simply called Christianity, and when they reached the New World, they planned to practice it in its purest form. Indeed, the Shakers landed in New York before the Revolutionary War was over, a month before the First Continental Congress was to assemble in Philadelphia. According to one early Shaker compendium, a divine voice had instructed the Shakers that a new church "would be established in America; that the colonies would gain their independence; and that liberty of conscience would be secured to all people, whereby they would be able to worship God without hindrance or molestation." Led by a redoubtable woman named Ann Lee Standerin, "Mother" Ann Lee to her followers, the Shakers set sail from Liverpool in May

1774 and landed in New York Harbor three months later. However, the pacifist cenobites had no sooner drained the swamp and built a log cabin in the woods of Niskayuna, New York, than they found themselves sitting in an Albany jail for "daily dissuading the friends of the American cause from taking up Arms in defense of their Liberties." This was not Mother Ann Lee's first incarceration.

Born in Manchester, England, in 1736, Ann Lees (she dropped the *s* when she arrived in America) was a blacksmith's daughter, a short, sturdy woman with blue eyes and chestnut hair. She never learned to read or write, and at age eight was sent to work in a cotton mill; later she sheared fur for women's hats. In 1761 she married a blacksmith, Abraham Standerin, and quickly gave birth to four children, none of whom survived infancy. After the use of primitive forceps nearly killed her as she delivered her last, stillborn child, the bereft young woman became convinced that her children's deaths were punishment for her own, as she put it, "concupiscence." Thereafter, she avoided her marriage bed "as if it had been made of embers." Instead, she spent her nights in anguished prayer, even sweating blood, she later testified, over the sins of the flesh. Her husband, for his part, complained to the local church authorities about what he perceived as his wife's unreasonable austerity. Finally Ann Lee sought refuge with a dissident group of Quakers whose Pentecostal fervor earned them the epithet "shaking Quakers." In such paroxysms, these Quakers received a vision that Christ was returning imminently and that theirs represented the only true religion. The Church of England had betrayed the true teachings of the Gospels and thus had abdicated any claims to the kingdom of God. One Sunday in 1770, when Ann Lee interrupted an Anglican service to inform the parishioners of this unwelcome news, she was arrested and delivered to the Manchester Gaol. She was kept there for weeks— without food or drink, she claimed—long enough for the shaking Quakers to turn her into a kind of martyr. One of her fellow apostates, James Whittaker, later said that he visited Ann Lee's cell each night and slid a straw through the keyhole so she could at least sip milk and wine from a bowl. But the Shaker historian Edward Deming Andrews has pointed out that inmates were kept on the second floor of the Manchester Gaol, so either Whittaker's straw was the length of a garden hose, or this tale marks the beginning of Mother Ann Lee's hagiography. In stir, she received a spiritual visitation. This time it came from a divine light that told her Christ would reappear to the world in a female form—and that *she* was that form. The world would be ready for this kingdom of God only after the Holy Trinity was squared with a female version of the Son of God. Hereafter, this divine quarternity would comprise Power (God), Wisdom (Holy Spirit), Christ (Jesus), and Mother (Ann Lee). And much to Mother Ann Lee's relief, this symbolic marriage would restore a spiritual unity between the sexes and thereafter make the actual, physical act of sex unnecessary. As joint parents of the new movement, Jesus Christ and Mother Ann Lee would restore humankind to the Earthly Paradise. It apparently didn't take much for Mother Ann Lee to convince a handful of the Shaking Quakers of her newfound vision. They christened themselves the United Society of Believers in Christ's Second Appearing and set off for America.

Soon after Mother Ann Lee was released from the Albany jail, a revival of Congregational separatists took place in New Lebanon, New York, right on the Massachusetts border, and it rivaled Shaker worship for its general atmosphere of shouting, moaning, and holy rolling. In such a heightened state, a few leaders of the movement, led by a man named Joseph Meacham, wandered out to the Niskayuna swamp to find the mysterious female prophet they had been hearing about. According to one of the first Shaker documents, *Testimony of the Life, Character, Revelations and Doctrines of Our Ever Blessed Mother Ann Lee*, the visitors were entranced by the herky-jerky convolutions of the Shaker service, after which Mother Ann Lee told them of her divine revelations. The Day of Resurrection would not arrive as a cataclysmic event, she said. Instead, any man or woman was personally resurrected on the day he or she confessed all sins and entered into the life of the spirit.

Meacham seemed almost convinced. "If you have attained to that of God, which we have not, we should be glad to follow you."

"We," said Mother Ann Lee, "are the people who turn the world upside down."

And by turning it upside down, they would set it right: they would call God's kingdom into being. These, as it turned out, were precisely the people Meacham had been looking for. If James Whittaker (of the long straw) was Mother Ann Lee's Peter, Meacham became her Paul. The three of them traveled all over New England looking for converts. Like Jesus, Ann Lee recruited mainly working people to her cause, and like her Mediterranean counterpart, she performed, or is said to have performed, miracles along the way. According to early Shaker accounts, Mother Ann Lee healed ax wounds, fever blisters, broken ribs, and even lameness. But like Jesus, the Believers also encountered considerable resentment and hostility. If the Second Coming of Christ was at hand, that nineteenth-century New Englanders could accept. Hundreds of different Protestant groups were preaching a similar millennial message. But that Christ had returned as a woman, a woman demanding celibacy, was another matter entirely. Mother Ann Lee was routinely accused of witchcraft, just as she had been in England. And while she was threatened with stoning back in Manchester, one night in 1784 she was seized at a worship service, tied to the back of a wagon, and dragged by her heels for several miles over icy roads. An account from the *Testimony of the Life, Character, Revelations and Doctrines of Our Ever Blessed Mother Ann Lee* goes on: "In the struggle with these inhuman wretches, she lost her cap and handkerchief, and otherwise had her clothes torn in a shameful manner. Their pretence was to find out whether she was a woman or not." She died at Niskayuna a few months later with her skull fractured in three places.

Mother Ann Lee left behind no codified set of doctrines. There were only these two precepts of the Shaker faith: celibacy was the only true path to God, and believers must confess all their sins, even if it took months, and it often did, to realize the kingdom of God. James Whittaker died two years after Ann Lee.

At that point the Shaker elders at New Lebanon received what they said was divine instruction that Joseph Meacham, from then on "Father" Joseph, should lead the Believers away from worldly persecution and into isolated communities where they would turn prayer into work and thus realize God's will on earth as it is in Heaven.

To that end, the Shakers raised their first meetinghouse, a white, barnlike building with a gambrel roof, at New Lebanon in 1785. Three years later, Meacham gathered most of the Shakers' American converts to New Lebanon. He seemed to use the Jewish temple and the Catholic Benedictine orders as his model for establishing three classes of believers: those mature in their spiritual lives, those who were still striving for perfection, and novitiates who had just embarked upon the Shaker way. Eventually these classes would be divided into spiritual families with their own houses and livelihoods. As new Shaker communities arose across the eastern United States, they essentially operated under a federalist system whereby the colonies would be self-governing while the ultimate spiritual authority rested with the elders at New Lebanon.

By 1800, eleven Shaker communities had formed throughout the northeastern United States. Over the next five years, a modest Presbyterian camp meeting in Kentucky, just north of here, in Bourbon County, swelled into one of the most outrageous revivals in the country's history. Part of the larger religious groundswell that became known as the country's Second Great Awakening, the Cane Ridge Revival began on August 6, 1801, twenty-seven years to the day after Mother Ann Lee and her followers landed in the New World. During that Kentucky Pentecost, Methodist circuit riders and Baptists of all stripes started preaching from the backs of wagons and the tops of tree stumps. By August 12, things had spun decidedly out of control. The famous Methodist evangelist Charles Finney, who witnessed the revival as a boy, recalled a crowd of twenty-five thousand people overcome by a single spasm of riotous piety that sounded like the roar of Niagara Falls. "My hair rose up on my head," he wrote in his autobiography, "my whole frame trembled, the blood ran cold in my veins, and I fled to the woods a second time, and wished I had stayed at home."

The Shakers would clearly have been in their element at Cane Ridge, and word to that effect gradually drifted back to New Lebanon: Kentucky was ripe for converts to the Believers' cathartic faith. In 1805, Joseph Meacham dispatched three envoys to Bourbon County, and within a year, fifty-nine Kentuckians (fourteen families and some single men and women) had pooled their property and gathered at one of the proselytes' 140-acre farm on Shawnee Run. Some of the original converts actually wallowed in the mud to "mortify" their flesh of sin, while others savagely destroyed their own furniture to show they had absolved themselves of the world's vanities. Such behavior soon attracted crowds. A few miles up the road, James Harrod and his party of longhunters had built Kentucky's first settlement in 1774; thirty years later, 124 people lived in Harrodsburg, and they became instantly suspicious of their shaking neighbors. Nevertheless, the insipient Believers began building their log cabin utopia down along that small creek. They wrote to Father Joseph's son, John Meacham, who was an elder at an Ohio Shaker community, and offered him a horse, saddle, and spending money if he would come to Shawnee Run and act as spiritual adviser. However, the new Believers had hardly settled into their modest cabins when one member added his upland farm to the communal experiment and the Shakers ventured to higher ground. There they built the first main dwelling on the rolling plateau they called Pleasant Hill.

One hundred fourteen years later, I pick up a key at what was originally the Trustees' Office, where all the community's financial matters were decided, and walk the short distance to the Kentucky Shakers' first permanent dwelling. Originally called the Centre Family Dwelling, it was later converted to a tavern for secular travelers, and then it became, as it is called today, the Farm Deacon's Shop, where medicinal herbs were tinctured. Long after the demise of the Shakers at Pleasant Hill, some Harrodsburg mechanics turned the structure into a gas station. But in 1963, a Kentuckian, Earl D. Wallace, secured a federal Economic Development Administration loan of $2 million to begin restoration of the entire village. Five years later, Pleasant Hill opened, for the first time ever, to the general public, and today the Farm Deacon's Shop looks very much as it did a century ago. The façade is Shaker plain: no crown molding around the cornices, and simple four-by-fours to frame the windows. Two chimneys stand on each end of the house, and there is a door on either side of the building that marks the separate entrances for men and women: brothers lived on one floor, sisters on the other. According to the architectural historian Clay Lancaster, the stonework itself is the finest in the state, but the only possible things you could call "architectural details" on the whole building are the voussoirs and keystones set above the doors. Yet this first Centre Family Dwelling embodies the absolute, unadorned symmetry that would be fundamental to the Shaker aesthetic, and that would make it famous. Inside, the original spline floors seem as hard as the two-foot-thick stone walls. Upstairs, a heavy chest of drawers stands beside the fireplace, and a classic wooden pedestal table stands between two slat-back chairs. The only secular concession in the room seems to be the mirror that hangs from one of the pegs, above the chest. The Shakers guarded against pride at every turn, so mirrors were forbidden, as were paintings. (Vanity, thy name is portraiture!) The white plaster walls of this room remain austere and unadorned, lined only with a row of pegs that run along all four walls. In their unrelenting pursuit of cleanliness and order, the Shakers hung everything: clothes, candle sconces, hats, bonnets, tools, brooms, and chairs (upside down, to gather less dust). It would be hard to imagine a religious community that took the "cleanliness equals godliness" equation more seriously than the Shakers. The women polished the floors to a shine every day. "There is no dirt in heaven!" Mother Ann Lee was known to say. The Shakers even committed whole days to "spiritual sweeping," during which they scoured the premises with imaginary brooms, eradicating every trace of sin. Around 1791, the New York Shakers began cultivating a species of corn with resilient bristles. They called it "broom corn," and with its dried stalks, they invented, to the great relief of housekeepers everywhere, the flat broom. "Every force evolves a form," Mother Ann Lee is reputed to have said. The spiritual force to create and keep clean their New Jerusalem gave form to the Shaker broom. When my teacher at the University of Kentucky, the writer Guy Davenport, was named a MacArthur Fellow, he built a writing studio with the award money, and in it he hung a Shaker broom with Mother Ann Lee's proposition inscribed along its shaft. And in a book that he titled *Every Force Evolves a Form*, Davenport wrote, "Previously the broom, such as Parisian street cleaners still use, was a fascicle of twigs, which one stoops to use. The Shaker broom *sweeps*. One's upright stance in using it has dignity." What both Davenport and Mother Ann Lee were saying, I think, is that art or artisanship, whether it be the Shaker broom or the Shaker dance, is the form we give to forces that we feel and struggle to articulate.

In giving form to those forces, the Shakers created what is arguably this country's most singular and elegant native aesthetic. With religious restraint and clean lines, they anticipated by over a hundred years modernist design movements such as the Bauhaus and De Stijl. The Trappist monk Thomas Merton, who lived cloistered not far from here, at the Abbey of Our Lady of Gethsemani, once said that Shakers built a chair as if they literally expected an angel to descend and sit upon it. And in some way, one did. They were designing and building for the millennium. Everything, from the candleholder to the pencil post bed, had to reflect their candidacy for the divine community, their rejection of the secular world's more tawdry economy. They were artisans of the very first order, and their craft seems purified because they did not believe in individual innovation or in the buying and selling of one's work. Their aesthetic was simply a manifestation of their dual devotion to God and to the communities they had formed. The Shakers called their own mode of production and exchange the divine economy. It was the opposite of a consumer economy based on planned obsolescence; the Shakers were building for all time, for a moment when history stopped and the eternal, holy present began. You can see it even in the splash blocks of hand-chiseled stone beneath the downspouts of the Farm Deacon's Shop. Unlike the plastic variety we now buy for five bucks, the Shaker splash blocks may still be sitting here when some pandemic or global catastrophe has wiped away every trace of what we modern Americans refer to, with a sense of hubris and inevitability, as "the economy." The Shaker economy was about the farthest thing from mass production one might imagine—which is perhaps the secret of what we might call the Shakers' artless art. By "artless," I don't mean clumsy, but rather unpretentious. While the world of the early nineteenth century was clambering for the elaborate scrollwork and intricate inlays of Thomas Chippendale, the Shakers were creating an aesthetic so pure, so free of the superfluous, that one of their chairs begins to look like some kind of Platonic archetype: the Original Chair.

One feels tempted to say that Shaker design is so beautiful precisely because the Shakers did not believe in beauty. They believed, rather, in perfection. That is what they were after in a chair as much as in their own lives. The New Lebanon elder Frederick Evans dismissed the very idea of beauty as "absurd and abnormal." He went on: "The divine man has no right to waste money upon what you would call beauty, in his house or his daily life, while there are people living in misery." (In fact, once when the ministry from New Lebanon visited Pleasant Hill, they made the Kentucky Shakers pull up the flower beds around their entryways because these were considered ornamental attempts at beauty.) Yet, like the fish who has no definition of water, the Shakers were everywhere surrounded by beauty. Their farms and fields were the very definition of what nineteenth-century landscape painters called the "picturesque." Every piece of furniture, every handmade object, from their split-wood boxes to their cane-bottom chairs to their clothes hangers, is a work of art. Like great artisans, they *erased* the boundary between beauty and utility, between the functional object and the objet d'art, between art and life. Since the Shakers saw beauty as superfluous, they instead made beauty so integral to their design that it could not be separated from utility. Because the Shakers didn't believe in anything so frivolous as "art," they ended up converting their entire lives, everything that surrounded them, into works of art.

The Pleasant Hill Shakers got quickly on the path to achieving the spiritual perfection they so badly desired. They cleared the land and planted orchards, a sixteen-acre garden, and fields of wheat, corn, flax, and hemp. They devised a three-story mill on Shawnee Run, equipped with three grinding stones that produced the highest-quality cornmeal in Kentucky. They built more stone and log structures to house their swelling numbers. They built a blacksmith's shop, a saddler's shop, a loom house, a sawmill, a tanyard, and a school. They bought a local ferry and built a landing from which they would ship goods down the Mississippi to Natchez and New Orleans. They built stables galore. Finally, deciding they were here to stay, the Pleasant Hill Shakers laid out a graveyard on the western side of the village.

This happened all before 1813, when Joseph Meacham finally did name his son John as the first "father" of Pleasant Hill; he sent a New Lebanon eldress named Lucy Smith to act as its "mother." All Shaker villages were divided into smaller, self-sufficient units (with their own kitchen, barns, shops, fields, and livestock) they called families. All biological families that joined the Shakers were split apart so they might become members of the much larger "spiritual families." Hadn't Jesus, after all, said that to be worthy of him a man must leave his own family? The new Shaker families were comprised of anywhere from forty to one hundred members. By April 1812, three communal families, the West, Centre, and East, were organized, and a fourth, North "gathering family" was established as the novitiate order for prospective members.

In June 1814, 128 brethren and sisters signed the first Pleasant Hill covenant. It read, in part:

The coming of Christ and the setting up of his kingdom on earth has been contemplated in all past dispensations as an event which would be productive of the most perfect union among the people of God . . .

The New Jerusalem or church of God in the latter day should consist of a people of one heart, one soul and one interest . . .

And believing according to the distinguishing faith of said Church that Christ has actually made his appearance the second time without sin unto salvation, and has begun to establish his kingdom of righteousness and peace on earth, which is free to all people and will stand forever.

Accordingly when Christ made his first appearance the first lesson he taught was to deny self and to love others . . .

It has been our faith from the beginning, that to be united in a joint interest according to the gospel is the most perfect order of God on earth.

The "dispensations" of which the covenant speaks derive from Father Joseph Meacham's earliest statement of the Shaker faith, *A Concise Statement of the Principles of the Only True Church According to the Gospel of the Present Appearance of Christ*, written in 1790. Up until then, the early Shakers had no written creed. They believed in the spirit, not the law. This was fundamental to who they were. They would have agreed with Ralph Waldo Emerson that the *intuitions* of the heart are more trustworthy than the *tuitions* handed down by the written word. The divine spoke to them, and they literally shook with the power of that Original Word made flesh. No rote reading from the Anglican prayer book could compete with that. So the Shakers rarely read the Bible. What's more, they had been founded, like the early Christians, by an illiterate day laborer. They weren't intellectuals; they were men and women who experienced, without the mediation of scripture, what they called the "Christ presence." As a result, Father Joseph Meacham issued only what he called "waymarks," principles of guidance, like the blazes made on trees in a forest to signal that one is still on the right path. But in 1790, Father Joseph did put forth his *Concise Statement*. In that document, he set down what he called the four dispensations of God's grace to fallen man. The first dispensation was God's covenant with Abraham. The second dispensation was God's law handed down to Moses, a dispensation that went unfulfilled when Moses and his followers proved unworthy of the Promised Land. The third dispensation was the appearance of Christ in the flesh of a carpenter. This, if we are to believe the New Testament, should have been the last dispensation. Jesus *was* the Messiah, after all. But the problem that has plagued Christianity almost from the beginning—indeed the problem that *marked* its beginning—was the uncomfortable fact that Jesus was a failed messiah. He didn't overthrow the Temple hierarchy; nor did he expel the Romans from Palestine. The only way the early Christians could get around this rather intractable problem in their messiah narrative was to change it: Jesus would return—"soon," he told his disciples—and *then* there would be hell to pay. Then he would judge the quick and the dead, and then he would set up for the righteous his kingdom on earth. Another problem: he didn't return "soon." Christians waited, and still wait. In his novel *The Brothers Karamazov*, Fyodor Dostoevsky imagines Jesus returning to earth at the time of the Spanish Inquisition, only to be jailed by the Grand Inquisitor, who tells the Mediterranean street preacher that Caesar's sword, not peacemaking, will establish a kingdom of God. The Shakers proposed a similar rereading of history, and the result was the same harassment suffered by Dostoevsky's Jesus. But in 1790, for the first time, Father Joseph put it in writing: Jesus had returned; he had made his "second appearance," only this time it was in the flesh of a Manchester mill worker, Mother Ann Lee. This would be God's fourth and final dispensation.

Benjamin Youngs, one of the three men who brought the Shaker message to Kentucky, would later, in 1808, contend in his *Testimony of Christ's Second Appearing* that the failure of Jesus to conquer Palestine with his message of peace was the very *reason* Ann Lee had to finish the job—and perhaps the reason the Shakers actually talked or wrote so little about Jesus. They did, however, invoke him to explain why Shakers would not observe the Lord's Supper. Jesus told his disciples to reenact the ritual feast until the day he returned, but since he already had returned in the body of Mother Ann Lee, the ritual no longer held purpose or meaning for them.

According to the Shakers, God Himself is not God Himself (a patriarchal deity) but rather a singular, generative force that is at once male and female. Therefore, it made sense that the kingdom of God couldn't be brought about until Jesus found his "bride"; the new paradise needed a corresponding female Eve to go along with Jesus' Adam. All Shakers would be their spiritual children. Then they would bring into being the fullness of time.

If the base sexual reproduction of the flesh had spawned an unregenerate humankind, then the spirit would impregnate the New Society of Believers with the consciousness of an indwelling divinity that would be the basis for Shaker communal life. John Dunlavy, the public minister at Pleasant Hill and the author of the only sustained theological treatise on Shakerism, put it like this in his 520-page *Manifesto*: "Jesus Christ, who was the first true tabernacle of God among men, which the LORD pitched, and who is the head of the body, the Church, had the fullness of the Deity dwelling in him bodily; so each and all of the members who, in union with the head, constitute the true body or church, which is Christ, are partakers of the same Spirit and the same divine nature, that God may be all and in all." It is a radical doctrine: that Christians don't need to worship Jesus Christ, but rather must strive to *become* as divinely embodied as Christ. That is to say: Christ is not their savior; they can *save themselves*. This is the logical working out of Mother Ann Lee's Second Appearing as Christ. After her, *all* Shakers should seek the Christ within their own hearts. The theologian and Shaker scholar Robley Edward Whitson has called this experience the "Resurrection Life," and he goes on: "This is the central experience of the Shaker Way: the full reality of Christ recognized in-through-with all who are called into his unity." What's more, Whitson argues (as have many others) that Mother Ann Lee was not and never claimed to be a second incarnation of Christ (despite the obvious official name of the Shakers). Rather, she simply realized, as did Jesus, the divine potential we all carry within us.

I am not quite convinced by Whitson's contention that the Shakers did not think of Mother Ann Lee as the actual reincarnation of Christ. There is plenty of textual evidence to the contrary. But I do admire his attempt to clear away that most problematic of Shaker doctrines (besides celibacy) to show how the Shakers lived in what we might call a realized resurrection. The early Shakers did not simply *believe* in the resurrection; they enacted it. They had not so much a doctrine as an experience, and that experience was of a divine presence, a presence that dwelt within the Believers and was made manifest in the communities they built. Unlike most mainline Protestant denominations, the Shakers were not future-oriented, waiting for Christ's Second Coming, waiting to be swept up into the Sweet Hereafter. They felt the holy in the present, and in their presence. They lived it every day because they believed that Christ *had* already come. They answered Mother Ann Lee's charge to "labor and make the way of God your own." They lived in a world redeemed from cruelty and poverty, war and rapacity. This, I think, was their greatness, their singularity of vision.

It reminds me of an epiphany Thomas Merton once experienced while standing on a downtown street corner in my hometown of Louisville. Merton was fascinated by the Shakers, and he liked to walk the grounds of Pleasant Hill back in the 1950s, when the buildings were empty of Shakers, before preservation efforts began. One day in 1958, Merton was wandering through a much different landscape, one of derelict motels, Laundromats, and liquor stores, when he stopped at the crowded corner of Fourth and Walnut. There, he writes,

> I was suddenly overwhelmed with the realization I loved all those people, that they were mine and I theirs, that we could not be alien to one another even though we were total strangers. It was like waking from a dream of separation . . . Then it was as if I

27

suddenly saw the secret beauty of their hearts, the depths of their hearts where neither sin nor desire nor self-knowledge can reach, the core of their reality, the person that each one is in God's eyes. If only they could all see themselves as they really *are*. If only we could see each other that way all the time. There would be no more war, no more hatred, no more cruelty, no more Greed. I suppose the big problem would be that we would fall down and worship each other.

That experience is the essence of John Dunlavy's vision of a human race that sees the divine dwelling in all and therefore overcoming all the separateness bred by our all-too-human fears and ambitions. Yet whereas Merton leaves off on the inspired possibility of men and women becoming gods, Dunlavy and the Shakers made this indwelling "fullness of the Deity" the basis of communal Shaker life. And from it finally arose the four pillars of Shakerism: celibacy, equality, peaceableness, and communal ownership of all earthly goods. Men and women who see the divine in all human beings would find no compulsion to deny equality to women. One of Joseph Meacham's first acts as the first Shaker Father was to establish a female line of authority equal to his own—one that reflected Mother Ann Lee's vision of a dual hermaphroditic godhead, and one that established for each Shaker community a spiritual mother and father. With that decision, gender equality became a fundamental fact of Shaker communities long before it was accepted into any other American institution, certainly long before it was accepted into any American churches. The Shakers also believed in equality for all races, and they welcomed as equals the few freed slaves who wanted to join their ranks. The Pleasant Hill Shakers bought the freedom for a slave named Jonah Crutcher, who was about to be sold south. (He died of dyspepsia and is buried in the Pleasant Hill cemetery.) What's more, men and women who believe in the divinity of all humans would obviously have no use for human warfare. (In fact, to follow the letter of the Gospels, all Christians must be pacifists. It's a rather unequivocal point in Jesus' Sermon on the Mount.) "As we have received the grace of God in Christ, by the gospel," wrote Joseph Meacham, "we cannot, consistent with our faith and conscience, bear the arms of war, for the purpose of shedding the blood of any, or do anything to justify or encourage it in others." Unfortunately, the Shakers of Pleasant Hill had barely signed their first covenant when Kentucky was pulled into the War of 1812. To avoid imprisonment, they paid a "muster fine." However, by the time of the Civil War, the elders concluded that even paying such a fine violated their pacifist principles, since it went toward hiring substitute soldiers. In 1863, the New Lebanon elder Frederick Evans was granted a meeting with President Lincoln, wherein he laid out his case for the constitutional right of religious conscience. More ingeniously, he pointed out that many Shakers, before joining the order, had fought in the Revolutionary War and the War of 1812; but because of Shaker doctrine, they had refused to draw their military pensions, which Evans figured to be exactly $439,733. According to Anna White and Leila Taylor's early work *Shakerism: Its Meaning and Message*, the president replied to Evans, "You ought to be made to fight. We need regiments of just such men as you." Yet in the end, Lincoln did not make the Shakers enlist.

As for communal ownership, the 1814 Pleasant Hill covenant makes clear that the kingdom of God is not financed by venture capitalists. Instead, the Shakers believed that common property would ensure spiritual union (one heart, one soul) among the members of the new community, and that union would finally usher in what they called the New Creation. The propertyless agrarian community of sinless Shakers would become an earthly reflection of the heavenly kingdom, like two spotless mirrors facing each other. Each would call the other into being. The Shakers' "communism," which caused immediate suspicion among their neighbors, was actually based on the very first Christian church, sometimes called the Primitive Church, as articulated in Acts 2:44–45: "All who believed were together and had all things in common; they would sell their possessions and goods and distribute the proceeds to all, as any had need." While I grew up in the

Baptist Church, which I was compelled to attend at least twice a week, I never heard a preacher quote this passage. As Americans, we greatly prefer a version of Christianity that, while it might "care" for the poor, advocates no structural economic changes that might actually decrease levels of poverty in the United States. And of course the United States has been waging some kind of military action since the Berlin Airlift of 1948. It is no wonder that, in hindsight, the Shakers found this country a rather inhospitable place to locate the kingdom of God. As we all know from Sunday school, American Christianity is founded primarily on one passage from the Gospels, John 3:16, the passage that promises everlasting life to anyone who believes that Jesus died as a blood sacrifice for that life. Yet this, simply put, was not the Shaker Gospel. The Shakers actually sought to realize fully the actual teachings of a Mediterranean street preacher named Yeshua. Were they the only Americans truly to answer Jesus' call in the Gospels to give up all one owned, to renounce violence, to abandon one's family, and to follow Him?

Perhaps what made their neighbors so uncomfortable and resentful was the awkward realization that the Shakers were far better Christians than they. When a new member joined the Society of Believers, a Shaker trustee documented every item the novitiate brought to Pleasant Hill and assigned it a monetary value. After that, all property was legally held by the trustees, who supervised all financial transactions in the community. Here is a typical inventory, conducted for Louisa Jenkins in 1841.

Feather Bed, Bolster and two Pillows	$11.67
Two Large Bed Quilts	11.00
Two Small Bed Quilts	7.00
Two Cotton Sheets	1.50
Cotton Under Bed Tick	1.00
Twill Blanket	3.00
Carriage and Harness	25.00
Colt	25.00
Cash	10.00

It is easier, said Jesus, for a camel to pass through the eye of a needle than for a rich man to enter the kingdom of Heaven. Unburdened of her possessions, Louisa Jenkins presumably crossed the threshold with ease.

The Farm Deacon's Shop is all that remains of the original village, which is why it alone faces the north–south road. In the same year it was completed, Benjamin and Elizabeth Burnett joined the Pleasant Hill Shakers, along with their eight children. The oldest was a seventeen-year-old boy named Micajah, who would soon prove to be a remarkable architect and, as we say today, city planner. While Shaker scribes were obsessed with the daily goings-on at Pleasant Hill, they didn't write biographies or autobiographies, so we know very little about Micajah. His testament is the village itself as it stands today. The only image that exists of Micajah Burnett is a pencil drawing done by the somewhat deranged botanical genius Constantine Rafinesque. (Rafinesque's ghost is said to haunt Lexington's Transylvania University, which drove him away in 1826 and then later exhumed his corpse to be interred on campus, only still later to find it had dug up the wrong set of bones.) Rafinesque, who discovered and applied Latin nomenclature to 6,700 plants (more than the great Linnaeus), was botanizing around the Kentucky River in 1822 when he came upon the Shakers and singled out Burnett as the subject for a quick profile sketch. In it, the thirty-year-old Burnett, with dark locks falling over his shoulders, looks like the actor Matthew McConaughey wearing a straw hat. Seven years earlier, Burnett had laid a plan before the elders to reorient the village along an east–west axis, probably so the main dwellings could face south and absorb the sun's heat during the day. His blueprint was accepted, and today all twenty-four remaining buildings— between 1809 and 1884, the inexhaustible Shakers built 270 structures at Pleasant Hill—face the east–west road, except for my current accommodation. Of course Pleasant Hill, like any Shaker village, was exceptional for what it *didn't* have: a jail, a courthouse, a police station, a lawyer's office, a bank. All these were symbols of humankind's fall from the Earthly Paradise: the very place Pleasant Hill was working to revive. Any civil dispute was handled by an elder or a deacon; any financial matter was left to the trustees appointed by the elders.

I head out for a stroll along Burnett's main thoroughfare, a wide gravel road lined with maples and sweet gum trees. James Fenimore Cooper once said he had never seen any "villages as neat, and so perfectly beautiful, as to order and arrangement, without, however, being picturesque or ornamented, as those of the Shakers." This Shaker village, restored in the 1960s to its original state, certainly resembles Fenimore Cooper's description. Geese sputter across a pond just below the cemetery in some kind of water dance that involves a furious flapping of wings and paddling of feet. Just across from the Farm Deacon's Shop, a tawny Scottish highland bull lazes in a small paddock, wearing what looks like a terrible toupee between its horns. One of the Pleasant Hill "interpreters" tells me the bull was a gift from the last active Shaker village, of Sabbathday Lake, Maine, where a handful of Believers still resides. The original Durham bull of Pleasant Hill was imported from England alongside Henry Clay's own livestock in 1832 and cost the Shakers one thousand dollars. The chaste Shakers quickly became obsessive breeders of cattle and seemed to notice no contradiction between their theology and their animal husbandry. So successful was the latter that the Pleasant Hill Shakers bought a steamboat, built a landing on the Kentucky River, and were soon shipping four thousand pounds of cheese down the Mississippi each year. By 1850 they had the largest shorthorn herd in the country.

Beside the paddock stands the white clapboard meetinghouse—the Shakers never called it a "church" because they considered *themselves* the church—and farther down the road are the impressive dwellings of the village's three church families. The white, marble-like limestone of the three-story Centre Family Dwelling is beautiful against the blue sky. It's the largest building at Pleasant Hill and the second-largest stone structure in Kentucky, after the State Capitol. An ell extends beyond the bedrooms of each family dwelling to the kitchen and dining area on the first floor and the meeting room on the second. In 1835 the Centre Family kitchen was the first in Kentucky to have running water. The Shakers tapped into a spring down at the tanyard and used horse power to pump the water through six hundred yards of iron pipe up to the main village. This was where the most spiritually advanced family at Pleasant Hill lived, in the middle of the village, right across from the meetinghouse. Above the jerkin-headed roofline, and between six chimneys, runs a long white parapet where elders and eldresses once walked and watched for any signs of secular dalliance between the sexes. When Micajah Burnett took over as the Pleasant Hill architect, he designed every major building with two front doors, one for men and one for women. Beyond the doors of the Centre Family Dwelling stretches a hallway built wide enough so that, when passing there, no one of either sex would risk touching someone of the other. The plaster walls are whitewashed, and the dark blue trim of the molding is original to the Shakers. Beautiful wooden arches frame the high thresholds that lead from room to room. Since there are no pictures on the walls, the interior feels decidedly austere, almost monastic. The overwhelming sense I get while moving through these interiors is of calm. The genius of Micajah Burnett, I realize, was to make manifest in architectural form the repose of the Shaker spirit.

As I climb the male staircase, I wonder, as many others no doubt have: Might the Shakers have succeeded much longer into the twentieth century if not for their intransigence about sex? Yet that intransigence was the foundation of the society. The Apostle Paul said famously that the love of money was the root of all evil. Mother Ann Lee said, no, it was sex. When human beings *were* perfect, back in the original Earthly Paradise, there had been no need for sex. Copulation and procreation were only the punishments of exile east of Eden. This is how one Shaker ballad recounts the story of the Fall, in Adam's voice:

I dropp'd my hoe and pruning-knife,
To view the beauties of my wife.

An idle beast of highest rank
Came creeping up just at that time . . .

Adam, we see, was a perfect Shaker, content to hoe and prune until the serpent and Eve conspired to show him the real forbidden fruit: coochie. And nothing good came of it. Sex begat pride, which begat jealousy, which begat violence, which begat war, which begat rapacity. Rearrange that list of deadly sins however you want— sex was still the cause of all the world's problems, or so preached Mother Ann Lee. Men killed their wives, or killed their neighbors over their neighbors' wives. The Trojan War had been waged over sexual jealousy and legitimized by the idea that women were the property of men. In Mother Ann Lee's time, women were caged inside corsets and bodices, hoopskirts and bustles. For Ann Lee the equation was simple: sex equaled power, and she did not believe, as did the utopian Frenchman Charles Fourier, that sex could be purified of its malignant power and turned solely to the good of society. As one Believer later wrote in the Society's journal, *The Shaker,* "Since the duties of maternity must necessarily restrict the actions of the female, and those of paternity as necessarily leave the male unrestricted; it follows, that whatever should subject the female, in any department of the animal kingdom, to male rule, must be productive of disorder. Shall we admit this, and thus easily account for the disorders of society?" This, the anonymous writer laments, is the woman's plight under the natural course of "generation." Because of the biological imbalance of sexual power—males of the animal kingdom don't have to stick around and accept responsibility—a cultural imbalance of power always exists. But, the writer goes on, in the Shaker utopia of "regeneration," a woman "has no cause to complain of the usurpation of her rights by the man; for the life of purity which, following Christ in the regeneration necessitates, places them precisely in the relation of brother and sister, where they are alike mutually dependent and mutually independent." Men could wield no sexual power over women because there was no sex, and just as Mother Ann Lee had predicted, the subtraction of sex allayed a number of other problems. She had intuited in a simple but remarkable fashion that nothing divided men and women of the Enlightenment more than gender and property. Abolishing both private property and the power imbalance between the sexes would bring about a new era of unity and wholeness, concepts fundamental to the Shaker vision of the Second Coming. In his *Manifesto*, which was printed at Pleasant Hill on paper made at the tanyard, John Dunlavy distilled Shaker celibacy into this sentence: "The love of God unites, but the lust of the flesh separates and divides." On a practical level, it simply isn't possible to cultivate a unified "spiritual family" if men and women are constantly pairing off to form biological families. According to the Shakers' beliefs, that wasn't a true church; it was something more akin to the suburbs.

It's easy (but a mistake) to ridicule the Shakers for lacking the foresight to see that vows of chastity would bring about their sect's demise and, if implemented worldwide, the extinction of the entire human race. The Society of Believers, after all, were millennialists (perhaps even postmillennialists), who believed that by building the New Jerusalem, they were actually bringing into being Christ's Second Coming. They didn't need to perpetuate the species; they needed only to perfect it. Like a secret code, that perfection would open the heavens.

Micajah Burnett mounted a 750-pound bell on the roof of the Centre Family Dwelling, and its sweet tone could be heard all the way to Woodford County, where I live. It woke all of Pleasant Hill at 4:00 a.m. in the summer and 5:00 in the winter. Shaker women began each day cleaning all the bedrooms while the men milked cows. After their chores, the Believers returned to their rooms for silent prayer, and then marched off in divided unison to a silent breakfast. The women cooked, washed, ironed, sewed, and tended poultry until noon, while the men worked the farm, shops, and mills, and hauled produce down to the river for export. The bell rang again at noon for lunch, and then it was back to work until dinner at five.

Like Jesus and his followers, the Shakers were working men and women. They could and did provide for themselves. Later reformers such as Robert Owen and Bronson Alcott would point to the efficiency and productivity of Shaker villages to prove that their own secular brands of communism could work. But these reformers didn't realize until too late that the Shaker work ethic was grounded in a belief that the brethren and sisters were bringing about the kingdom of God on earth as it is in heaven. As a result, the Shakers were driven to work by something far more compelling than the profit motive or the belief in some secular brotherhood of man. For them, work was a kind of prayer, a very manifest way to praise what was holy. "The Shaker idea was that in consecration, not compulsion, lay the secret of a successful economy," wrote Edward Deming Andrews. And the Pleasant Hill Shakers were successful. In one year before the Civil War, they sold seventy-nine thousand packets of seeds, seventeen thousand jars of preserves, and eleven thousand brooms to the cities downriver.

They did not, like the Amish, resist technological advances simply as a way to avoid change. In fact, they were inveterate tinkerers, inventing the circular saw—Tabitha Babbitt of the Harvard community imagined it while working at her spinning wheel—cooling fan, stickpin, threshing machine, chair tilter (exactly what it sounds like), common clothespin, silk reeling machine, apple corer, and condensed milk. They invented, in essence, the dump truck: a four-wheel wagon with a flatbed that could be elevated like a cart. The Shakers invented a mechanical shucker and sheller that allowed them to mill, at Pleasant Hill, four hundred bushels a day. But the Shakers patented almost none of their inventions, believing the patent to be a sign of hubris and greed. Likewise, a Shaker craftsman never signed his work.

They were generalists in their approach to work. When they

mastered something such as broom making, they might move on to animal husbandry or coopering. The elder Harvey Eades of the South Union, Ohio, village was a tailor, shoemaker, teamster, seed collector, sheet metal worker, printer, hatter, even a dentist of some stripe. It was a way to avoid drudgery, and from all accounts, Shaker work was never that. Moving from one occupation to another was also a way to reject any stigma attached to certain jobs. It was a leveler. The New England minister Theodore Parker wrote approvingly to one Shaker village, "None of your community think work is degrading while, in society at large, many men are ashamed of work, and, of course, ashamed of men (and women) who work, and make them ashamed of themselves."

The trick, of course, to avoiding "work" is not to see it as work at all. We can see it as pleasurable, we can see it as rewarding, we can see it as a benefit to someone else, or we can see it as a higher calling. God knows the Shakers probably worked harder than any other American utopian community. At Pleasant Hill, they built forty miles of stone fencing to corral their livestock and delineate their sacred garden from the rest of the fallen world. But if they worked hard, they never seemed, as we say, pressed for time. They worked deliberately, and a task simply took as long as it took. There were no stockholders or foremen calling for "greater productivity." There was no abuse of workers, as when today's meat-packers lose fingers when disassembly lines are run too fast. There was no inequality of pay between the sexes because, of course, there was no pay at all. There was no menial labor because there was no work that wasn't useful to the community. All work was appreciated, and all work brought with it some sense of self-respect on the part of the worker. In short, all the things that can make contemporary work miserable the Shakers eliminated.

After dinner, each family adjourned upstairs to conduct its own worship service in its own meeting room; only on the Sabbath did all of Pleasant Hill gather across the street at the main meetinghouse. On Tuesday and Friday nights, each family dispensed with worship and held instead a series of "union meetings." These two hours were the only time during the week that men and women were allowed to speak with one another. In 1793, Father Joseph Meacham decided that, since some "correspondence" between the sexes was inevitable, rather than seek to restrict all communication, he should sanction it with small after-dinner commingling. For an hour, five to ten men and women sat across from one another and actually talked (for a time, the Pleasant Hill Shakers even smoked while they talked). Heavy political or spiritual matters were discouraged; chitchat was the name of the game. One visitor to a union meeting recalled the great lengths to which a Shaker brethren praised one of the sisters' johnnycake recipes.

The Shakers, who slept six to a room, were in bed by ten in the summer, nine in the winter. An herb sack filled with yarrow, tansy, wormwood, and lavender hung on each bedpost to keep insects out of the straw mattresses.

While I'm admiring the ancient beehive oven in the Centre Family Dwelling kitchen, one of the male interpreters gives a hard tug on the hemp rope that drops down through the floors and ceilings from the bell tower. The ringing announced Shaker song to commence in the meetinghouse, across the street. Walking into the white clapboard building feels a little like entering a three-dimensional painting by the Dutch abstract artist Piet Mondrian. As with Mondrian's rigid bars and spare use of color, the downstairs of the meetinghouse is a large white room framed with vertical and horizontal blue lines. Mondrian was so rigid in his aesthetic that he broke with the modernist De Stijl movement when his fellow Dutch painter Theo van Doesburg introduced a slanted line into his own work. As if following Mondrian's uncompromising ethos, even the stovepipes in the meetinghouse stand at severe right angles, and just as Mondrian reduced his palate to the primary colors, the only paints used at Pleasant Hill are yellow, blue, and red (though the red is always a maroon). Indeed, Shaker principles of design sit comfortably beside Mondrian's ambition to strip art down to its elemental, and therefore universalist, nature. If art has evolved, as Mondrian believed, from "the individual to the universal," the Shakers represented society's evolution from acquisitive individualism to a pure, spiritual communism.

Inside the meetinghouse, before a small audience, an African American interpreter with a deep, full voice sings some hymns written at Pleasant Hill by a freed slave named Charlotte Tan. Then she whirls as she sings the famous Aaron Copland adaptation of "'Tis a Gift to Be Simple." The acoustics are incredible and the music bounces off the walls as the skirt of the singer's violet dress rises to the motion of her solitary dance. As if the celibacy and joint ownership were not odious enough in the eyes of the Shakers' neighbors, the Shakers also had to contend with the well-known Baptist aversion to dancing. (Joke: Why don't Baptists have sex standing up? Because they're afraid it will lead to dancing.) The Shakers argued that there was no opposition to dancing in the Bible. Did King David dance before his Lord, as did the virgins of Shiloh? In *The Testimony of Christ's Second Appearing*, Benjamin Youngs pointed to nineteen passages in the Bible that "speak *of dancing as the worship of God*, and not one passage in the whole which speaks against it *as sacred devotion*." Another Shaker elder justified dancing this way: "God has created nothing in vain. The faculty of dancing, as well as that of singing, was undoubtedly created for the honor and glory of the Creator." Of course, based on that logic, one could argue: so was the faculty of fucking. Certainly Shaker dancing functioned to sublimate the sex drive into something that made the sacred out of the profane. Father Joseph Meacham also wanted to in some way normalize the Shakers' ecstatic worship. In 1792 he claimed to receive an angelic vision of what he called the "square order shuffle," a simple up-and-back, side-to-side four-step. That soon evolved into the "ring dance," in which two concentric rings of men and women dance a counterdirectional circle around a small group of singers or whirling female dancers. The *New-York Tribune* editor Horace Greeley dismissed Shaker dancing as "penguins in procession," but the Currier and Ives illustrations of the Shaker dance make it look like a real hoedown. The Shakers may have been chaste, but they weren't altogether prudish.

Once, when the dancing at Pleasant Hill became too rigid and formal, the Lord Himself appeared (so wrote one of the village scribes) to chastise the Believers: "Such proud, delicate motions I cannot accept, so ye must limber up your bodies as the limber willows." A group of angels then appeared and presented the Shakers with four willows—whether real or imaginary, we're not told—to be planted at each corner of the meetinghouse as emblems of the supple, organic dance that is most pleasing to God.

Not so discreetly placed beneath the stairwells on each side of the meeting room is a portal, one foot square, from which elders and eldresses watched carefully to make sure the Believers' dances of spiritual devotion remained that and only that. The idea of couples dancing together was anathema not only to Shaker celibacy but to the belief that the dance was the central force holding the whole community together. It was both a symbol and an enactment of unification, wholeness, solidarity. The Shaker dance erased the individual and the urge to act on selfish, biological instincts.

Since in their dancing the Shakers moved with one will, like a school of fish, they needed to move unimpeded by stationary objects such as columns. The main meeting room, therefore, had to be clear of the usual architectural supports. What's more, the building would have to sustain decades of jumping, stomping, and the general carrying-on that gave the Shakers their name. Micajah Burnett's genius was to invert the laws of gravity in his framing of the meetinghouse. He built interlocking cantilever trusses in the attic that extended joists down to the ceiling of the meeting room. These connect to dark blue beams that run across the ceiling, thus suspending it from the attic rather than propping it up from below. Burnett notched and wedged the trusses together in the attic—not a nail was used—so they could better spread the internal weight out to the external walls. The meetinghouse was finished in 1820, and the Believers thought they might belay some of the criticism aimed against them by inviting the skeptics from Harrodsburg to attend their Sabbath meetings. And the curious did come, by the thousands, to watch the Believers mortify the flesh with their ritualistic whirling and shouting. However, something happened in 1837 that made even the unself-conscious Shakers close their Sabbath services to the public.

From the beginning, the Shakers were spiritualists, people thoroughly convinced that the dead communicate with the living. What separated them from the mesmerists and necromancers of the nineteenth century was the explicitly religious content of their spiritualist visitations. And from 1837 to 1844, the spirit world rode a great wave through the meetinghouses of all the Shaker communities. It began one August afternoon, when three girls from the Gathering Order at Niskayuna, New York, were playing near a creek and heard beautiful music coming from the trees. That night, during the family meeting, the girls started to shake and whirl uncontrollably. Then one of them began to chant:

> *Prepare, O ye faithful,*
> *To fight the good fight;*
> *Sing, O ye redeemed,*
> *Who walk in the light.*
> *Come low, O ye haughty,*
> *Come down, and repent.*
> *Disperse, O ye naughty,*
> *Who will not relent.*

The girls later reported that their spirits had been transported into the celestial kingdom, where they were given a grand tour by Mother Ann Lee herself. The elder James S. Prescott of the North Union Society recalled years later that when the girls stopped spinning, they suddenly fell into a bizarre Q-and-A with Mother Ann Lee:

> "What city is this?"
> "The City of Delight."
> "Who lives here?"

"The colored population."

"Can we go in and see them?"

"Certainly."

"Who are all these?"

"They are those who were once slaves in the United States."

"Who are those behind them?"

"They are those who were once slaveholders."

"What are they doing here?"

"Serving the slaves, as the slaves served them while in the earth life. God is just; all wrongs have to be righted."

So began the strangest decade of the Shakers' existence. When the spirit world opened up, it visited upon the mediums not only the disembodied personage of Mother Ann Lee, but also Jesus, former slaves, dead Shakers, Benjamin Franklin, George Washington, Turks, Arabs, Eskimos, and American Indians by the score. When Mother Ann Lee led the three original mediums first to a "blue city" inhabited by Native Americans, one asked her why it was the most accessible on the tour. She replied, "Because the Indians lived more in accordance with the law of nature in their earth life, according to their knowledge, and were the most abused class by the whites except the slaves."

This new era became known as "Mother Ann's Work." Girls and young women were often seized as the "instruments," as the Shakers said, of the advice-dispensing dead. The messages from the spirit world were often admonitions against vanity, slovenliness, and lust. At the Enfield, New Hampshire, colony, two mediums arrived from another sect and told the men and women to each form a circle around them. Then, as one of the brethren, Harvey Elkins, later wrote, the entranced women went around the circle "reading the condition of every heart." Onto some members they cast aspersions; to others, they offered solace. Everyone was given an ethereal spiritual "gift."

"I recollect," wrote Elkins, "that the first spiritual gift presented to me was a 'Cup of Solemnity.' I drank the contents, and felt for a season the salutary effects. I soared in thought to god, and enjoyed him in his attributes of purity and love. I explored the beauties of ineffable bliss, and caught a glimpse of that divinity which is the culmination of science and the end of the world." Since the eighteen Shaker villages had not made much discernible progress in awakening the rest of the country to Christ's Second Coming, Mother Ann's Work at least seemed to revive the communities and imbue them once more with some sense of relevance and purpose.

In September 1838, a cook named Sarah Poole became the first Shaker at Pleasant Hill to be made an instrument of the spirit world. She was escorted to heaven by occupants of the Pleasant Hill cemetery, and when she returned from her tour, Poole brought with her new songs to be copied down and performed at meetings. Those were the first of many thousands of gifts bestowed upon the Kentucky Shakers by the heavenly throngs. The song gifts usually took the form of quick recitations that the medium delivered and that a more lucid member transcribed. Yet most of the gifts were ephemeral in nature, and they always followed a formula: an x (concrete though invisible object) of y (some abstract virtue or admonition). Above all, the dead were forever presenting the Shakers with gift balls—balls of prayerfulness, simplicity, resolution, freedom, wisdom, you name it.

Last winter, I spent some time at the Harrodsburg Historical Society, poring over the original leather-bound *Spiritual Journals* that scrupulously record daily miracles. It is compelling if repetitive reading. For instance, on May 14, 1843, the apparition of John the Divine presented the Shakers with "a cage of birds and vines placed a round our necks of heavenly fruits with a request to open our mouths and let the birds feed us." (The Shaker scribes were luckless spellers, and I have transcribed their words as written.) Anyone who refused was given instead "a cup of mortification." Not every visitor brought council; some sought absolution. American Indians were always appearing at the meetinghouse door, begging to be admitted and forgiven their pagan ways. Once they brought gourds and "asked to drink with us of the pure stream," after which they proclaimed, "We are now at peace with you."

Another time, two chiefs, Willowith and Blewjacket, brought "a bufalow skin filled with love." On November 25, 1843, Issachar Bates noticed a "large canoe full of the natives" paddling through the meeting room. Their chiefs made "lamentable interception for their own tribes and beg shiney white people to take them in." Elder Issachar had spoken a few words when George Washington piped up and asked the Lord to "call forth these poor savages from their prisons of darkness to learn the way of peace & salvation."

The Shakers' sympathy for the natives seemed to outrun any actual understanding of their history or culture. The native spirits that visited themselves upon the Shakers did so in the most stereotypical of ways: dog-sledding through the meetinghouse if they were Eskimos, simulating the war path if they were American Indians. On November 22, 1843, one instrument fell to her knees and channeled this native plea: "Ho ho ho ho poor me poor me just from eternity. Seeking seeking here for a crumb. Me fall upon my knee me trimmer at the sight. To see the shiney whites all marching in the light. Me poor Indian stand here in demidst leaning on my staff loaded down with sin & condemnation me beg entrance in some shiney white man me poor and needy me want to help my sin and make peace." The Indian then produced a "pipe of friendship," and the brethren all smoked with him.

So it went. If the Shakers had fortressed themselves away from the secular world, here was a spiritual counterpart every bit as raucous as a Harrodsburg saloon. And that realm seemed to become a vicarious portal through which the Shakers themselves could pass into a world that wasn't all work and repudiation. The *Spiritual Journals* got so crazy that women started rising into the air and wafting back to their rooms like the great levitating saints of the seventeenth century.

Mother Ann's Work spread to all eighteen Shaker villages and lasted for eight years. Modern neurologists have given a name to this phenomenon of collective mania: they call it mass psychogenic illness. The strangest recent case happened in 2011, in Le Roy, New York, where twenty high school girls, mostly cheerleaders, began twitching, shaking, and shrieking uncontrollably for months. Doctors suggested environmental causes, traumatic triggers, even strep infections. But nothing proved conclusive, and in the end, the malady slowly went away (conveniently, right before the prom). As with the Shaker mediums, mass psychogenesis happens mostly to girls and young women. And as the name implies, it seems to be contagious. Many observers accused some of the Le Roy girls of faking their fits, just as many suspected the Shakers of simply imitating departed races rather than channeling them. And yet the accounts in the *Spiritual Journals* seem as convincing, in their own way, as video of the Le Roy girls compulsively flailing and stammering. Whether outsiders believed they were under some influence, the Shakers and the girls from Le Roy understood the reality of their involuntary spasms.

Many people have puzzled over how the Shakers could be at once so silly and so resourceful. How could they hop around like third-graders playing make-believe at night, and then produce the finest furniture in the country by day? It's true, the Shakers were an impossibly unironic people. They believed as uncritically in the spirit world as they believed in a chair. Both were real because both could be experienced—at least by them.

And before Mother Ann's Work was over, a final spectacle occurred that once more convinced the Shakers of their chosenness before God.

In 1842, New Lebanon sent down word that each Shaker satellite should designate a sacred piece of ground for a new kind of worship, the "mountain meeting." On July 10, the Pleasant Hill scribe reported (in exactly this way), "We was privileged this evening with hearing read a couple of communication from the heavenly Parents. One of them gave an account and described the Location of a Spiritual Pool or fount of holy waters and a large burning Altar in the East part of our dwelling house yard with beautiful fruit trees growing round its borders also a large white pillar of marble where on the Angles sit to guard the sacred spot." So a half mile from the meetinghouse, the Shakers set about grading and fencing this half-acre ground and sodding it with bluegrass. They built a lower, hexagonal fence around the immaterial fountain and called the spot Holy Sinai's Plain.

On September 26, 1844, the Believers gathered at the meetinghouse and marched in two columns, four abreast, out to Holy Sinai's Plain. They paused at the river and were told through an instrument that "there is a bower over our heads filled with heavenly fruits that we might gather and eat, and we received heavenly bread and wine from Moses." Then John the Divine "spoke a few words through some of the inspired, and said these were the waters"—these Kentucky streams—"that he had seen in a vision hundreds of years ago, bursting forth from the Eternal God and spreading through these lovely plains." The prophet Jeremiah chimed in that he, too, "had seen this lovely sight in the visions of God in ages long past; he had seen a living fountain in a pleasant plain." The sisters and brethren marched on to the holy spot, where "celestial inhabitants" welcomed them and presented each with a lamp of holy light. They marched around the fountain, then "little David (the King) brought out the Ark of God, and said we might now show our simplicity by dancing before the ark as he had done." The Shakers "took from off our heads golden trumpets and sounded seven short blasts in union with the trumpet sounding angels who stood upon four snowy white marble pillars." At one point, Elder Isaachar Bates said that the Native Americans should be invited to participate, and "this was done with a blast from our trumpets." The natives dutifully appeared with "a sack of love" and told the Shakers that "they had once inhabited this land in their wigwams." Then the Believers knelt before Mother Wisdom and prayed for the lost children of the world. Mother Ann Lee appeared and chided her followers not to spend their days in idle recreation. "After exhorting us a little on this subject," she introduced God Himself, sitting on a chariot of fire above the Believers' heads. He "showered down sparks of living fire for every one to gather and be filled." They "leaped and rejoiced in thankfulness for our privilege." Holy prophets and patriarchs appeared and told the Shakers to gather "seeds of righteousness from the bushes around the pool and fruits from the tree of peace which stands in the midst of the pool." Then Gideon reminded the Shakers that when he commanded the armies of Israel, "he was told to take none but such as would lap like a god, and with them few he conquered." The Shakers poked their heads through the real fence and lapped at the imaginary waters. Next, "ancient Noah placed lamps of oil on their heads, that when they felt too much found & pinched up they might shake their heads and it would flow all over them." Finally, the Creator spoke through a medium, saying, "Lo, Lo, hear ye my voice, for I have come with my comforting blessing for the children of my love; and I have caused this holy fountain to boil up in this lovely plain for my chosen people, for the purpose of purifying & making clean this holy City, and preparing it for a place of refuge & a shining light for millions yet unborn." The Believers danced like "the trees of the forest when shaken with a mighty wind." The "celestial company sailed around with their ships" and escorted the Shakers back home. It was a good day.

Back outside the meetinghouse, I wander up the road to a beautiful vegetable garden that spreads across an acre of land directly across from the East Family Dwelling. There are long, well-tended rows of red and green summer lettuce, green beans, beets, chard, tomatoes, onions, and several varieties of kale. I spot a young man bent over a row of potato plants, picking pill bugs from each individual plant. He stands, shakes my hand, and introduces himself as Zach Davis, a recent graduate of the University of Kentucky's sustainable agriculture program. He's a lanky young man with an infectious enthusiasm for this, his first job out of school.

"I started with a rusty grubbing hoe," he says. "That was the only tool out here." He invested in a small tiller and a ton of chicken fertilizer—in the Shaker way, Zach doesn't use any pesticides, herbicides, or chemical fertilizer—and now he's trying to get as much produce as possible from this garden into the dining hall, next door. He has just picked a hundred pounds of peas for tonight's menu.

"Do you like raw broccoli?" Zach asks. When I say I do, he pulls out a pocketknife, cuts off two heads, and hands me one. "We can snack while we talk," he says as he shows me the specific varieties he has growing. When we reach a small paddock, we find four goats and a few attending kid goats making short work of a tall hay bale. A few are eating from its flank while others treat it more like a jungle gym. When two of the billy goats finally manage to climb to the top of the bale, it collapses and the rest of the drove leap into the bed of hay.

From time to time, one of the seemingly disapproving goats looks over the stone wall at Zach as if to say, "Are you seeing this?"

"They should be out grazing right now, not cooped up in here eating hay," Zach says. "But, you know." I take "you know" to mean that there were concessions even an idealistic farmer like Zach had to make to the tourist trade. Free-ranging goats obviously aren't as entertaining as this.

"Each family—the West Family, the Centre Family, and the East Family—had its own kitchen garden. And this is part of what used to be the East Family garden." Zach points to the head-stone set into the brick above the front doors of the East Family Dwelling that reads: 1817. "It's cool to be growing a small farm out here, but it's even cooler and more meaningful to be partici-pating in that series of generations in this one place."

Zach tells me he thought seriously about going to divinity school, but finally decided that enacting a Shaker-like steward-ship of the land could be its own kind of ministry. Last week, he says, an older couple carefully examined his garden rows for thirty minutes; then they approached Zach, and the husband told him, "I feel like I'm walking in a sacred space." That, in fact, had been Zach's design from the beginning. "I draw a lot of strength from the metaphorical significance of the word *garden*, which is an enclosure," he says. "Eden was a paradise garden. A paradise in Persian was an enclosed pleasure space, so it all kind of goes back to this idea of our original condition in the Garden." He points to the white plank fence surrounding his garden. "The frame is very important, because within that frame, the garden creates a sense of wholeness and harmony." Whether he knows it or not, this is almost exactly the kind of sacral and spatial thinking that inspired the Shakers' "mountain meetings" and the building of Holy Sinai's Plain. But I suspect he knows it. While Zach explains he wasn't hired to act as an interpreter—he was simply brought on to tend the garden—it's clear his theological leanings veer close to the beliefs of the Pleasant Hill Shakers. And it's clear he's done his reading. "I think," he goes on, "the best lesson is Mother Ann's saying, 'We should do everything as if we had a thousand years to live and as if we were going to die tomorrow.' I think about the Shaker ideal that they were practicing and believing in a realized eschatology. The Shakers weren't really a dogmatic people. But the Shaker system was lived. I think that's an important lesson to remember. It's the doing that counts. It's working out your salvation in the context of a community. The practice becomes the faith. So here we are in heaven on earth. I might not necessarily believe that we are living in heaven on earth, but we could act as if we were. There's nothing keeping us from believing that and developing a close relationship with the earth."

The word *eschatology* concerns the end-time for Christians. But here Zach seems to be using it, as did John Dunlavy, to emphasize the Shaker belief that the end-time, the New Creation, is now; and Shakers acted on that belief: they *built* heaven on earth. And even if we no longer believe in the Shakers' Second Coming, how radically different might our actions be, as Zach says, if we behaved as though we did?

There are, after all, American farmers and writers who still do. Zach mentions Wendell Berry, for one, and Wes Jackson, for another. Both have written about the problems of modern American agriculture in explicitly religious terms. In his essay "Two Economies," Berry remembers asking Jackson what kind of economy would be comprehensive enough to eliminate "the causes of the modern ruination of farmland." Jackson "hesitated a moment, and then, grinning, said, 'The Kingdom of God.'" I ask Zach what he sees as the link between the Shakers and today's prophets of more humane land management.

"It's an eyes-to-acres problem," he says, echoing Jackson, whose team of researchers at the Land Institute in Salina, Kansas, is growing mixed perennial grains in a manner that emulates the natural diversity and soil conservation of the Great Plains. "It's been our policy to move people off of the land, and if they're still on the land, alienate them from it as much as we can." Because of that alienation, according to Jackson, a third of the world's arable land has been lost to erosion, and over the last hundred years, the United States has abandoned three-quarters of its agricultural crops. We have destroyed the life of the soil with herbicides and pesticides, and destroyed soil structure with nitrogen fertilizers. "It's a big problem for the earth," says Zach, "that its chief steward can't take care of it." Waving his hand over the East Family garden, he goes on: "This I take care of with an assistant, so we have four eyes to one acre, whereas in the western part of the state, you might have two eyes to ten thousand acres. How can you take care like that?"

The answer, unfortunately, is that we haven't. One solution, says Zach, quoting Jackson again, is to become native to one place. Of all the Europeans who came to America, Zach maintains, "the Shakers made the best effort of trying to develop an indigenous narrative in this land. They created a mythology around this place"—their millennial, realized eschatology—"which we don't have. Throughout the nineteenth century we turned away from the place and turned toward the mechanization and industrialization of our landscape. We never wanted to settle here. We imported Europe to America."

In my experience, you don't run into a lot of twenty-two-year-olds who have thought through the whole history of this country's attitudes toward the land and who have decided upon both a practical and the spiritual way forward. But I think Zach is right in tracing the causes of our current farm crisis. It's precisely

Alexander Hamilton's idea of the American Dream that Thomas Jefferson warned against: importing a European economy based on manufacturing instead of building a native economy based on small farms. Without probably knowing it, the Shakers followed Jefferson's agrarian—many said utopian—dream, and here at Pleasant Hill, they made it last for one hundred years before the tide of mass production proved too much for a community of artisans, for a people who farmed and built as if they had a thousand years to live, and as if they would die tomorrow.

I duck into the Cooper's Shop, where a young man is using a drawknife to shave an angle into a thin piece of cedar. He wears a loose-fitting cotton smock that looks vaguely Shaker period, and jeans that do not. The original Shakers wore whatever clothes they brought to Pleasant Hill. Only later, in 1842, did elders dictate a more regimented uniform of plain cotton shirts and linsey-woolsey trousers for the men; and for the women, long blue or gray dresses pleated at the waist. The men wore broad-brimmed straw work hats and the women straw poke bonnets. The female interpreters at Pleasant Hill still wear the plain cotton dresses, but given the scarcity of linsey-woolsey gabardines, the men wear jeans.

Barrel hoops and drawknives of all sizes hang from the white walls of the shop. All the modern interpreters at Pleasant Hill seem to possess an encyclopedic knowledge of the men and women they impersonate. (Over in another shop, the broom maker rattles off a bewildering slew of facts—"In 1869, the Pleasant Hill Shakers shipped 74,400 brooms to New Orleans and points south"—as he feeds a bundle of straw into the black iron press.) The young man in the Cooper's Shop asks me if I know what a cooper is, or was.

"A barrel maker," I hazard. As the world's leading producer of bourbon whiskey, Kentucky has probably been, or so I surmised, the leading producer of barrels ever since the Baptist minister Elijah Craig invented the stuff not far from here, on Hickman Creek.

"*Not* a barrel maker," the cooper says, stopping his work to educate. "A cooper is a maker of *staves.*" Staves, I knew, were the wooden planks that, fitted together and fastened with metal hoops, formed a bourbon *barrel.* "But a stave," the cooper went on, "is the main component of any wooden *vessel,* not just a barrel." And the Shakers traded in a whole line of tubs, churns, piggins, and noggins. I tell the cooper I take his point, then head back out to the main road.

It is one of the precepts of postmodernist theory that nothing is really real—reality least of all. Everything in contemporary life is a simulation of something that was once real. Airbrushed supermodels replace real women, Taco Bells replace real Mexican cantinas, fantasy football replaces the real game. And on and on. After a while, the simulacra seem more real to us than the real, and eventually, says the French social theorist Jean Baudrillard, the *hyper*real replaces reality—*becomes* our reality. We, as a result, turn into quiescent spectators of our lives: we want the reality only of reality TV. So goes the theory. And since it is a French theory, the force behind all this banal simulation is, predictably, America and American popular culture. The problem isn't so much that Americans love the simulacra of Disneyland, writes Baudrillard; the problem is that "Disneyland is presented as imaginary in order to make us believe that the rest is real, when in fact all of Los Angeles and the America surrounding it are no longer real, but of the order of the hyperreal and of simulation." Like a lot of French theory, this one is constantly forcing a square peg into a round hole, and then we only have to kick Dr. Johnson's rock to refute it thusly. Or in the case of Pleasant Hill, kick the limestone splash blocks outside the Farm Deacon's Shop—no simulacra there. But since Pleasant Hill does function, on some level—say, the level of the cooper in jeans—as a simulation of the Shaker past, I must ask myself: How do the simulacra of Pleasant Hill speak to, or reflect back on, the larger culture? Am I traveling through, and away from, one hyperreality (mainstream America) just to discover another ersatz simulation of some American past? And if so, what's the point of that?

Perhaps the danger of the Pleasant Hill simulation is that it compels us to say: how quaint, how old-fashioned, how *historical*. The masterful and thorough restoration of this nineteenth-century utopia convinces us how far away it really stands from our own century, our own architecture, our own manufacturing, our own economy. We see the Shakers as a people completely *other*, a culture lost to us except as an amusing footnote in a much larger narrative of this country's manifest destiny. As Baudrillard might say, we smile at this simulation so as not to see how inauthentic our own culture has become. At Christmas, you can take a horse-drawn carriage ride, even a sleigh ride if there's snow, around the village at night, and it's a great time. The buildings are beautifully candlelit. You pretend for a moment that this isn't 2016. But then you get in your car and go home to watch TV. Both experiences are forms of escapism, I can hear Baudrillard smirking.

Yet since I, in general, prefer German social theory to French, this is how I choose to read the tableau of Pleasant Hill: The village as a whole represents what Walter Benjamin would call a dream image, a sleepy scene from our collective past. It rests on the pile of wreckage that the Angel of History contemplates as the storm of progress sweeps the angel farther into the future. Pleasant Hill is, in Benjamin's theory of history, a ruin, but one that still bears great import. Because the future has no image, the utopian imagination must reclaim, must resurrect, past ruins and transform them into wish images that still carry a revolutionary potential for change. "The utopian images that accompany the emergence of the new always concurrently reach back to the ur-past," Benjamin theorized. Because the original dreams of the ruin were never realized, it still bears a dormant potential to reroute the path of history. In thinking this way, Benjamin was greatly influenced by the scholar of Jewish Kabbalah Gershom Scholem, and from that influence he developed the theory that a "messianic age" could suddenly open like a trapdoor released on the stage of history. "At opposite poles, both man and God encompass within their being the entire cosmos," wrote Scholem. "However, whereas God contains all by virtue of being its Creator . . .

man's role is to complete this process by being the agent through whom all the powers of creation are fully activated and made manifest." Certainly no human impulse could be more utopian than that. One way to make those powers manifest is through the wish image, or Benjamin's "image of redemption," which acts as a portal, releasing the utopian present onto the stage of history. Then the storm of progress might stop, the terrible estrangement end, and humankind might be unified with its Creator in the fullness of time. The wish image—in this case, the collective image of Pleasant Hill—jams the works of history; it ceases to be a mere simulacrum and instead releases us from our sleepwalking dream of hyperreality. That, at least, is how I like to imagine Pleasant Hill. The genius of the Shakers—their artisanship, their stewardship of the land, their culture of absolute equality—still lies dormant here. It simply wants to be released again into a present that can escape its own catastrophes and stop the storm that goes by the name of progress.

It took little more than a decade for the experiment at Pleasant Hill to quite literally transform a small Kentucky farm into a city on a hill—an almost entirely self-sufficient community of 491 members housed in three main dwellings and surrounded by a constellation of shops, barns, mills, and the meetinghouse. Widows and women fleeing oppressive, sometimes violent home lives arrived at Pleasant Hill, and their ranks quickly outnumbered the brethren. And when the fervor of the revivalist and millennialist movements finally waned, the cholera epidemic of 1833 provided the Shakers with a growing number of orphans. Micajah Burnett brought thirteen foundlings back from a trading trip to New Orleans. The Shakers set up a school for these and the other children at Pleasant Hill, emphasizing what today we call experiential learning. During the spring and summer, the children learned agriculture, animal husbandry, and herbal medicine alongside Shaker adults; then, from November to February, they studied reading, writing, arithmetic, geography, "moral science," and religion. The usual paternal allowances seemed to have been extended to Shaker children. Though separated from their biological parents (if the parents were still alive), the children were taken on picnics, sleigh rides, and berrying parties. The cooks made them peppermint and checkerberry treats, while the shop men fastened together corncob dolls and wooden toys. Still, it could not be said that all the Shaker children turned into amenable Shaker adults. The Shaker journals are full of hilarious invective aimed at thankless orphans who abandoned Pleasant Hill. Some were called "dead limbs," "flesh-pots," "puffs of trash." According to the anonymous history *The Origin and Progress of the Society at Pleasant Hill*, one orphan, Fanny Hutton, "left this Society for the whole [*sic*] and pit from whence she was dug." Another orphan, fantastically named Lucy Lemon, "was kindly invited to go to the world" when she was found in violation of Shaker chastity laws. "She went!" a scribe dutifully wrote. Another annalist described a certain Caroline Whittymore as the "Harlot of Harrodsburg." In 1846 she was driven from the village—"REPROBATE CREATURE," reads the journal—only to return "under the influence of liquor" and brandishing a horse pistol. She collected the man with whom she had committed the alleged infractions and, as the journal reads, "James made no resistance but walked willingly along with her."

In the early evening, I meet Melissa back at the Deacon's Farm Shop, and I, too, make no resistance as I walk willingly along with her on our last night together. The Shakers' original sidewalks were intentionally made with stones cut too narrow for a man and a woman to walk side by side. But the current stone paths are more accommodating to those from that heathen place the Shakers disparaged as "the world"; it is, I suppose, a tacit admission that the secular world of tourists, with their biological families, has finally overtaken the Shaker vision of spiritual perfection.

However, when we enter the last major building completed at Pleasant Hill, the Trustees' Office, it's as if, in 1840, at the age of fifty, Micajah Burnett threw off all Shaker austerity to create what the historian Thomas Clark rightly calls "an almost intoxicated spasm of romance." While the exterior is classic Shaker simplicity, the interior is something altogether different. Two spiral staircases frame the center hall and wind up three flights in a sumptuous display of white plaster and cherry rails and banisters that Burnett bent and sanded himself. The stairs spiral in opposite directions, forming a double helix that resolves itself in an elliptical dome ceiling. Indeed, it looks as if Burnett were channeling, and releasing, all the community's sexual restraint into these stairways that seem to follow the curves of a woman's hips and breasts, and that frame the entrance into the dining hall. Even the two indoor sprinklers, affixed to the white plaster at the upper curve of the stairs, seem curiously well placed.

At dinner, Melissa notices that the teenage girl serving us has a hickey on her neck. Of course no one "kindly invites her to go back into the world." After all, that's where she came from tonight.

For starters, she serves us a large bowl of snap peas from Zach Davis's garden. Melissa's allergies are bad tonight, so I quote for her the Shaker rule that says, "If you are obliged to sneeze or cough, don't bespatter the victuals." Then we gorge on the platter everyone recommends at Pleasant Hill: the fried chicken.

Melissa says, "Did you see that church sign on the way here that said 'If evolution were true, mothers would have three arms'?"

"Indeed."

"Well, why wouldn't they have four arms? I mean, wouldn't that be even better?"

"You make an excellent point," I say. "Of course the Shakers didn't believe in evolution or mothers."

"That's crazy. Why build something this beautiful and then tell people they can't have sex here. It's not natural."

Melissa and I are both in our midforties, and neither of us has any children. She is less happy about this than I. I see it as a victory of self-control and family planning; Melissa sees it as a series of missed opportunities.

"They didn't want people pairing off," I say. "Then you'd have private families and then private property, and then there's no more utopia."

Melissa shakes her head, unconvinced.

"Up in Oneida, New York," I continue, "that community solved the problem by saying you could have sex with everyone. I mean, it's the same principle in a way; there's still no private property."

"That sounds like something a guy thought up."

"Yeah, it was a guy."

"And a woman founded the Shakers, right?"

I nod slowly.

"So if a woman starts the utopia," Melissa continues, "they have no sex, and if a man starts it, they can have all the sex they want."

"I hadn't really thought about it that way."

Melissa purses her lips and gives me a look that says, "Maybe you should."

After dinner, we walk over to the somewhat-neglected cemetery to watch the sun set. For a moment, I think I might search the headstones for Micajah Burnett's initials—that's all the Shakers used to commemorate the mortal coil. But the markers were so badly weathered that all the dead Shakers had faded into the individual anonymity to which they once aspired. Yet while the Shakers, like another matriarchal Protestant sect, the Christian Scientists, distrusted modern medicine, they tended to live a very long time. For decades they relied solely on herbal medicine, a field in which they are said to have made great advances. Throughout the year at Pleasant Hill, the sisters would walk down along the banks and slopes of the Kentucky River gathering horehound, lobelia, sarsaparilla, liverwort, snakeroot, bloodroot, kohosh, and mayapple. In their herb gardens they cultivated sage, mint, thyme. They even grew opium poppy for their own medicinal uses, though some of the northern communities sold it as well. In the early 1840s the Shakers dried and shipped downriver almost three thousand pounds of medicinal plants. When a "Cansor

Doctor" appeared at Pleasant Hill in September 1816, the village scribe groused that he was paid one thousand dollars for cures that didn't work, and besides, the Shakers had to repair his carriage and do his family's washing. Yet the best health care the Shakers ultimately provided was what today we call, as if it were something new, preventive medicine. When you eat well, engage in physically demanding work and worship, avoid strong drink and tobacco, and feel a psychological certainty that you are one of God's chosen people, health will tend to be the rule of the community. In 1846, Micajah Burnett undertook a mortality study and found that, contrary to popular belief at the time, hard work did not shorten one's life. On average, the Shakers at Pleasant Hill lived to seventy-one, almost twice the national average at the time.

"Clean living," Melissa says.

We lie back in the grass and watch the day's last orange light reflect across the goose pond.

In the morning, Melissa and I pack our bags into our respective vehicles.

"Don't get arrested or wind up in the hospital," she says as a team of draft horses slowly plods past us.

This is a line from one of our favorite novels, Richard Russo's *Straight Man*, in which the narrator's wife issues that same edict on her way out of town, only to return and find her husband has landed in jail *and* in the hospital. Unfortunately, past bad behavior on my part has rendered the Russo line more than just an inside joke, so I try to assuage Melissa's fears.

"You're thinking of the old Erik Reece," I say.

"Good," she says with a kiss. "Let's keep it that way."

Before leaving Pleasant Hill, I decide to go look for the remnants of Holy Sinai's Plain. Several interpreters tell me it stood on a small hill in the pasture that now lies on the other side of Route 68. I walk once more down Micajah Burnett's boulevard, past the Centre Family Dwelling, where the date stone reads:

Actually, due to a decade of strife, the building wasn't finished until 1834. On September 16, 1826, eight years after he finished *The Manifesto*, John Dunlavy died from malaria. That marked a serious loss of leadership at Pleasant Hill. Younger members seemed to resent what they saw as the sanctimonious decision making of the aging and infirm eldress Lucy Smith. One member of the Gathering Order, John Whitbey, had come under the influence of the Welsh social reformer Robert Owen. At that time, Owen was crisscrossing the eastern United States, spreading his message of a secular, utopian socialism. Whitbey began agitating to name deacons and elders of Pleasant Hill through a popular vote instead of by decree from New Lebanon. Whitbey convinced one of the founding members, James Gass, to "run" for the office of Centre Family elder. When his bid for the post succeeded, the ministry at New Lebanon descended upon Pleasant Hill to set matters right. The elder Benjamin Youngs stripped Gass of his eldership and sent him and Whitbey packing. Gass sued for compensation, but lost his case before the Kentucky Court of Appeals in 1834. That decision, in effect, legitimated the Shaker covenant of joint ownership and guaranteed that communal life at Pleasant Hill had a future. Much damage, however, had already been done. Forty-two of the original covenant signers seceded from the Society of Believers, and a number of second-generation members fled after them. Several of the apostates were married within a few weeks of leaving Pleasant Hill. As the amateur historian Patricia Goitein has discovered, many moved to Peoria, Illinois, where they reformed their community—into one in which celibacy played no part.

After the golden age of Mother Ann's Work, retaining and recruiting members at Pleasant Hill became increasingly difficult. In 1869 the trustees of Pleasant Hill paid for fifty-four Swedish converts to immigrate to the United States and join the Kentucky Shakers. The experiment was not a success. An April 7, 1873, entry in the church records reads, "Absconding Swedes—Seven left today. Quite a waterhaul, those Swedes." In fact, the Shakers' fishing hole for followers had been drying up for quite some time. The country had long since moved beyond its millennial passions and expectations; people got tired of waiting. The commercial culture became increasingly seductive to the younger Shakers.

Many have blamed the Civil War for destroying the repose of Pleasant Hill. While it's true that Rebel soldiers made a colossal nuisance of themselves on their way to the battle of Perryville—one scribe called them "bipeds of pandemonium"—they wreaked no permanent damage. That came from the industrial economy of mass production that followed the war, leaving the Shakers unable to compete in the market for seeds, brooms, and canned goods. Nor were there any longer enough Believers at Pleasant Hill to sustain the group's earlier, self-sufficient ways. The scribe lamented, "The older brethren are dying off rapidly, and the young ones are running off more rapidly." Instead, Pleasant Hill was increasingly overrun with "winter Shakers," mostly men who converted to the faith during the cold months, when work was light and the rooms and food warm, and then absconded back into the world come spring.

In 1873, fires set by the Swedes seriously damaged barns and shops at Pleasant Hill. Micajah Burnett died in 1879. In the 1880s, the elder Benjamin Dunlavy, son of John Dunlavy, made a disastrous investment of Pleasant Hill assets in a Nevada gold mine that went bust. By the turn of the century, there remained fewer than sixty members at Pleasant Hill, and most of them were too elderly to perform basic chores, much less keep the village running. In 1910, the last twelve Believers deeded the remaining eighteen hundred acres of Pleasant Hill to a George Bohon of Harrodsburg, with the agreement that he would pay for their care for the rest of their lives. In 1923, Mary Settles, the last Shaker of Pleasant Hill, died in the front bedroom of the Centre Family Dwelling.

I see Zach Davis again working in the garden, and he says he wants to give me a bushel of vegetables for the road. I tell him I won't really have any way to prepare them, so he hands me a sack of cucumbers instead. We shake hands, and I climb a set of three stairs that has been thoughtfully built into one of the stone fences at the eastern boundary. Then I cross the road that today acts as the southern boundary of Pleasant Hill. I climb a white wooden fence and start walking through a pasture that today Pleasant Hill leases out to a local farmer. I look around for any clues of where Holy Sinai's Plain might have been, but all I find are a few troughs sitting beside some rotting fence posts that surely were set long after the Shakers abandoned their sacred site. Finally, I decide, it doesn't much matter. What ultimately makes any place sacred is the rituals that men and women perform there, or believe were once performed there. Walt Whitman wrote in "Song of Myself," "there is no object so soft but it makes a hub for the wheel'd universe." The entire world could constitute sacred space if our imaginations were capacious enough. The history of religions is the history of such objects and places—places deemed so sacred as to be the center, the axis, of the world. But in most religious experiences—and the sacred is above all an *experience* of intense being, as the Shakers demonstrated on Holy Sinai's Plain—the sacred symbol or liminal space must be defined against the profane world. The Shaker dream was gradually to transform the American continent, and then presumably the world, into the Earthly Paradise. But early abuses at the hands of their neighbors convinced them that first they had to establish a paradise wholly separate from the profane world of promiscuity, inequality, and violence.

The romantic poet William Wordsworth would have understood the Shakers' attitude toward Holy Sinai's Plain. He experienced a similar sense of the sacred in 1798, while sitting on the banks of the Wye River, overlooking the ruins of Tintern Abbey. When I was in high school, I had a humanities teacher who compelled us to memorize large chunks of Wordsworth's poem "Lines Composed a Few Miles Above Tintern Abbey." My teacher wanted us to appreciate, I think, the inspiration the poet drew from the natural world; he wanted us to appreciate the sentiment that "Nature never did betray / The heart that loved her." Years later, in graduate school, I learned that while visiting the Wye Valley, Wordsworth could see a mill just beyond Tintern Abbey, polluting the skies of his pastoral subject. Unlike his contemporary William Blake, who famously included the "dark Satanic mills" in his poem "Jerusalem," Wordsworth ignored the encroaching evidence of an industrial age. Standing in the pasture where Holy Sinai's Plain once stood, I would like to ignore it as well. Unfortunately, two tall smokestacks are unavoidable just over the rise, belching out the effluents of a coal-burning power plant at Dix Dam. That dam, built on the Kentucky River in 1927 in the name of flood control, was meant to generate only hydroelectric energy. But like the Tennessee Valley Authority, Dix Dam began buying cheap strip-mined coal in the late 1950s, and the results are the mercury, sulfur dioxide, and nitrogen oxide that alone killed thirteen thousand people last year in the United States.

Standing in the pasture between the smokestacks and Pleasant Hill, between these emblems of an industrial and an agrarian utopia, I think about how, as a country, we so often choose the smokestacks and mass production over the agrarian, artisanal dream of the Shakers. For a moment, I turn my back on Dix Dam and look instead, for one last time, at Pleasant Hill. And this is what I think: I can't imagine a better place to *conceive* a utopian dream and try to bring it into being than here on this verdant tableland high above the Kentucky River.

What is amazing about Pleasant Hill is the degree to which the Shakers really did re-create, for one hundred years, their spiritual utopia beyond the reach of the fallen world. Whole nations have failed in far less time. And there is simply no criteria by which we can say that the Shakers of Pleasant Hill failed. They became diminished and eventually died, but we cannot say they failed. We might say, in retrospect, that the larger American culture failed them and, in doing so, lost a great deal. What we lost with the Shakers was a kind of spiritual materialism that transformed their Kentucky farm into an agrarian paradise where craft replaced commodity, where quality of the object trumped quantity of goods, and all distinctions vanished between the beautiful and the useful. We left behind the biblical injunction that cooperation would create a more just—a more Christian, if you like—society than a culture based on gender, class, and racial inequality. We left behind—far behind—the Shakers' guiding principle that the kingdom of God is here.

Monk's Pond

The idea of human pilgrimage is probably as old as the human idea that we should bury our dead. A friend of mine once drove to Louisville to stand at the corner of Fourth and Walnut, where Thomas Merton experienced his epiphany of oneness with humankind. Traffic whizzed by, and a steady stream of people gathered, and then crossed at the light. My friend simply stood there, waiting to feel for all those people something similar to what Merton had felt. But it didn't happen, and gradually he noticed another man standing beside him who also was making no effort to cross the street. After another set of pedestrians had moved along, the man slowly turned to my friend and said, "Merton?"

I read into this story a cautionary tale about the idea of pilgrimage. It says: only Thomas Merton can have a Thomas Merton epiphany at the corner of Fourth and Walnut, so go conjure your own moment of spiritual intensity, or whatever it is you came for. It says: you probably won't get what you came for. It says: prepare to be let down. And still we go. When Merton was accidentally electrocuted in Thailand in 1968, he himself was on a pilgrimage to the East, a journey so far into Buddhism that many feared he would never make his way back to Catholicism.

I myself am heading west. Indeed, one could make a geographical argument that when you take a left turn out of the Pleasant Hill parking lot, you are leaving the South for the Midwest, grits for bratwurst, tobacco fields for waves of corn and grain. As I head out, I see wild chicory and bull thistle blooming along the roadside, in front of field after field of corn, which, though it's the middle of June, is still only two feet tall due to a cold, wet spring. Redwing blackbirds dive at the corn from power lines, and suddenly the pulsing orange plumage of an oriole flashes against my windshield. I pass in the vicinity of the only Kentucky cave (inaccessible to the public) where we know for a fact Daniel Boone sought refuge in the winter of 1770, when he was spying out potential real estate investments for the North Carolina judge Richard Henderson. Henderson, apparently, had paid some of Boone's debts to keep him out of prison, and in return wanted a rough survey of the terrain beyond the Cumberland Gap, where Henderson hoped to make a fortune in land speculation.

Under a cloudless sky I decide to stop by the Civil War battlefield at Perryville to eat a couple of Zach Davis's cucumbers for breakfast. I pull up under some cedars beside a nearly dry creek bed in what has become known among Civil War historians and reenactors as the Valley of Death. Here, because of the rolling terrain, the Union army descended on the unsuspecting Rebels from two fronts, north and west, and mowed them down with a hailstorm of lead. Dying soldiers crawled to this creek for water, which they soon turned red with their own blood. But, just as in Herman Melville's "Shiloh," a poem about visiting that Civil War battlefield four years after the fight, the only sound I hear today is birdsong. Of the dead at Shiloh, fought six months before Perryville, Melville wrote,

> But now they lie low,
> While over them the swallows skim,
> And all is hushed at Shiloh.

All is hushed as well here at Perryville, where, alone, I toss cucumber peels into the now-dry creek bed. While the Battle of Perryville raged, forty-three Benedictine monks were building the Abbey of Our Lady of Gethsemani about forty miles from here, crow-wise. Trappists of the Order of Cistercians of the Strict Observance, they had been led to Kentucky from France by Father Jacques "Eutropius" Proust in December 1848. The next day, the monks chanted their order's seven offices, and they have been doing so every day ever since.

At a parking lot in Bardstown, a small city known far more for its bourbon than its devotion to monasticism, I ask a cop how to get to the abbey. She seems confused and pulls a map down from behind her visor. But she locates the town, gives me directions, and soon I'm heading up a country road past chicken coops, trampolines, and shade tree mechanics. Nothing about the drive suggests that a monastery, home to the twentieth century's most famous monk (with the exception of the Dalai Lama), is right around the corner. But after passing Whiskey Run Road, I see the tall white walls of Gethsemani rise up from rolling meadowland.

I've come briefly to Gethsemani in the hope that the monks' prayers might sanction my travels and offer Godspeed. I've also come to think about the four points on my mental compass: the utopias of escape and reconstruction, solitude and solidarity. Thomas Merton spent twenty-seven years at Gethsemani struggling to find a balance among all four.

Above the gate that closes the public off from the monastic gardens are the words GOD ALONE. Behind that gate, the Trappists practice their version of utopia, which has much in common with that of the Shakers: they're cloistered, celibate, and taciturn, and they own few worldly possessions. Individually, these monks don't have a dime to their names. Their days consist of work—making cheese, fruitcakes, and bourbon balls—study, and constant prayer. Like the Shakers, the Trappists embody both the utopia of escape and the utopia of solidarity, yet over the years their most famous member found himself reaching for at once more solitude and a more active, political role in the world.

I've arrived in time for the office of sext. With a dozen others, I enter the abbey church and stand behind the waist-high glass that separates the monks from us. The basilica is long and narrow, with thick brick walls painted white. When bells peel over the monastery grounds, the Trappists, who take the strictest vows of all monastic orders, enter the church from two side doors, dip two fingers in holy water, cross themselves, and then assume their places on two sets of wooden risers that line the long walls. They wear white cowls and black cloaks held together with brown leather belts. The average age of the monks seems to be about sixty. Only a few look to be in their twenties. Most, but not all, have shaved heads, and a few wear beards. As they sing and chant, I try to read their faces. How do years of constant prayer, silence, and contemplation manifest outwardly? I see calm certainly, perhaps something I would call contentment. They don't look like saints, whatever a saint looks like, but they do seem to move with a certain assurance that has nothing to do with arrogance, much less with all the postures of daily secular life.

Today they chant from Psalm 124: "Jerusalem! The mountains surround her; so the Lord surrounds his people both now and forever." I've read that Thomas Merton used to quote this passage and tell young monks that, as in Jerusalem, they themselves were surrounded at Gethsemani by the horseshoe-shaped knobs of Kentucky's outer bluegrass. They were safe from the same ungodly "world" that the Shakers feared and disparaged. Born in France to artist parents, Merton once said this about his adopted homeland: "If ever there was a country where men loved comfort, pleasure, and material security, good health and conversation about the weather and the World Series and the Rose Bowl, if ever there was a land where silence made men nervous and prayer drove them crazy and penance scared them to death, it is America." According to his friends and biographers, Merton loved the world of sex, booze, and jazz a great deal while he was a student at Columbia in the early 1940s—so much so that it brought on a spiritual crisis that landed him at Gethsemani on Easter weekend in 1941. At Columbia, Merton had aspired to be a famous novelist.

At Gethsemani, he resolved to renounce that self-serving aspiration and devote his life to silence and prayer.

There is, Merton maintained, a freedom that comes with giving up your will to the will of the abbot, the monastic community, and ultimately, it is hoped, to God. "We become contemplative when God discovers himself in us," Merton would write years later. That divine inhabitation was what Merton was searching for behind these high white walls. But writing, to Merton, was like breathing, and he couldn't give it up. The abbot, Dom James Fox, told him he didn't have to; he simply should use his pen to deepen his spiritual life and serve the monastery. Merton, whose monastic name was Father Louis, wrote prayerful poems for himself and devotional pamphlets for the monastery. Then, at the abbot's urging, he wrote his own version of St. Augustine's *Confessions*, an autobiography that, to the surprise of everyone, including his publisher, became a bestseller. When *The Seven Storey Mountain* was published in 1948, Gethsemani was nearly broke. Merton's royalties, none of which he saw, almost single-handedly saved the abbey from dissolution. It also brought a lot more novitiates to Gethsemani, whose population doubled. Merton took on the role of master of novices, but he was also becoming restless. Silence, the voluble Merton had slowly come to appreciate; now he needed more solitude as well. Dom James told him to find *inner* solitude, but Merton was chafing from too much solidarity in the crowded monastery, and the abbot relented to the point of allowing Merton two hours alone each day in an abandoned garden shed.

Merton had a problem: he was now famous for his humility. Whereas in his early years at the monastery he was allowed four letters a year, now he received hundreds a week. He had become, in the most improbable way, the famous writer he had once wanted to be. There was another problem: in the public's imagination, Thomas Merton was now the name of one of Catholicism's most pious exemplars.

He enjoyed the fame that *The Seven Storey Mountain* brought him, but Merton also realized that fame was a threat to his spiritual life. As he saw it, his only recourse was to retreat further into solitude, into a life of meditation and prayer. In 1950, Merton was, for the first time, allowed beyond the walls of Gethsemani. He began exploring the woods and ponds that surrounded the monastery, and his journals took on a decidedly pastoral tone. "In the woods I can think of nothing except God," he wrote. As for Thomas Merton the somewhat sanctimonious model of Catholicism, that idol had to be smashed. Merton did so by taking up causes that greatly troubled his religious superiors: racism, war, and nuclear proliferation. While the Second World War raged, Merton had occupied himself with writing his spiritual autobiography. But as race riots and the Vietnam War unfolded outside the walls of Gethsemani, he could no longer, in good conscience, simply maintain the role of a monk praying that God's will be done. He could no longer live content in this utopia of escape. So, in the face of relentless censorship from his order, Merton sent into the world what he called conjectures of a guilty bystander. He accused "the West" of greed, cruelty, dishonesty, and "above all *its unmitigated arrogance towards the rest of the human races*. Western civilization is now in full decline into barbarism (a barbarism that springs *from within itself*) because it has been guilty of a twofold disloyalty: to God and to Man." This was not what the Catholic Church wanted to hear from Merton, who, for his part, gloated in his journal that he had killed the author of *The Seven Storey Mountain*. If he could not march in Selma or at the Pentagon, he could at least commit to these movements his writing and his reputation. Finally, in 1962, Dom James officially silenced Merton from writing any more on the subject of war and peace. Merton acquiesced, but continued sending private letters of encouragement to activists all over the world. In March 1968, Merton urged Martin Luther King Jr. to come to Gethsemani for a spiritual retreat. King's secretary wrote back to say that while the civil rights leader very much wanted to meet and pray with Merton, first he was needed in Memphis.

By that point, there were rumors circulating around the monastery and larger Catholic circles that Merton himself was on several hit lists—maybe even the CIA's—because of his political views and his influence, especially over young activists. Some crackpot had shown up at the gates of Gethsemani waving a gun and demanding to see Merton. A teacher of mine at the University of Kentucky, Guy Davenport, told me he once talked to an officer in the John Birch Society who solemnly informed him that Martin Luther King, Jr., was the president of the American Communist Party and that Thomas Merton was the leader of the party's Kentucky cell. When Guy told Merton about this encounter on a visit to Gethsemani, the monk who Guy thought looked like a cross between Picasso and Jean Genet howled with laughter. Merton later wrote in his journal that he had been visited that day by "three kings from Lexington"—Guy and the photographers Ralph Eugene Meatyard and Jonathan Williams. Meatyard (whose work would earn him a posthumous international reputation) and Williams (whose work wouldn't but is still deserving) took, on that day, some of the best portraits that exist of Merton. Both photographed him in front of a white outbuilding, wearing a large denim barn jacket. Its large pockets bulge with Merton's journal and other slim books, and a PEACE button is affixed to the collar. In one of Williams's portraits, Merton has his hands crossed and his eyes closed. He looks like a man incredibly comfortable in his own skin, in the fields of his monastery. His is the face one would want to see in a mirror: warm, unself-conscious, and completely alive. But of course it was the face of one who *didn't* look in mirrors, and as such, Merton's expressions seem to well up from some deeper place.

By then, Merton was at the end of his long struggle with Dom James over his desire for solitude and the abbot's demands that he maintain solidarity among all his monks. Merton felt he had paid his dues to the community as the master of novices for twelve years, and he certainly felt that, given the millions of dollars he had brought into Gethsemani through his books, at the very least the abbot could build him a small hermitage a short distance away. Unlike the Shakers, Merton never mastered the spiritualization of work, at least not the kind of work performed at Gethsemani. He didn't want to make cheese and fruitcake, and his satirical poem "Chee$e" ends, "Poems are nought but warmed-up breeze, / Dollars are made by Trappist Cheese." Merton clearly wanted to be paid for his poems, not his cheese. Perhaps sensing that the restless Merton might leave the order altogether and take his book royalties with him, Dom James finally relented, and in the summer of 1964, Merton officially took up residence in the two-room cement-block hermitage—think International Style on the lowest of budgets—about a mile from the main edifice.

The Shaker scholar Edward Deming Andrews sent Merton a collection of Shaker hymns, and Merton sang some of them in the morning in front of the hermitage. He said Mass, he prayed, he meditated, he wrote. He scolded himself: "The bad writing I have done has all been authoritarian, the declaration of musts and the announcement of punishments."

He was moving further away from church doctrine, toward some spiritual space where words fall away and one feels the immediate presence of one's own participation in the being that is also simultaneously God—not a being, but Being itself. That, at least, is how Merton understood it. He had also fallen under the spell of Zen Buddhism, which preached no doctrine at all, only the direct grasping of reality without the mediation of words and their inevitable prejudices. "High up in the summer sky," he wrote, "I watch the silent flight of a vulture, and the day goes by in prayer. This solitude confirms my call to solitude. The more I am in it, the more I love it. One day it will possess me entirely and no man will ever see me again."

But many did see Merton at the hermitage, and he liked it that way. Everyone, it seemed, wanted to meet him, and if Joan Baez asked to sit at his feet, who was he to object? (In fact, Merton asked Baez to take off her shoes so he could see her feet; it had been so long.) Merton possessed what Guy Davenport called "a complicated roundness." He craved solitude and company; he took a vow of silence but, beyond earshot of the abbot, never stopped talking; he was a Catholic monk (and a priest) who seemed to be on the verge of converting to Buddhism.

Merton had a large and devoted following in my very Catholic hometown of Louisville. Though I wasn't raised Catholic, I was brought up in a very regimental Protestant home. When I wound up in the throes of my own crisis of faith, I, like Merton and many others, went searching for answers and alternatives in the literature of Eastern religions. That reading quickly led me to Merton, particularly to his book *Zen and the Birds of Appetite*. There he suggested that if Christianity was only an ideology, a theology of revelation and salvation, then it had come up short. It needed to learn from Zen Buddhism that *experience* was the core of any vital religion. Christians had to get over their sense of piety and superiority, their "sense of security in one's own correctness," and find "the pure unarticulated and unexplained ground of direct experience." Christians had to move beyond their religion of the word, the Logos, to discover a deeper level of communion with their Creator. Merton was pointing a way past the rigid, self-flagellating Christianity I had grown up with and toward a new kind of spirituality that borrowed the best from all religions without expecting adherents to abandon their own traditions.

After Dom James retired from his post as abbot to become a hermit himself, Merton was finally free to travel, to leave Gethsemani for an extended period. In 1968 he set off on a long pilgrimage through India, Tibet, and Thailand; he called it, curiously, a "coming home," though he had never been to Asia before. At a spiritual summit at Darjeeling's Temple of Understanding, Merton told the Eastern monks who had come to hear him: "My dear brothers, we are already one. But we imagine that we are not. And what we have to recover is our original unity." That was the great epiphany visited upon Merton at the corner of Fourth and Walnut in Louisville, and he was still thinking about it halfway around the world.

In the mountains of Tibet, Merton met the Lama Chatral Rinpoche, who looked to him like "a vigorous old peasant in a Bhutanese jacket tied at the neck with thongs and a red woolen cap on his head." The lama, whose rugged Himalayan hermitage must have looked like the ultimate destination in any search for solitude, made a strong impression on Merton, and he contemplated staying on to study with the Tibetan guru. Yet in the end the Western monk flew to Bangkok, where he was scheduled to speak at another ecumenical conference. In his talk, "Marxism and Monasticism," Merton suggested that a monastery offers the only practical example of Marx's famous tenet "From each according to his ability, to each according to his need." He might have cited the Shakers as well; the sentiment had certainly once applied at Pleasant Hill, as Merton well knew. When he finished the talk, Merton said he was tired from traveling and would take questions later that night. He took a shower and went back to his room for a nap. With a hand still wet, he plugged in a fan with faulty wiring and was electrocuted. He died on December 10, 1968, twenty-seven years to the day after he arrived at Gethsemani.

Today, only a steel black cross, identical to a hundred others, marks Merton's grave. Wandering among all the crosses of the cemetery, it takes me some time to find the one that simply reads FATHER LOUIS MERTON. The only thing that distinguishes Merton's grave is a string of faded plastic prayer beads someone has wrapped around his cross. If in life Merton's reputation dominated and perhaps distracted the monastery, in death he is simply another monk of the Order of Cistercians of the Strict Observance. His hermitage lies behind the monastery walls, closed off to the public, so I take a walk instead through the woods and fields that lead to Dom Frederic's Lake, where Merton met with the three secular magi from Lexington. In an essay memorializing his friend, Davenport noted that Merton lived out the utopia of solitude twenty-five years longer than Henry David Thoreau stayed at Walden Pond. Still, there were similarities. "They were both," Davenport wrote, "men suspicious of man's wisdom but in awe of and in search of God's." Perhaps that foundational wisdom can be found only in solitude. For all Merton's urgency not to be a guilty bystander to the world's injustices, in the end he was a contemplative, and any action he took could come only out of a place of deep, private meditation. In that, too, he and Thoreau were in agreement: One could not truly work for the world's reconstruction without first escaping into the quiet chambers of one's own heart. Or to a small pond.

This pond, much smaller than Thoreau's, is surrounded by thick stands of oak and pine. I take a seat at the base of a large oak, pull from my book bag a copy of Merton's journals, and begin reading from the last years. Of his massive body of work, these entries are my favorite. All sanctimony and self-seriousness have vanished. In fact, Merton hardly seems to trust writing at all—he *finally* seems on the verge of silence. In the summer of 1965 he wrote a "Sermon to the Birds": "Esteemed friends, birds of noble lineage, I have no message to you except be what you are: *be birds.* Thus you will be your own sermon to yourselves." And the birds reply, "Even this is one sermon too many!" It sounds like something a Zen master would tell novice monks, but it also sounds like Merton's sermon to himself: *no more sermons.* Instead, Merton turned to the natural scripture all around him. There he found the real impulse of the Gospels, quite literally written on the wind: "Up here in the woods is seen the New Testament: that is to say, the wind comes through the trees and you breathe it." To breathe in that earth-borne spirit, just as the birds do, is to abandon tuitions and return to the profound intuitions that drove a Mediterranean wanderer out into the wilderness beyond Palestine to find his own god in his own utopia of solitude.

I look out over Dom Frederic's Lake and watch water striders— around here we call them Jesus bugs—darting like electrons across the surface of the pond. It's an ordinary enough miracle for an insect that uses surface tension to walk on water. I go back to Merton's journal and am somewhat struck when I read this: "I am coming to see clearly the great importance of the concept of 'realized eschatology'—the transformation of life and of human relations by Christ *now* (rather than an eschatology focused on future cosmic events)." *Realized eschatology*: it's the same term the Pleasant Hill gardener Zach Davis used to describe the Shaker theology. It's the same immanent theology of the birds and the Jesus bugs. It says simply that we can transform our own lives, right now, into the kingdom for which the whole Christian world waits. Merton believed that such a transformation could begin only with one individual, alone in prayer, discovering the face he had before he was born. From that realization—the realization that he is one with his god, and the realization that such unity binds him to all other living things—everything else would follow.

A Beautiful Failure

NEW HARMONY, INDIANA
Mile: 000268

I had resolved before beginning my trip that I would, as much as possible, stick to two-lane roads. I was, after all, in no hurry. I had destinations but no itinerary. And after leaving Gethsemani, as I follow the dips and turns of Kentucky back roads, this feels like the right decision. Driving fifty miles an hour, I can roll down the window, get a left-arm tan, and leisurely assess the puns of in-home beauty parlor signs: SHEILA'S SHEAR DELIGHTS and RONDA'S SUCH A TEASE SALON. Careening along the interstate highway, I never would have seen the garage covered with five different colors of tin roofing, or the county line liquor store with this dire warning painted on its side: DRY AHEAD! I certainly wouldn't have tasted the fantastic cheeseburger and fried okra at Norman McDonald's Country Drive-In, a log cabin converted into a roadside diner. This is a landscape, a countryside, with texture. It retains at least remnants of a native imagination, a vernacular intelligence.

That all disappears when I reach the outskirts of a city such as Henderson, Kentucky. My spirit of exploration sinks to sullenness as I plod from light to light in this dingy low-rise town. I could, of course, be driving into one of a thousand American towns, because it's all the same chains, all the same disposable architecture, all the same heat rising from the blacktop. The last, I'm sure, is partly to blame for my foul mood as I try to navigate through Henderson's afternoon traffic. And of course it's the vehicle I'm driving that made Henderson this way, so I can hardly complain. When I finally do spot something verdant on the edge of town, the John James Audubon State Park, I take a hard right into the dense shade of that small forest. It's a welcome respite. I park my truck at a trailhead and walk up among the pawpaw and large polar trees, some surrounded by ancient, coiling grapevines. The air is much cooler here, and zebra swallowtails flit in the spaces where light filters down through breaks in the canopy. Most of the birds Audubon is famous for painting are quiet now, except for a few Carolina wrens calling back and forth high in the canopy.

In 1775, Richard Henderson, the same North Carolina judge who sent Daniel Boone prospecting into the bluegrass region of Kentucky, tried to buy all the land between the Ohio, Cumberland, and Kentucky Rivers from the Cherokee. His Transylvania Company arranged for twelve hundred Cherokee to gather at Sycamore Shoals, Tennessee. Henderson and his fellow speculators convinced the indigenous council to deed over seventeen million acres, but in the end, the Virginia General Assembly rejected the deal, claiming sole right to purchase Indian land. As a concession, the assembly granted the Transylvania Company two hundred thousand acres around the confluence of the Green River and the Ohio for its trouble. Henderson again sent Boone to survey the country and report back on the best real estate prospects, but Henderson died twelve years before a surveyor laid out the plans for the town that would come to be called Henderson.

John James Audubon arrived in this small river town with his new wife, Lucy Bakewell, in 1810. He had designs on setting up a general store and, in his leisure hours, hunting and drawing the prodigious number of birds that lived and migrated along the Ohio River. Audubon was born in 1785 to a French chambermaid who worked on his father's Saint Domingue sugar plantation and died during childbirth. At the beginning of Toussaint Louverture's slave rebellion, which changed the country's name to Haiti, Audubon's father, Jean, brought his bastard son to France, only to send him abroad again twelve years later, this time to Pennsylvania, to escape conscription into Napoléon's army. The young man named Jean-Jacques became John James, and in a new country he made up his mind to reinvent himself as a woodsman, a bon vivant, and the first man to draw, in a naturalized setting, every North American bird. The staggeringly handsome Audubon—tall, with a mane of red hair that was the source of some vanity—married the beautiful daughter of a Pennsylvania-via-Derbyshire plantation owner. They set out to start a family and a business in my hometown of Louisville, but Audubon found the competition too great there, so he and Lucy pushed farther west, down the Ohio. They rented a log cabin in Henderson, where Audubon set up a general store selling whiskey, gunpowder, and other necessities on the frontier. Lucy raised a garden and two sons (a daughter died in infancy), while John James hunted and fished for the family's sustenance. In the evenings, while Lucy read—her favorite book was Erasmus Darwin's long poem, *The Botanic Garden*—Audubon mounted dead birds on a wooden board hung with wires and pulleys, to give them the effect of movement, and he drew. "The pleasures which I have felt at Henderson, and under the roof of that log cabin," Audubon later wrote, "can never be effaced from my heart until after death." By all accounts, from the early Henderson days, the Audubon marriage was its own kind of utopia. Together, he and Lucy swam across the Ohio River every morning and were known in the village for their expert dancing. Townspeople were enamored with Lucy's sophistication and Audubon's skill in shooting contests. And while Audubon's life would soon prove to be an operatic swing of highs and lows, it was his marriage to Lucy that sustained him until his death.

In the summer of 1818, Audubon was walking along the banks of the Ohio when an odd, hunched man emerged from a keelboat in a long yellow coat "stained all over with the juice of plants," as

Audubon would later remember. With what looked like a bundle of dried plants on his back, the stranger approached Audubon and asked where he might find the man who drew birds. When Audubon announced that he was the very man in question, the stranger presented him with a sealed letter of introduction. The letter began, "My dear Audubon, I send you an odd fish, which you may prove to be undescribed . . ." Folding the letter, Audubon asked the stranger to see the fish. The stranger smiled and said, "I am that odd fish, I presume, Mr. Audubon." The stranger standing before the embarrassed Audubon was Constantine Rafinesque, the naturalist who, back at Pleasant Hill, sketched the portrait of Micajah Burnett. A hunched, squirrely-looking individual with sunken cheeks and a sallow complexion, Rafinesque was also a lexicographer and was fluent in ancient cultures and modern finance. Like Audubon, he had arrived at Henderson via France and Philadelphia. By that time, he had already infuriated much of the international scientific community by taking it upon himself to rename hundreds of North American species that he claimed earlier taxonomists got wrong. He also had the maddening habit of creating new species that violated Linnaeus's binomial system of nomenclature. Here along the Ohio River, he was gathering new species for his seminal work, *Ichthyologia Ohiensis*, which would introduce readers to one hundred new fish of North America. Audubon, who seemed to be the only person ever to like Rafinesque unreservedly, invited the wanderer to stay with his family for as long as he wished.

One night, when "the eccentric naturalist," as Audubon later called his visitor in a comic biographical sketch, was flipping through Audubon's portfolio, he informed the artist that there existed no such plant as the one he had placed beside a particular bird. When Audubon walked his accuser down to the river and pointed to the flora in question, Rafinesque "danced, hugged me into his arms, and exultingly told me that he had got not only a new species, but a new genus." Perhaps the childlike pleasure Rafinesque took in this discovery, along with his reputation as an omnivorous classifier, prompted his host to begin describing incredible river species that existed only in Audubon's mind. (It might also be that Audubon was a little steamed that his guest had tried to kill a bat in his bedroom with an expensive violin and had consequently smashed the instrument to pieces.) Most outlandish of these imaginary creatures was the "Devil-jack diamond fish" (half alligator, half paddlefish) that Audubon drew for his guest, who then convinced himself he had actually seen this creature, "but only at a distance." Rafinesque included the fictional fish as a fact in his *Ichthyologia Ohiensis*, and scientists already suspicious of Rafinesque's prodigious taxonomy pounced on this ruse as evidence of his unreliability. One later biographer, Leonard Warren, blames Audubon's "sadistic exercise" for ruining an already unstable man, but in truth, Rafinesque, who invented entire mythologies about indigenous people and then passed them off as archeology, was wholly capable of irreparable self-sabotage. Warren goes so far as to ascribe motive for Audubon's prank: namely, that he was frustrated over his failing business in Henderson. While this seems improbable, it is true that a few months later, when regional banks were forced to call in loans to pay off the Louisiana Purchase, Audubon went bankrupt almost overnight, and even spent one night in a debtor's jail in Louisville. In the end, all that he and Lucy owned was seized, and their family left Henderson with nothing but Audubon's portfolio and drawing supplies. Rafinesque, for his part, had a contract with a Pittsburgh publisher to produce a map of the Ohio River. So he abandoned the Audubons with no word of farewell—an alarmed John James set up a small search party—and then continued down the Ohio, on his way to its confluence with the Wabash River in Indiana.

That is where I'm headed now. Back in my truck at dusk, I cross the river at Evansville and point my headlights into the cornfields of Indiana. When I reach the small town of New Harmony, it takes me a few passes along Church Street to locate the Old Rooming House, my lodging for the night, because it is almost entirely obscured by the golden rain trees growing in its small front yard. The tree, which Thomas Jefferson introduced to this country, has become something of a symbol of New Harmony, and I have arrived at the height of its blooming. Thousands of tiny yellow flowers shoot forth in what looks like a small fireworks display at the end of almost every branch. And when a breeze pulls the flowers from their stems, the effect, to some, is that of a golden rain.

The Old Rooming House, which shed its paint long ago, is the cheapest place to stay in New Harmony ("Ideal for artists and writers," according to its website), and I find my own door unlocked, with a note from the proprietor, Jim Stinson, compelling me to make myself at home. The room is nautically themed, with paintings and models of ships, shell lamps, a porcelain marlin, and a shelf of maritime books. An incongruous set of roller skates sits by the door, below a sign that reads TO LIFE BOATS. I settle in and read the navy's *Song and Service Book for Ship and Field*, which contains any religious service or hymn you might need performed on an aircraft carrier or helicopter gunship, until I fall asleep.

In the morning, I meet the loquacious hotelier, Jim Stinson. He looks to be in his sixties, with untamed gray hair and the face of a man who has spent a lot of time in the sun. He wears faded jeans and a brown shirt that at some point had an unfortunate encounter with bleach. Jim tells me he used to travel the Southeast buying and selling discontinued china before he settled down in New Harmony thirty years ago and began managing some properties around town. In the late 1990s he ran for mayor and lost by two votes.

Jim untangles a couple of old bicycles from the Virginia creeper that is indeed taking over one side of the house, and then says, "If you don't mind parking your male ego, we can go for a ride on these."

He quickly pumps up the tires of both bikes. Egos in check, we start off swerving down the road. In 1814 the German millennialist George Rapp bought seven thousand acres in this bend of the Wabash River and, with five hundred of his followers, built the town of New Harmony on a five-block-by-three-block grid that still defines the town today. The streets were wide, as they still are, and many of the Rappites' brick or frame houses still stand alongside twentieth-century cottages and bungalows. With a population just under eight hundred, contemporary New Harmony is actually smaller than when Rapp's community was at its largest, and since the town hasn't grown much beyond the original settlement, the automobile is about as pointless there today as it would have been two hundred years ago. Tourists walk or bike, and locals, whose median age seems about the same as that of the monks at Gethsemani, tool around in customized golf carts with names such as ROCKY AND VERA airbrushed on the side. Almost all the businesses in New Harmony are locally owned and Jim says the community has worked hard to keep it that way. When we ride past a Fifth Third Bank that a few years ago replaced a local lender on the corner of Main and Church, Jim tells me, "They painted over an original mural inside the bank the first week they got here."

On the corner across from the bank stands the original house that George Rapp built for his own large family. His theology and his community so closely resembled that of the Shakers that to tell their story in full would be to repeat much of what I said back at Pleasant Hill. Rapp himself was to the German Lutherans what Mother Ann Lee was to the British Anglicans: a separatist thrown in jail (in Rapp's case, in Württemberg) for claiming that the established church had abandoned the true mission of its founder. What's remarkable is that such similar apostasies grew at the same time out of two very different European soils. Like the Shakers, George Rapp and his followers believed that the fall of man occurred when the female element of the Divine was separated from its male counterpart. The Rappites practiced celibacy, confession of sin, and common ownership of property as first advocated in the Book of Acts. In fact, their beliefs were so closely aligned with those of Mother Ann Lee's people that they contemplated merging with the Shakers of South Union, Ohio, in 1816. The main difference between the two sects was this: whereas the Rappites built a place to wait for the kingdom of God, the

Shakers built the kingdom itself, or so they thought. The Rappites took as their symbol the woman clothed of the sun of Revelations 12:6, who "fled into the wilderness, where she hath a place prepared of God." But the Shakers lived that Second Coming every day. Still, the Rappites were every bit as industrious, and as successful in business, as the Shakers. By the time George Rapp sold New Harmony a decade after its founding, to the Scottish socialist Robert Owen, there stood over 150 buildings, surrounded by a vineyard, an orchard, and a five-acre garden. Today, descendants of Owen still live in the original brick house that George Rapp built for his family. It is surrounded by a tall brick wall with green wooden gates. When Jim Stinson and I ride by, the front gate is open, something that apparently surprises Jim. He quickly doubles back and pulls up on the sidewalk. Two women, one older than the other, are sitting on the front porch, near the gate.

"This is probably a real violation of your space," Jim calls up to them, "but do you mind if we look at Gabriel's footprint right quick?"

"It's too faded to see now," the older woman replies.

Undeterred, Jim goes on: "Could we have a look anyway?"

"Um, no," she says, and both women quickly retreat indoors.

"What was that about?" I ask.

Jim explains that there is a slab of limestone behind the house that looks to be embossed with two human footprints. In 1819, George Rapp claimed that the archangel Gabriel paid him a visit and, as proof, left those footprints in the limestone.

According to Jim, "Rapp told his followers, 'Gabriel spoke to me, and here's the proof, so you guys need to get in line.'"

Robert Owen's son, the geologist David Dale Owen, concluded years later that the footprints were carved by indigenous people, and Rapp's own records show him hauling the slab by oxen from the bluffs of the Mississippi River near St. Louis. Apparently Rapp worried that, as the hard work of building New Harmony came to completion, idle hands might soon do the devil's dealing. (Indeed, as Robert Owen would learn the hard way, there was substance to Rapp's premonitions.) He had other problems. While, as with the Shakers, the Rappites' goods (from linen to cotton to rope to leather to whiskey) were synonymous with quality, the community, again like the Shakers, still suffered the abuse of its neighbors. George Rapp even went so far as to build the New Harmony granary to such a massive scale that it would double as a fort. Jim and I park our bikes outside to go have a look. Indeed, with two-foot-thick sandstone walls, imposing oak beams, and tall windows only a few inches wide (presumably to hang a musket through), the granary still has to be the sturdiest building in Indiana.

Yet by 1824, George Rapp had had enough of the American frontier, so he decided to relocate his flock to Pennsylvania, where they built it all over again. This new community, just outside Pittsburgh, Rapp called Economy, in reference to "the Divine Economy" of communal sharing—the exact phrase the Shakers used.

Jim and I ride south out of New Harmony proper, up to a hilltop cemetery where many of Robert Owen's descendants are buried, and then we climb a bit higher, to a suburban street called Plank Road, the modest route by which the father of British socialism arrived in New Harmony to begin his and this country's first experiment in secular communism. Owen was a fifty-four-year-old cotton magnate when he first surveyed New Harmony, believing that the true work of his life was finally about to begin.

Born on the Severn River in North Wales on May 14, 1771, Owen was a bookish child, often found lurking in the personal libraries of local clergy, physicians, and lawyers. At age twelve he wrote to the prime minister, pleading for stricter laws for observing the Sabbath in his hometown, and to the astonishment of everyone, a government proclamation to that effect was issued a few days later. However, by age fourteen, Owen had already carried out an extensive inventory of the major world religions and found that they had all originated from the "same false imaginations of our early ancestors." That each religion considered itself the only path to God seemed, in Owen's mind, to cancel out the others, so that the only true religion remaining was one based solely upon "universal charity" for the whole human race. Demonstrating a kernel of the philosophy he would later elaborate, Owen also chafed at the religious idea of free will. We could not be wholly responsible for our actions before God because the human constitution was determined partly by nature and partly by society, neither of which could be decided by one's own choosing.

Soon Owen was serving as a draper's apprentice in London and pondering Seneca's moral precepts in his spare time. When his apprenticeship ended in 1790, he moved to Manchester, a decade after Ann Lee and the Shakers had fled. There he bought three power looms, hired three employees, and went into the cotton business. At the time Owen was born, Great Britain imported about six million tons of raw cotton. By 1790 that number had risen to over thirty-one million tons. The recent invention of a steam-driven loom called Crompton's mule was upending a six-hundred-year-old English guild system and forcing independent tradesmen to abandon their private shops for factory work. It also meant Britain could buy far more cotton from the American South, where the arrival of more and more slave ships made cotton the driving force behind the transatlantic Industrial Revolution. The world had changed in Owen's eighteen years, and cotton was king.

Owen took on partners, and his business quickly grew. By 1795 there existed two main objects of Owen's affection: a young woman named Anne Caroline Dale and her wealthy father's cotton mill in New Lanark, Scotland. So as not to appear a man with ulterior motives, Owen planned to buy the mill first, and then persuade David Dale to give Owen his daughter's hand. The deeply Presbyterian Dale had caught wind of Owen's unconventional personal theology, however, and he was reluctant to surrender his daughter to such a man. Still, after several years Dale acquiesced on both matters, and in 1799, Owen took possession of Dale's cotton mill and married his daughter.

At that time, many in New Lanark refused to work at David Dale's mill, where the air had to be kept hot so the fabric would stay malleable, and as a consequence, diseases spread easily. Since the adults refused to submit to the factory's conditions, five hundred of Dale's eighteen hundred employees were children, some as young as five. They worked from six in the morning to seven in the evening, the same hours as the adults. The children's small hands were useful in threading and cleaning the machines, even if it meant an epidemic of lost fingers.

When Owen took over the New Lanark mill, he cut two hours off the workday without reducing pay and raised the age children could work from five to ten. Today, that doesn't sound terribly revolutionary, but at the time it was exceptional. Owen wanted to shorten the workday more, but he had partners who would hear no more of his squishy ideas. So, instead, he started a factory school for the children, and when the partners balked at that, he bought them out with the help of some Quaker businessmen and the British philosopher Jeremy Bentham, who was just beginning to formulate his theory of utilitarianism, a straightforward political philosophy that argued for the greatest happiness of the greatest number of people. Owen's earliest and most thorough biographer, Frank Podmore, recalls that in 1800 the education of poor children was "neglected more in England than any other civilized country." So, for the first time in the English-speaking world, Robert Owen invented kindergarten, or what he called the "infant school." It would become the core of his emerging philosophy that all people will be good and moral if trained early and properly. It was up to Owen, of course, to define what "properly" meant. He named his school the Institute for the Formation of Character, and in it, children would be neither scolded nor praised. They "were not to be annoyed with books," but allowed to handle all the maps, geodes, and mounted animal specimens Owen provided. Students shouldn't be bothered with the secondhand knowledge gained from reading until they had fully absorbed the primary experience of these objects and maps. Curiosity was to be the sole motivation for learning. And Owen believed children were most curious about the natural sciences, geography, and history. After Owen shortened the workday, he also offered night school for the working children. About four hundred of them actually shook off the weariness of a ten-hour shift so they could handle Owen's exotic specimens and sometimes dance to an orchestra.

As for parents at New Lanark, Owen insisted on temperance and cleanliness within his factory town. He improved the worker housing and cleared trash from the streets. He also exhorted his workers to "make everyone happy with whom they have any intercourse." Partly to that end, he mounted a square block of wood on a wire over each man's or woman's workstation. It looked like the top of an obelisk, and each side was painted a different color, from black to blue to yellow to white, to signify a different level of "character." Each day, a worker's conduct was displayed—black for poor and white for excellent, with blue and yellow somewhere in between—and recorded in a "book of character." Owen himself, in a condescending and self-congratulating tone that would become typical of his adult discourse, likened this idea to "the recording angel marking the good and bad deeds of poor human nature." After 1800, Owen seemed almost always to be at once generous and patronizing, large-hearted and boorish. In New Lanark, he also instituted curfews, random body searches, and home inspections. Even so, he won the workers over to his cause of compulsive self-improvement when the 1906 American embargo on cotton exportation brought all international trade to a standstill; Owen continued to pay his idle employees a full wage until work resumed. He also supplied a public store for his workers, but unlike the company stores of American coal camps, where prices were jacked up and miners had to shop there using company scrip, Owen sold everything at cost. As a result, philanthropists and reformers from all over the world (about thirty per day) came to view Owen's school and factory. In 1816, Czar Nicholas of Russia paid New Lanark a visit, and when the czar observed at dinner that Owen's filial crest resembled the Russian coat of arms, Owen bestowed upon him (much to his wife's dismay) some of the family silver. Buoyed by such attention, Owen began writing several essays "on the principle of the formation of the human character." They were published in 1816 under the title *A New View of Society*, and that small book became the platform from which Owen would disseminate, almost thirty years before Karl Marx met Friedrich Engels, the germinating political philosophy we now call socialism.

The overarching goal of human culture, Owen maintained, should not be the pursuit of happiness, as the American Declaration of Independence states, but rather its *realization*. Moreover, Owen wasn't talking about happiness merely for the individual, but "happiness of the community," a definition of democracy that Jeremy Bentham first put forth as the cornerstone of utilitarianism. Contrary to the beliefs of Adam Smith, whose *The Wealth of Nations* appeared the same year as the American Declaration of Independence, Owen claimed that a man's "individual happiness can be increased and extended only in proportion as he actively endeavours to increase and extend the happiness of all around him." He argued that Adam Smith's culture of competition, which rewarded cruelty and punished poverty, which "brings ten thousand evils in its train," had to be replaced by a new culture of cooperation. The supremacy and dominance of Smith's political philosophy were due, Owen believed, to the West's nearly unshakable belief that humans are responsible for their own actions. The poor, therefore, deserve what they get, as do the rich. This, said Owen, was "the greatest of all errors," and as long as societies believed it, there would be no chance for "sincere love and extended charity." So Owen proposed, in *A New View of Society*, a guiding principle that became the mantra for the rest of his life: "It is of all truths the most important, that the character of man is formed FOR—not BY himself." Since all Owen's thinking, all his utopian scheming, rises out of that conviction, any success must ultimately rest on the education of children, the "passive and wonderfully contrived compounds" onto which Owen could graft his principles of human character. The best government was one that directed its chief attention to the formation of character, and that meant a program of universal education, or as Owen would have it, reeducation.

He looked around him and found that all the West's dominant institutions (the church, the banks, the police and prisons, and even private property and marriage) conspired against happiness and cooperation. They all, in one form or another, sowed discord and disharmony. They repressed, from infancy, our better natures. The world's religions served only to turn whole nations against one another. By extension, marriage, Owen wrote (much later, after his wife had died and after he refused to attend her funeral), "is the Satanic device of the Priesthood to place and keep mankind within their slavish superstitions, and to render them subservient to all their purposes." The exclusivity of marriage encourages "falsehood, secrecy and deception," he said, adding that it leads to prostitution. The banks encourage misery by ensuring a disparate distribution of wealth and, thereby, power. Prisons punish the poor and the powerless for crimes they committed only because an inhuman system kept them poor, and poorly educated. Rather than punishing crime, Owen argued, society should be reconstructed in a way that would never create criminals in the first place. He called this reconstruction the New Moral World.

Owen made quick work of the perennial nature-versus-nurture debate simply by declaring there was no nature—there was only good nurturing and bad nurturing. All we had to do, as a society, was identify the causes of evil and eliminate those causes through proper, rational conduct. The role of government was to encourage the "sentiments and habits" that would advance the happiness both of the individual and of the community. Encourage education and cooperation, abolish lotteries and gin shops. "You can," Owen promised, "if you will, train man to be a social animal, and to obey only social instincts; and with men so trained a community such as I propose cannot fail of success." In this way, Owen was a radical behaviorist a century before B. F. Skinner invented the term as a school of psychology. The superiority of this new "social system" was so compelling, so rational, so innately obvious that Owen believed it would trigger an immediate velvet revolution. Governments would cringe at their own obtuseness, and when the new system was adopted, "no complaints of any kind will be heard in society." Owen possessed the self-confidence of the self-made man, and critics who disagreed with him were ignorant, irrational, "mere children in the knowledge of the principles and economy of social life." Or they were charlatans.

By 1816, the end of the Napoleonic Wars and the mechanization of labor had created an unemployment crisis in Britain. Parliament formed a Select Committee on the Poor Laws, and that committee asked Owen for a few recommendations. What he gave them instead was a blueprint for a workers' utopia, a plan to right all the wrongs of the modern world. From that point on, Owen was no longer an industrialist with progressive views about workers' rights; he was the self-appointed messiah of modern socialism. He was about to birth upon the world nothing less than "the second creation or regeneration of man."

That process could begin with the problem of unemployment, which existed, in Owen's mind, because the poor labor for the wealthy instead of for themselves. But to Owen, the only honest, natural standard of value was labor. If one actually worked for something, or created something, then he or she should be remunerated, plain and simple. But to shift that value onto gold, as Britain had done, was to let loose all manner of corruption and graft. The few would unfairly accumulate a disproportionate amount of wealth, and because the measure of that wealth was an arbitrary metal, it could easily be manipulated to the advantage of the powerful, the nonworkers. Meanwhile, the working classes "were made slaves of an artificial system of wages, more cruel in its effects than any slavery ever practiced by society, either barbarous or civilized." Long before Marx and Engels, Owen established the fundamental economic principle of socialism: workers would control and profit from the means of production. Or, as Owen put it, in his own italics, *That which can create new wealth is of course worth the wealth which it creates.* The worker who creates the wealth, be it food or manufactured goods, justly deserves a large proportion of that wealth, not just wages or, worse, a pink slip. This, said Owen, would be the basis for a village devoted to communal well-being and cooperation. Under such a system, individuals would simply exchange for what they needed at cost, which would be based on the amount of labor that went into any particular thing.

Owen situated this new political philosophy—it became known simply as "the Plan"—in what he called a Village of Unity and Mutual Cooperation. This fortress-like quadrangle would stretch a thousand feet long on all four sides and rise three stories high. Three of the outer walls would house the adults in apartments with bedrooms that overlooked the gardens and orchards outside the village walls and sitting rooms that opened onto an inner square. Children would be bunked in dorms along the fourth wall in an effort to keep their impressionable minds free from the adult, pre-utopian prejudices of their parents. In the inner courtyard, "leaving free space for air and light and easy communication," there would stand the schools, kitchen, library, museum, dance hall, and even, Owen reluctantly conceded, a church.

Beyond the village walls would spread farms and manufacturing shops. Owen estimated it would take between three hundred and two thousand men, women, and children to make one unity village self-sustaining, but a population of eight hundred to twelve hundred would be ideal. The Owenites would eat together in an effort to build community and break down class lines, and because it was more efficient than placing a kitchen in every apartment. Owen also recommended that they dress alike in the comfortable, versatile manner of the Scottish Highlander. The purpose again was efficiency of production and minimization of class difference. Eventually, Owen suggested, his dress code would prove so successful that "fashion will exist only among the most weak and silly part of creation."

Owen's Plan had many admirers, including the founder of "free trade" economics, David Ricardo, who allowed that it could produce "considerable happiness, comfort and morality" for the lower classes. But Owen also had enemies, most notably church elders who resented that the Plan was not based on religious principles. Owen, possessing what Frank Podmore called an "instinctive aversion to reticence," responded to his critics in the most un-ameliorating tone imaginable. On August 21, 1823, he stood before the committee and pondered its understandable question: If Owen's Plan was indeed the cure for all the world's ills, why hadn't it been tried, or why hadn't it succeeded, before? The reason, Owen announced, was religion, pure and simple. Religion had perpetuated the ignorance and the superstition that kept all men and women, particularly the poor, in bondage to the powerful. What's more, religion had turned man into a "weak, imbecile animal," a "furious bigot," a "miserable hypocrite." While Owen had held up the Rappites and Shakers as proof that communism of property could work—they certainly were not hypocrites—now he seemed to be suggesting that those societies worked only because of their monolithic adherence to one doctrine. But for his plan to be scaled to an international level, the level of all humankind, religious sectarianism had to be abolished. "Therefore," he concluded,

> unless the world is now prepared to dismiss all its erroneous religious notions, and to feel the justice and necessity of publicly acknowledging the most unlimited religious freedom, it will be futile to erect villages of union and mutual co-operation; for it will be vain to look on this earth for inhabitants to occupy them, *who can understand how to live in the bond of peace and unity;* or who can love their neighbour as themselves, whether he be Jew or Gentile, Mahomedan or Pagan, Infidel or Christian. Any religion that creates one particle of feeling short of this, is *false;* and must prove a curse to the whole human race!

Owen would later refer to that speech as the turning point in his life. He had finally announced his religious views plainly, and the world could either join or condemn him. For the rest of his life, the world would do both.

Owen did attract to his cause the Duke of Kent, son of George III and father of Queen Victoria. So, in 1821, his proposal finally went before the House of Commons. All he asked was that one unity village be built and supplied with as few as five hundred men and women from the ranks of the unemployed. Then all would see the genius of his Plan, and the entire world would voluntarily adopt it, one unity village at a time. Some legislators feared that Owen would deprive his workers of private property or insinuate among them his heretical views on religion, but the overall objection to Owen's Plan was that it would turn men into lab mice. Lord Londonderry said the scheme was "by no means agreeable to the freelings of a free nation," and Joseph Hume added that it would reduce men to brutes "ranging the four corners of a parallelogram." The motion did not carry.

So Owen packed up his six-by-six-foot scale model of the unity village (he had paid a great deal to have it built) and began traveling the world, looking for a government willing to finance his grand experiment in social engineering. In 1823 he told an enthusiastic Dublin audience, "I will now disclose to you a secret, which till now has been hidden from mankind." The secret was Owen's unshakable belief that man is shaped only by circumstance: change the circumstances and you change man. And really, his philosophy was about that simple. Everything else (the infant schools, cooperative societies, common property) flowed from his blank-slate theory of human nature. Owen possessed the irritating habit of, once he hit upon an idea, loudly proclaiming himself the only person in history ever to have had that idea. But he was a powerful public speaker, and Ireland's House of Commons appointed a committee to study Owen's proposal. The result was the same as back home: because the plan was "so irreconcilable with the nature and interests of mankind," the committee found it "impossible to treat this scheme as being practicable."

Yet if Owen failed to start a Village of Unity, he hadn't failed to start a movement. Enthusiasm for that movement reached—if it can be believed today—to the highest offices of American governance. In *Backwoods Utopias*, the most reliable study of Robert Owen's influence in America, Arthur Bestor observed that "Owenism was more gospel than theory, and it needed to be preached rather than explained." In 1824, Owen came to preach it. During the five-week voyage from the Old to the New World, the loquacious Owen converted most of his shipmates to "the social science," or at least they led him to believe he had done so. Once ashore, he met with leading educators in New York and Philadelphia, and then proceeded south with a letter of introduction to President James Monroe. On his way west to purchase New Harmony from the Rappites, he dined with Thomas Jefferson, whose encouragement put the wind at his back. Then the indefatigable Owen met with Choctaw and Chickasaw chiefs, and with the man who would send the natives off on the Trail of Tears, General Andrew Jackson.

On Christmas Eve, Owen sat down with Frederick Rapp, George Rapp's son, in Albion, Illinois, and purchased twenty thousand acres and the entire village of New Harmony for $125,000. Word spread quickly through newspapers that the country's first secular experiment in utopianism would soon begin. Owen's scale model of the Village of Unity was put on display at the Rembrandt Peale museum in Philadelphia. On February 25, 1825, Henry Clay granted Owen access to the Hall of Representatives in the nation's capital so he could extol the virtues of his new system. President-elect John Quincy Adams attended, as did members of James Monroe's Cabinet, the Supreme Court, and Congress. Owen had arrived in this country at a time when his own agenda for social reform did not seem terribly at odds with the populist appeal of Jeffersonian and Jacksonian democracy. The word *socialist* certainly wasn't used as the bludgeon it is today to attack anything that threatens the current economy; in fact, it wasn't used at all until Owen arrived. He had not come to this country to attack its aspirations of life, liberty, and the pursuit of happiness. Rather, he had come to show a better path to such noble aims. Thus he explained his Plan to the Washington luminaries: "It is scarcely to be supposed that any would continue to live under the miserable, anxious, individual system of opposition and counteraction, when they could with ease form themselves into or become members of one of these associations of union, intelligence, and kind feeling." Today such words sound like an attack on a whole number of American values, but in 1825 they sounded to many like a bolder path to real democracy.

When Owen arrived at New Harmony, it was as if the Rappites had turned over an entire movie set to a director with a new cast and script. Looking back, many blamed the failure of New Harmony on Owen's first decision: to accept anyone (besides "persons of color"; even a classless utopia, it seems, could not violate the race barrier in America). When he had addressed Congress and the president in February 1825, Owen invited all "industrious and well-disposed" men and women to join him in New Harmony and begin "a new empire of peace and goodwill to men." Within six weeks of Owen's arrival in America, more than eight hundred collectivists had answered his call and found their way to the banks of the Wabash River. Who actually arrived, according to his son Robert Dale Owen, was a "heterogeneous collection of radicals, enthusiastic devotees to principle, honest latitudinarians and lazy theorists, with a sprinkling of unprincipled sharpers thrown in."

Owen could not immediately shape his ideal society out of such raw material. First these men and women had to be weaned from the evils of individualism and private property. On May 1, 1825, the Preliminary Society of New Harmony was formed; Owen, of course, wrote its constitution, whose preamble reads, "The society is instituted generally to promote the happiness of the world." It goes on to say that there will exist no "artificial inequality" at New Harmony, but since Owen bought and paid for the town, he would appoint a committee that would manage its affairs for that first year. Everyone would be given accommodation in return for rendering "their best services for the good of the society." Members of the society should always be temperate and kind. Using a credit system, they could exchange their labor for goods at the general store, and could run a debt, up to a point. Prices would be determined by the committee. Children could live with their parents or, as Owen recommended, they could live at a communal boardinghouse.

A month after everyone signed the constitution, Owen left the community's incubation in the hands of his son William, while he sailed to New Lanark on business, and then embarked on another propaganda tour of the United States. "While time ticked away," observed one commentator, "he turned his back upon the reality which was New Harmony in order to chase the phantom which was public opinion." Many of the Rappite shops had been taken over by new coopers, cobblers, tanners, butchers, and bakers, but more hands were still needed in the fields, where the planting had really begun too late. The official roster of workers listed only thirty-six farmers and two gardeners. Of the more than 800 residents at New Harmony, only 137 were employed in the numerous trade shops the Rappites left behind. What were the other 600 Harmonians up to? Apparently, not much. The only crop they seemed truly intent on cultivating was winter barley with which to make beer in the coming year (Owen's rule of prohibition notwithstanding). Overall, it seemed, New Harmony had attracted more theorists and sharpers than it had farmers and craftsmen. By the time Owen returned from New Lanark, consumption was greatly outrunning production, and the benefactor had to open his coffers again to keep the town afloat.

The Wabash is an unruly river that often jumps its banks, and as a result, a series of sloughs fill a dip in the terrain between the main body of water and the town itself. A pair of flat-shelled terrapins called cooters drop reluctantly from a fallen tree and into the stagnant water as Jim and I ride by on a gravel road that runs parallel to the river. Jim is telling me about plans he has (and that the town, he claims, ignores) for bringing more people to New Harmony. The rickety one-lane bridge to Illinois we pass under has been recently condemned as unsafe, which it surely looks to be, so there went five hundred travelers a day, according to Jim. Nor is there any boat traffic down here on the river. But on January 18, 1826, everybody from the newly formed town gathered on these banks to meet the venerate passengers of the flatboat *Philanthropist*.

Two months earlier, the eighty-five-by-fourteen-foot vessel had departed Pittsburgh for New Harmony, convening, in Owen's words, "more learning than ever was before contained in a boat." For once, he wasn't exaggerating. In his seven months away from New Harmony, Owen had persuaded a number of Philadelphia's leading intellectuals to join his experiment on the western frontier. First, he convinced William Maclure, who had presented the first comprehensive geological map of the United States to the American Philosophical Society in 1809, to invest part of his fortune in the New Harmony venture. Maclure, like Owen, was a Scotsman who had accrued early wealth and then abandoned his businesses for the realm of science and education. On the surface, the two men had much in common. Maclure had first visited Owen at New Lanark and had been intrigued by his efforts to "drown the self in an ocean of sociality." Owen's radical politics also appealed to Maclure, who believed the world was unfairly divided between the powerless working class and a nonproductive class who unjustly held all the power.

Such common purpose also convinced Philadelphia's most progressive educators, William S. Phiquepal and Marie Fretageot, to move their schools to New Harmony. Though married, the latter also set sail determined to become Maclure's mistress. (She succeeded.) The eminent zoologist Thomas Say decided to join the migration, as did the French naturalist-artist Charles Lesueur, who had executed the engravings for Say's classic *American Conchology*. Owen was right: the *Philanthropist* would convey by far the greatest concentration of scientists and intellectuals in the then-western United States.

In *Backwoods Utopias*, Arthur Bestor argued that Owen was so successful in attracting such a prominent group of educators west because there existed then—it's almost impossible to imagine now—such a strong link between progressive education and communitarian idealism. Education was the natural ally of radical social reform. Outside of a military coup, it had the potential to incite the most significant cultural change. Besides, what was a progressive school if not its own self-contained utopian experiment? When the French utopianist Charles Fourier set out to found his own phalanx, he wrote to Napoléon and requested five hundred children that the emperor's wars had just turned into orphans. Waiting down in New Harmony were not orphans, exactly, but rather hundreds of frontier children who knew nothing of a formal education.

The narrow flatboat was lined with four cabins for the crew, the men, the women, and the children. (Lesueur dryly designated the women's cabin "Paradise" and the children's "Purgatory.") On the second day, they all woke to find the hull ensconced in ice. Owen and Maclure quickly abandoned the river for a land route, but the other scientists on board busied themselves catching and stuffing fish for the natural history museum they would soon build in New Harmony. After a thaw, the *Philanthropist* followed a leisurely course downstream. Maclure rejoined the voyage, and the passengers passed the time reciting Byron and discussing the works of Charles Fourier. When the *Philanthropist* reached New Harmony five weeks later, Owen rechristened it the *Boatload of Knowledge*. Here was the cargo that would transform the children of New Harmony into perfect citizens of Owen's socialist utopia.

So buoyed was Owen by that prospect that he announced upon landfall that New Harmony's Preliminary Society had come to an end. The people, he declared, were now ready for a true state of socialism, and therefore the New Harmony Community of Equality should commence. Residents immediately elected seven men to draw up a new constitution. Owen and Maclure exempted themselves from participation, but two of Owen's sons, William and Robert Dale, took part in drafting the document, which began:

OUR PRINCIPLES ARE:

Equality of rights, uninfluenced by sex or condition, in all adults.

Equality of duties, modified by physical and mental conformation.

Cooperative union, in the business and amusements of life.

Community of property.

Freedom of speech and action.

Sincerity in all our proceedings.

Kindness in all our actions.

Courtesy in all our intercourse.

Order in all our arrangements.

Preservation of health.

Acquisition of knowledge.

The practice of economy, or of producing and using the best of everything in the most beneficial manner.

The constitution went on to paraphrase the Owenite philosophy of character formation by universal education. It blamed private property for creating a culture of competition, jealousy, poverty, and slavery, and then stated that humankind could be truly happy only in a state of "cooperative union." The new communards would (eventually) share similar food, clothing, housing, and education. Everyone would render his or her best service to the good of the whole, and everyone would partake in the fruits of that collective labor. To achieve these ends, the community would be divided into six departments: agriculture, manufacturing, literature-science-education, domestic economy, general economy, and commerce. Anyone over sixteen years of age could apply for work under one of these units. Meanwhile, all real estate would be held in perpetual trust, by Owen and Maclure, for community use.

For a while New Harmony must have been a convivial place. There were dances on Tuesday nights, public lectures and discussions on Wednesdays, and concerts on Fridays. An excellent bandleader named Josiah Warren had moved down from Cincinnati to teach music and conduct the makeshift orchestra. Participants also remembered a commodious street life in those early days as everyone tried to embody the motto on the *Gazette*'s masthead: IF WE CANNOT RECONCILE ALL OPINIONS, LET US ENDEAVOR TO UNITE ALL HEARTS.

Today, that sentence is set in concrete and mounted in the brick wall at the corner of Main and Church Streets. Dodging golf carts, Jim and I pedal past it as we head back into town, and then veer off onto a side street that dead-ends into a rather derelict one-story school building. Because of dwindling enrollment, Jim explains, the Indiana Board of Education closed the New Harmony Public School last year.

"That seems ironic," I say, "considering New Harmony had the first public school in the country."

"That's what we were all pissed off about!" says Jim, growing shaky on his bike.

He and other residents fought to keep the school open, but in the end, New Harmony had to pay the price for becoming what it essentially is: a retirement community. When an influx of well-heeled retirees moved to New Harmony, they made expensive improvements to the houses they bought. This drove up the property taxes, which kept younger families away. When Jim explains all this, I suddenly realize how quiet and sedate New Harmony feels. It's beautiful, of course. There's hardly a piece of vinyl siding to be found in the whole place, and the many Greek and Gothic Revival bungalows, combined with immaculately kept gardens, make a strong argument for New Harmony's continuation, in some modest form, of Robert Owen's communal aspirations. But it also has the effect of making New Harmony feel a little like a toy town, an ersatz version of the original dream. The town that once so directly hitched its utopian promise to education today has no school.

In 1826, however, both Owen and Maclure seemed convinced they could create a secular religion out of education, a communal enterprise that would replace the millennial theologies of the Shakers and Rappites. Only later did they realize how incompatible were their theories of education. Maclure's governing ambition was to level the world's class system, beginning in America, by making education available to all the working class and their children. Only through education could wealth and power be taken from the hands of the few and democratically distributed, he argued. Education was the great leveler. It would succeed because, as he wrote in *Opinions on Various Subjects*, there exists a "strong propensity of nature to equalize property, and consequently, knowledge and power, when not counteracted by force or unjust laws." Under Maclure's guidance, New Harmony quickly instituted this country's first infant school, its first kindergarten, its first higher school for children under twelve, and its first trade school. At New Harmony, this country's public education movement was born. And in 1851, twenty-five years after New Harmony failed, Robert Owen's son Robert Dale Owen, an Indiana legislator, became instrumental in writing public education into law.

Maclure based much of his thinking about education on the work of the Swiss reformer Johann Heinrich Pestalozzi. Under that system, children learned by doing and observing, not by reading or being lectured to. The individuality of the child was regarded as sacred. Children developed the power of the mind instead of merely acquiring knowledge through memorization. They were taught *to* think, not what to think. Almost incredibly, while the *Boatload of Knowledge* was passing through Louisville, Maclure found Joseph Neef, a prominent European Pestalozzian teacher who had retired to America to farm. Maclure convinced Neef to sell his faltering farm and join his crew in New Harmony.

Maclure was adamant that a practical education should replace a classical one. He lamented that "the absurdity of my own classical education launched me into the world as ignorant as a pig of anything useful," and he could be caustic about any literary subjects that involved "the delusions of the imagination." (Drawing for scientific purposes was allowed.) Classes concentrated on math, science, writing, languages, and music. The scientists who had arrived on the *Boatload of Knowledge* gave lectures in mineralogy, zoology, and natural history. Yet in a sense, the curriculum was secondary. In the Pestalozzian fashion, Joseph Neef insisted that "education is nothing else than the gradual unfolding of the faculties and powers which Providence chooses to bestow on the noblest work of this sublunary creation, man." The point of education was self-invention and self-discovery, and through that process, students would gradually learn to take on the roles of freethinking citizens, not merely servile workers.

It's easy to see how this approach veers far from Owen's idea that the child is an empty vessel into which virtue is easily poured. That tension would soon enough spell the demise of the Owen-Maclure partnership. Education would become both the great legacy of New Harmony and the thing that ultimately drove Owen to pull the plug on his utopian incubator. He wanted a classroom that, from the earliest ages, would provide a laboratory for his behaviorist model of character formation through passive indoctrination. Maclure stressed experiential learning and the development of a critical intelligence. Because there was an imbalance of power and property in the world, Maclure argued, working people should be taught not simply to be good Owenites, but actively to take back political power through the use of knowledge. To that end, he started at New Harmony the Working Men's Institute, in essence a library and meeting space for the common man and his family. Ultimately, 160 such institutes spread across the Midwest. Today, only New Harmony's still exists. Yet Maclure's idea was the germ of our modern free library system.

At its momentary height, nearly four hundred children attended Maclure's schools and one hundred of them boarded at the Harmonist Community House Number 2. Unlike the rest of the United States, New Harmony educated its girls as well as its boys. Sarah Cox Thrall, who attended the infant school, remembered many years later, "We went to bed at sundown in little bunks suspended in rows by cords from the ceiling." Sometimes the child at the end of the row would start swinging her cradle and set off a chain reaction of knocking cradles. "I saw my father and mother twice in two years," Thrall later told George B. Lockwood. Which was exactly what Owen and Maclure wanted: children loosed from the influence of their unenlightened parents—"the handicap of ignorant and immoral homes," as Maclure indelicately put it. With the biological parents out of the picture, Maclure believed he could inculcate an early egalitarianism in the children. At one point, the New Harmony teachers even planned to let the children form their own republic within the school.

What Maclure and Owen did agree on was the ancient Spartan model of education whereby educators took responsibility for a nation's children at a very early age. Studies published this year reveal how right Owen and Maclure were to emphasize what today we call early childhood development. They were also right that, as the Nobel-winning economist James. J. Heckman recently wrote, "Cognitive skills and character skills work together as dynamic complements; they are inseparable. Skills beget skills." A study called the Perry Preschool Project offered intensive two-year instruction to disadvantaged three- and four-year-olds from 1962 through 1967. The instruction emphasized cognitive skills, self-control, and perseverance. The participants were randomly assigned to treatment and control groups. Four decades later, children from the treatment group far outperformed the others in terms of education and general success in life. A similar study, the Carolina Abecedarian Project, offers similar instruction along with health care. Today, the students from the treatment group have higher IQs than the other participants and dramatically lower blood pressure, hypertension, and obesity. While Congress has steadily cut funding for what New Harmony called its infant schools, Heckman estimates, "The economic rate of return from Perry is in the range of six percent to ten percent per year per dollar invested, based on greater productivity and savings in expenditures on remediation, criminal justice and social dependency."

This suggests that nearly two hundred years later, we as a country still haven't quite caught up to Owen and Maclure.

Jim tells me he needs to replace some gutters on one of his rental properties, but that he could tour me around some of the more modern sights of New Harmony later in the afternoon. Left to my own devices, I decide to check out the archive at the Working Men's Institute. A large brick turret above the entrance dominates the two-and-a-half-story building. The original Working Men's Institute was housed in the Rappite church—the bricks from that church now form the wall around the Rappite cemetery—and its current home was bankrolled by a local physician, remembered only as Dr. Murphy. He was an Irish waif brought to Louisville by a brutal uncle in the early 1820s. The boy escaped to New Harmony, by boat, one supposes; he arrived starving and was taken in by the Owenites. Murphy's gratitude extended over many decades, and in 1893 he helped finance and furnish the current Working Men's Institute with books, paintings, and artifacts. Today, a nearly life-size, vaguely Pre-Raphaelite painting of George Rapp signing New Harmony over to Robert Owen dominates the stairwell (though the two men never actually met). The second floor functions as an archeological and natural history museum. A five-foot-long alligator gar lies stuffed in one case, a fish so menacing-looking that Audubon might have made it up for the unsuspecting Rafinesque. In another display case sits one of Robert Owen's fire-damaged Scales of Human Faculties. The numbers one through ten run across the top of this copper sliding scale; down the right side are listed the standards by which the character of each Harmonian should be measured, according to Owen: strength, courage, excitability, perception, reflection, memory, imagination, judgment, affection, self-attachment. Judging from the community's jaundiced response to Owen's other schemes for moral improvement, it can't be an accident that this artifact ended up on some bonfire.

The downstairs is part historical archive, part local library that seems to cater mainly to the children, or grandchildren, of New Harmony. I ask the librarian if I can look at some original issues of the community's propaganda organ, the *New Harmony Gazette*. When she retrieves the leather-bound volumes from a locked vault, I take a seat at one of the diminutive tables meant for much younger and smaller scholars.

The *Gazette* was an eight-page quarto weekly. Beneath the masthead run three columns of small, bunched type. There are no images in the paper, and the one bit of levity comes on the last page, where one column was reserved for "Songs for Children." The masthead of the July 12, 1826, edition reads on the left, FIFTY-FIRST YEAR OF AMERICAN INDEPENDENCE, and on the right, FIRST YEAR OF MENTAL INDEPENDENCE. Below is printed Robert Owen's Fourth of July address in the Public Hall, "A Declaration of Mental Independence." Owen himself hailed the speech as the most important American oration since the signing of the Declaration of Independence fifty years earlier (and he unknowingly delivered it on the day that both John Adams and Thomas Jefferson drew their last breaths). The political liberty granted by the founding fathers in 1776 had paved the way, announced Owen, for throwing off the mind-forged manacles that still held men and women in bondage. This "TRINITY of the most monstrous evils that could be" was "PRIVATE OR INDIVIDUAL PROPERTY—ABSURD AND IRRATIONAL SYSTEMS OF RELIGION and MARRIAGE, FOUNDED ON INDIVIDUAL PROPERTY COMBINED WITH SOME ONE OF THESE IRRATIONAL SYSTEMS OF RELIGION." Extrapolating from an old theme, Owen railed that religion had robbed man of his rational faculties and made him a slave through fear of "nonentities created solely by his own disordered imagination." Men, for example, claim this Being is all-powerful and good, and then profess not to understand why the All-Powerful allows evil into the world. As for marriage and private property, Owen hazarded that they came into the world simultaneously so that the powerful, propertied classes could claim, through marriage, all the beautiful women for themselves. The women, for their part, would "barter their feelings and affections for wealth" and end up tragically unhappy. Only when property and marriage were done away with could people truly choose their mates based only on their "highest happiness." This three-headed "HYDRA OF EVILS" was the real and only cause of all the world's crime and misery. Soon this truth, from Owen's lips to the Harmonists' ears, would spread across America by word of mouth, and "almost as fast as it shall be conveyed, human nature will recognize and receive it." Problem solved. Or so the self-deluding Owen believed. In reality, all he succeeded in doing was to bring down a storm of vituperation and condemnation on his fledgling town. "One great brothel," the *Indiana Journal* called New Harmony. The problem with boors is they never seem to recognize when they're being boorish.

What's more, it must have seemed obvious to the New Harmonians who listened to this declaration that Owen himself had not given up his own private property or his marriage—a marriage founded on property, if one wanted to argue that Owen courted Catherine Dale to more easily gain control of her father's cotton mill. The residents of New Harmony could make use of Owen's land, but ultimately he held the deed.

Still, in fairness to Owen, he was trying (though the point could have been made more persuasively) to call attention to the scandal that, in nineteenth-century America, a married woman must surrender many of the rights she enjoyed when single. Of course no woman could vote or hold political office, but a married woman in Indiana had to relinquish all she owned, including real estate, to her husband, who also retained legal control over any wages his wife might earn. Such women lived what the Indiana historian Timothy Crumin has called a "civil death." All this Owen would set right by abolishing not only marriage but private property. In that, his philosophy was no different from that of the abstemious Shakers, but whereas the Shakers set out to purify religion, Owen aimed to eviscerate it.

Robert Owen ended his own Fourth of July speech by calling on the people of New Harmony to "do away with individual money transactions by exchanging with each other your articles of produce on the basis of labor for equal labor." I flip through the bound pages of the *Gazette* until I find a prospectus, by a certain "C. S. Rafinesque," on how to do just that. The same man who bedeviled Audubon and supposedly put a curse on the Transylvania University president Horace Holley for firing him—Holley died a year later from yellow fever—had flirted with the idea of joining Maclure's scientific collective at New Harmony. After abruptly taking his leave of the Boones back in 1818, Rafinesque had journeyed west to visit the Rappites, and apparently, seven years later, he was still thinking he might lend his considerable intellect to the New Harmony experiment. However, it wasn't his knowledge of the natural sciences that Rafinesque offered up to Owen and Maclure—the latter had already tried to buy for New Harmony Rafinesque's extensive inventory of species—but rather his recent excursion into the realm of finance. In August 1825 the indefatigably curious Frenchman had patented a new method of banking that he called the Divitial Invention. "Divitial" meant, according to Rafinesque, "leading to wealth," and his new system would level the way lending worked at the beginning of the nineteenth century, and rein in irresponsible speculators. In Rafinesque's bank, a client could deposit any form of wealth and receive, in turn, Divitial Tokens, which, unlike standard certificates of deposit, could be divided to function as actual currency. They also would continue to earn interest while they circulated, and clients would be paid a 6 percent dividend at the end of each year. Under Rafinesque's system, loan companies could no longer pay depositors 6 percent but could charge 36 percent interest on loans, while the companies themselves ("usurious pawnbrokers") put up no capital to secure the risky loans. It seemed as if Rafinesque could already see from twelve years away the seeds of the financial Panic of 1837—or, for that matter, of 2008—and he could see that speculation and uncollateralized loans would bring the country to its knees. (In 1819, Rafinesque thought it risky that a bank could issue three paper dollars for every one dollar of capital in its coffers; when Lehman Brothers collapsed in 2007, it was leveraging thirty-five dollars for every dollar it held in equity.) Rafinesque's bank would force such speculators out of the game and invite in anyone, rich or poor, who could offer up some form of real collateral.

The Divitial Institution of North America and Six-Percent Savings Bank did open in Philadelphia in 1835 and was still succeeding on its founder's principles when, five years later, Rafinesque died a pauper, having been cut out of the bank's profits by a board of trustees that—the pattern continued to his death—didn't like him. Fourteen years earlier, though, our transient polymath saw an even more radical application for his Divitial Invention. In May 1826 the *Gazette* published one of his letters to "Wm. Maclure." In it, Rafinesque praised Owen's aspirations but suggested that the Scotsman had tried to do too much too fast and had let his own personal prejudices get in the way of what could have been a relatively simple exercise in "mutual cooperation" for "each other's good and happiness." Rafinesque had a plan that would "leave to every one a home and the fruit of his exertion; while it will remove all the evils for which the social system is a remedy." This plan would take money out of the equation entirely (except when dealing with strangers) and replace dollars with the Divitial Token, which its inventor now referred to as a ticket. What immediately had to be fixed in Owen's system was its allowance for shiftlessness. As Rafinesque wrote, "Our comforts are to be proportionate and commensurate with our exertions." Those who don't work don't eat. "The vicious, intemperate or dissolute will have no claim nor influence on the society (and as soon as known as such may be expelled)." But anyone who was willing to work would receive tickets that could be exchanged for anything in the community. These tickets would also be awarded for any property from land to hand tools. All "moveable property" would be deposited at a general store that would function like a massive pawn shop where anything could be deposited or withdrawn with tickets. A small group of trustees would determine how much everything was worth, and tickets would be distributed accordingly. Land could be rented with the tickets for farming, and individuals could choose to buy a house in town, if they had enough tickets, or rent a room in one of the Rappite boardinghouses. Perhaps most important of all, everything would be sold and exchanged at cost: there would be no profit margin or surplus value. In other words, "money" would no longer be a commodity, but only be a symbol of wealth, a ticket of exchange. And while the wealthy could certainly move to such a community, there would be no financial system in place whereby they could create more wealth through usury and speculation while adding no actual value to the town. The advantages of such a plan, argued Rafinesque, was that "every man, woman or child will be allowed to exert their talents, industry, or skill in any way, and receive at once an adequate compensation for the same in a medium of exchange." Given the fairness of that proposition, "There will be no longer any poor, since any one being able to obtain materials to work with at the common store, will do some work at home and provide for themselves."

Apparently nothing came of Rafinesque's proposal until a few years later, after New Harmony's collapse, when one of its members started the country's first cooperative store by inventing something akin to the Divitial Token: the labor note. But that's on down the road. For now, as I close the thick volumes of the *New Harmony Gazette*, the great eccentric Constantine Samuel Rafinesque finally drifts away from this story.

When I rise from my Lilliputian table and chair, I decide it's time for a late lunch and an early drink. The vernacular wooden façade of the Yellow Tavern is indeed very lemony. It stands in a row of businesses on Church Street, around the corner from its original location. That Yellow Tavern, built by the Rappites in 1815, burned down in 1908. In the resurrected version, a long oak bar runs down one side of the tavern's dark interior. At three o'clock the place is empty except for two middle-aged women who look to be five or six drinks ahead of me. I take a seat a couple of stools down from them and order a beer and a cheeseburger.

One of the women in particular has a list of grievances that she is ticking off to her companion.

"We're sorry we're being so loud," she calls down to me, over the music.

I shrug and say it's not a problem.

"This has just been a shitty day," she continues.

I nod.

"We're working our way up to hard liquor," she explains as a Stevie Nicks song begins to fill the empty space around us.

"Oh my god," she says, turning back to her friend, who is studiously peeling the label from her Bud Light. "I sang this song at our high school graduation. You remember?"

The friend nods morosely. I don't know Stevie Nicks's solo work well enough to identify the song, but it sounds vaguely aspirational.

"I was going to make something of my life," the woman laments. Then back to me: "I'm sorry we're being so loud!"

"It's a bar," I say by way of allowance.

"We want shots!" she calls down to the bartender. "Shots to celebrate a fucked-up day."

"A fucked-up life," her friend adds.

"A fucked-up life!"

Such intemperance Robert Owen hoped to stamp out of his original community, but he had little success, and these two middle-of-the-day drinkers would not have looked all that out of place in Owen's quickly unraveling town.

In early 1826 a certain Count Charles Bernhard of Saxe-Weimar-Eisenach, better known as the Duke of Saxe-Weimar, was touring the New World and writing a book about his impressions. When he reached New Harmony, the duke went straight to the original Yellow Tavern and fell into conversation with a man "plainly dressed, about fifty years of age, of rather low stature." When the duke finally asked where he might locate Robert Owen, his companion announced himself as the very man, at his lordship's service. Owen gave the new arrival a two-day tour of New Harmony, attendant with a running commentary. The duke took in a "surprisingly good" concert, and dinners and dancing. He toured the schools and George Rapp's distillery, which Owen said would soon be torn down in his failing quest for temperance. The duke learned that Owen "looks forward to nothing else than to remodel the world entirely; to root out all crime; to abolish punishment; to create similar views and similar wants, and in this manner to abolish all dissension and warfare." But the duke's keen eye noticed fissures in Owen's Plan. Attending a ball one night, he observed how all the pretty girls formed "a little aristocratic clique." One young woman, "delicately brought up, and appearing to have taken refuge here on account of an unhappy attachment," was reduced to tears when told it was time for her to leave the cotillion and milk cows. Her remaining companions "turned up their noses at the democratic dancers," the young workingmen who had the temerity to ask them onto the floor. Another woman complained, "If you could see some of the rough uncouth creatures here, I think you would find it rather hard to look upon them exactly in the light of brothers and sisters." In the end, like many before him, the duke observed of Owen, "He was so unalterably convinced of the result to admit the slightest room for doubt." Then he added, "It grieved me to see that Mr. Owen should be so infatuated by his passion for universal improvement as to believe and assert that he is about to reform the whole world, and yet that almost every member of his society with whom I talked acknowledged that he was deceived in his expectations." Owen seemed good at turning a blind eye to the realities that did not square with his own social theories. "The enjoyment of the reformer," he later confided to his private journal, "is much more in contemplation, than in reality."

The selfless virtues of New Harmony's second constitution proved so hard to implement that two weeks after its signing, the executive committee asked Owen to assume directorship of the community for one year, in effect making him the benevolent dictator he always wanted to be. Many of New Harmony's day laborers grew to resent the intellectuals who had arrived on the *Boatload of Knowledge*. An hour's work in the fields seemed as if it should count toward more than an hour of sitting and thinking. The intellectuals, for their part, thought just the opposite. Owen even reverted back to installing his "silent monitor" device—the four-color wooden block sits in a display case on the second floor of the Working Men's Institute—in the workshops to try to show who was and wasn't carrying his weight. But back in New Lanark, for all Owen's benevolence, he was still the employer, and the workers *had* to respond to his compulsive character-building schemes. And while everyone at New Harmony knew Owen was bankrolling the town, many felt free to ignore his heavy-handed attempts to bring production in line with consumption.

In the beginning, Owen had partly silenced critics of his Plan by pointing to the examples of the Shakers and the Rappites. Their only mistake, he said, had been to found their villages on the "superstition" of religion rather than on his social science. Now it was finally Owen's turn to learn some hard lessons about human nature versus nurture. As it was turning out, the genius of both Father Joseph Meacham and George Rapp was their belief that *only* religion could unify a community around a purpose higher than one's self or one's biological family. Years later, one former Harmonian, C. A. Burt, made this clinching distinction: "There are only two ways of governing a Community; it must be done either by law or by grace. Owen abolished law, but did not establish grace." However irrational the Shakers' and Rappites' theodicy may have seemed to Owen, their "social science" turned out to be far sounder than his. As in the Gospel miracle of the loaves and fishes, they provided for their own and had much left over to share or, in their case, sell. Owen's utopia, on the other hand, was running low on both social and monetary capital.

In the summer of 1826, two factions decided to form their own communities. One, called Macluria (though not founded by William Maclure), separated mainly due to religious differences with Owen; and the other, arbitrarily euphonious Feiba Peveli (so named by Stedman Whitwell, who, in lieu of performing any actual work at New Harmony, gave the world a system of naming towns by coordinating certain letters of the alphabet with certain latitudes and longitudes), was made up of English agrarian families who seemed to resent the condescension directed at them by Maclure's intelligentsia. Owen actually viewed the smaller communities as a good thing inasmuch as they resembled the smaller Shaker families within the larger village. It must have become clear by then, even to the myopic Owen, that like preferred like, and that he had made a mistake to think he could so quickly eliminate division of class, occupation, and religion. Meanwhile, the central community continued to flounder amid accusations of sloth, malingering, and outright subterfuge.

Finally, Maclure proposed that those who hadn't yet splintered off should be divided into three communities based on occupations: the Education Society, the Agricultural and Pastoral Society, and the Mechanic and Manufacturing Society. Maclure would lead the first society, and he paid Owen $37,000 for the property and buildings it would occupy. By this point, Maclure's priority was to disentangle his interests (the success of the New Harmony schools) from Owen's inept attempts to salvage his own utopian dreams. Owen, who probably didn't realize the extent of Maclure's defection, consented to the new plan, and the final configuration of his experiment got under way.

With the followers he had left, Owen instigated Sunday night meetings meant to further inculcate the community to his version of the Great Leap Forward. But these quickly broke down into acrimony.

"Suppose," said Paul Brown, a man most wedded to a purist interpretation of Owenism, and therefore Owen's thorniest critic, "one-third of the population should pledge themselves to go the whole way with you (into communistic association), would you be willing to go the whole way? Would you be willing to make common stock of your property?"

"Yes," Owen replied, "I am ready and will join you whenever there shall be a sufficient number who follow and understand the principles, and who will honestly carry them into effect."

But that day never came. The most productive members of New Harmony either were working to build Macluria and Feiba Peveli or were members of Maclure's Education Society. Gardens and fields were almost entirely neglected. According to Paul Brown, a pilfering spirit pervaded the place. At the end of the year, when Owen sold fifteen hundred acres of New Harmony to a land speculator named William Taylor, the last true believers knew that the grand experiment was over. Bitterly, some decided to hold a mock funeral for the town, complete with a casket and a procession down Main Street. Such a pantomime was obviously meant to embarrass Robert Owen, and the night before the wake, someone stole the coffin that symbolically held the corpse of America's first secular attempt at socialism.

On May 6, 1827, with three-fourths of his personal fortune spent, Owen announced that the parent community of New Harmony was officially dissolved and all who remained must either join one of the smaller communities or support themselves independent of Owen's largesse. The founder delivered a farewell address on the twenty-sixth. In it, he scattered blame to all but himself. The families who had joined him at New Harmony had been "trained in the individual system" and therefore had "not acquired those moral characteristics of forbearance and charity necessary for confidence and harmony." What's more, William Maclure had hijacked his educational system so that the children of New Harmony and, by extension, their parents were not molded into the unquestioning, servile masses that Owen needed for his scheme to work.

Owen hadn't failed New Harmony; New Harmony had failed Owen. So he lit out for Mexico to try to convince the future Mexican president Santa Anna to grant him a large swath of Texas to begin the experiment all over. That, like all Owen's later utopian projects, would come to nothing. For the rest of his life, he would continue writing and lecturing around the world; he would publish, in effect, the same book over and over again, keeping to his behaviorist beliefs and his conviction that the religiously sanctioned biological family—that "den of selfishness and hypocrisy"—

was the root of human unhappiness. By the end of his life, it was in fact Owen's biological sons who were paying their father an annual remittance that was his only source of income.

The reasons for New Harmony's failure are legion. Almost everything that could go wrong with Owen's experiment did. The charismatic leader spent too much time away from his flock, preaching the abstract virtues of socialism without actually sticking around to oversee their implementation. He didn't screen the applicants to his new moral world, and therefore ended up with a largely unskilled labor force and an even larger coterie of layabouts. He couldn't find a way to overcome deep cultural differences among his New Harmonians. Finally, his obsession with abolishing religion and marriage blinded him to more substantial causes of nineteenth-century poverty and inequality: namely, speculators, unscrupulous banks, industrialization, and chattel slavery.

It is perhaps irony or perhaps simply causation that New Harmony started to thrive almost as soon as Robert Owen left. His wealth had created a class of parasites in the town, and when the money disappeared, so did they. Macluria and Feiba Peveli continued on for some years, before converting to communities of privately owned family farms. Robert Dale Owen and the feminist Fanny Wright took over the *New Harmony Gazette*, rebranded it the *Free Enquirer*, and transformed the community newsletter into an important abolitionist paper and a champion of suffrage. William Maclure, no doubt relieved finally to be shed of Owen, started his own New Harmony periodical, the *Disseminator of Useful Knowledge*. The scientists he had brought to the edge of the American frontier began to publish some of the most important research of the early nineteenth century. The one school that survived the collapse was Maclure's School of Industry, where every pupil learned a trade that Maclure hoped would both bring some financial support to the school and serve the student later in life. While students learned everything from farming to taxidermy, the main trades emphasized were drawing, engraving, and printing. Students from the school produced copperplate engravings for Thomas Say's *American Conchology*, François André Michaux and Thomas

Nuttal's *The North American Sylva*, and Charles Lesueur's *American Ichthyology*. All told, the students produced more than thirteen hundred copperplates and printed works. This makes me wonder: What if a bankrupt John James Audubon had not been forced to flee Henderson, Kentucky, in 1818 and had instead printed his magisterial *Birds of America* right here in New Harmony? In 1826, just as the School of Industry was setting up, Audubon was sailing for Liverpool on a merchant ship to find a British engraver for his life-size bird drawings. In England, Audubon was greeted as a real-life Natty Bumppo, and he became famous. But some part of me—and some part of Audubon—wishes he had never left the shores of the Ohio. With his 435 paintings of American birds, the likes of which the world had never seen, he might have made the New Harmony experiment memorable for something other than its early demise.

Another inadvertent success of the Owen legacy is that when the frustrated reformer left New Harmony, he left behind almost his entire family. All his sons chose to remain in that fertile bottom-land on the American frontier. His only surviving daughter, Jane, married and settled there as well. David Dale stayed to complete Indiana's first extensive geological survey, and in 1839 he was appointed the U.S. geologist. Richard, an excellent geologist himself, eventually became the president of Purdue University. But it was Robert Dale Owen who made the most lasting impression on the state. He became a six-term legislator in the Indiana General Assembly and supported President Lincoln's Emancipation Proclamation when it was far from fashionable to do so in the western territories. In 1851 he wrote the final draft of the state's constitution, and later, as a member of Congress, he was instrumental in creating the Smithsonian Institution. More than anyone else in the state, he pushed legislation that eventually led to an Indiana public school system. In that, he fulfilled William Maclure's dream for New Harmony, if not his father's.

In the late afternoon, I wait for Jim Stinson at North Street and Main, beside one of the original public bread ovens the Rappites built on every street corner. Each morning, one person would bake enough bread for her or his block. By the looks of it, this sturdy stone oven could be brought back into operation. When Jim does come tooling along on his bike, its seat having fallen so low that his knees almost hit him in the chin, we leave historical New Harmony behind for the decidedly postmodern world of the architects Philip Johnson and Richard Meier. First we pedal past the Roofless Church, a rectangular brick fortress that Johnson built in 1960. Two massive iron gates open at one end, and at the other stands a three-story dome covered in cedar shingles and built to resemble an inverted rose. Just past the Roofless Church, near the banks of the Wabash, looms Meier's Atheneum, a sprawling circuitry of staircases, ramps, and skylights, all sheathed in the architect's trademark white enamel panels. I ask Jim how New Harmony could afford commissions by two of America's most famous architects?

"I like to say Prozac built New Harmony," Jim avers as we watch two young men with long-handled brushes scouring the Atheneum's countless panels. Or, to be more precise, it was built with the profits from Indiana antidepressants and Texas crude. In 1941 a Houston oil heiress named Jane Blaffer married Kenneth Dale Owen, a descendent of Robert Owen. When the two were in New Harmony, they stayed at the original Rapp House, where this morning Jim tried to talk our way in to see Gabriel's footprints. Jane Owen quickly took New Harmony on as a personal project, and her preservationist zeal continued for the next seventy years, until her 2010 death at age ninety-five. In the 1960s and '70s she convinced Eli Lilly and Company of Indianapolis, the maker of Prozac, to match millions of its dollars with millions of her own. The Lilly Foundation took a particular interest in supporting state projects, and money flowed into New Harmony.

The Atheneum—its name comes from a Greek temple dedicated to the goddess of wisdom and the arts—sits on a small bluff just out of the Wabash floodplain. "Some people ask why we put the sewer plant in such a conspicuous place," Jim says with a laugh. Certainly one can see how a visitor might mistake the Atheneum's spiderweb of industrial stairs and walkways for something other than world-class architecture. There is a strange, almost puritanical beauty to the Atheneum. With its absence of color and its hard angles, the structure seems at once to absorb and resist the lush landscape around it. As we circumnavigate the building on our bikes, I decide that it is best seen from the river, where a sinuous wall evokes the curves of the Wabash itself. Yet what I find ultimately frustrating about the Atheneum are the signs at the base of every outer staircase that read UNLAWFUL TO PROCEED BEYOND THIS POINT. If, as the architecture scholar Ben Nicholson writes, the Atheneum "is really *the* essay for the United States of movement," what does it say that visitors are prohibited, by law, from moving through much of it? The longest set of stairs stretches from the river toward the town itself, suggesting, in the words of the American Institute of Architects, "a gleaming gateway between what is and what might be." That's fine: I like this idea that the stairs harken back to the arrival of the *Boatload of Knowledge* and the decamping of the men and women who came to build this midwestern utopia. Yet today's "gleaming gateway" is closed to the public. Those same stairs also wind up to an observation deck at the top of the Atheneum, which Meier meant as an homage to the rooftop balcony over at the Rapp House, where, as with the Shaker elders, the Harmonist founder liked to observe (and enforce) the chaste comings and goings of his followers. No one can get up there, either. A cynic might say this is indeed one of the most utopian buildings in the country in that it seems an almost complete divorce of form and function. Useless stairs, utopian stairs.

Since the Atheneum functions as the visitor center for New Harmony, Jim and I go inside to ask the woman at the front desk about all the building's prohibitions. She seems surprised by the question, claims not to know, and then says something vague about safety concerns. When she turns away, Jim confides in a whisper,

"A friend of mine calls it the Ass-eneum." All around us, light, broken into grids, pours into the vaulting emptiness. Up the ramp, on the second floor, stands a diorama of the original Rappite village, and against the curved wall overlooking the river are display cases sparsely furnished with a few fossils from the times when massive four-legged megafauna ruled these parts. Yet, really, the interior of the Atheneum constitutes what my mother would call a poor use of space. Then it occurs to me that perhaps the Atheneum really isn't supposed to be an embodied space at all. On the wall closest to the entrance, muted gray letters spell out the question WHAT'S YOUR VISION OF UTOPIA? The Atheneum, in its absolute white purity, stands as its own answer. It is not so much a building as an idea—or the embodiment of an idea. If the meetinghouse back at Pleasant Hill looks like an architectural manifestation of a Piet Mondrian abstract painting, it is still a beautiful melding of form (outward asceticism) and function (a place for the Shakers to dance). Yet the Atheneum has virtually no function beyond selling postcards in its gift shop. It is, or so it seems to me, a self-referential monument to the impossibility of utopia. Bleached of even the meetinghouse's most primary colors, it stands as a monument to, and a parody of, the abstract severity of Robert Owen's great Plan.

It is a relief, then, to coast next door to Philip Johnson's Roofless Church. The stark, rectangular brick wall that frames the "church"—that wall *is* the church—owes something to the less-is-more aesthetic of Johnson's mentor, Mies van der Rohe. The shingled dome (the inverted rose) inside the church does not. "Unto thee shall come a golden rose . . ." reads the inscription on the cornerstone, a line from the prophet Micah that foretold the coming millennium, or so believed George Rapp, who adopted said rose as a symbol of the Harmonists. The tips of Johnson's vaulting cedar petals are anchored with footers cut from the same local Oolitic limestone in which Rapp claimed to have found Gabriel's footprints.

When Jane Owen first met Johnson in the 1950s, she decided that he had "the poetry in his soul" to carry out her vision of a church in which "only one roof is wide enough, broad enough, for all worshiping humanity: there has to be the sky as our roof." Jane Owen, who studied in New York with the theologian Paul Tillich, seemed determined finally to bring religion, or at least spirituality, to Robert Owen's godless utopia. Yet apparently the heretical gene was strong in the Owen line, because Kenneth Dale shared none of his wife's ecumenical aspirations for New Harmony.

"He was a farmer," Jim tells me; "he was grounded in the business of breeding cattle. This church was too much pie-in-the-sky for him." So on the day of the Roofless Church's official dedication in 1960, Kenneth Dale Owen hired a truck-mounted steam calliope to drive around the church and play circus music during the ceremony. His wife was mortified, and soon afterward the Owens took up residences in separate houses across the street from each other. Still, for many years to come, Jane Owen, in her golf cart, was a fixture on the streets of New Harmony, and according to Jim, the town returned her affections. She brought to New Harmony a first-class restaurant and inn, along with a contemporary art gallery where, in 2007, she could be seen cavorting among Andy Warhol's silver Mylar balloons. Townspeople readily accepted her reinterpretation of New Harmony if it meant free outside money and the attendant tourists who followed.

Kenneth Dale Owen died at ninety-eight in 2002, but at the fiftieth-anniversary dedication of the Roofless Church, some locals rented a calliope from the Evansville Hadi Shrine Temple. "We had it playing very softly," one of them said in a local article, "as a tribute to Kenneth. And Jane thought it was a fun touch." She died that fall at age ninety-five. By then, New Harmony was filled with prayer gardens and meditation fountains and a granite labyrinth that replicates the one carved into the stone floor in the Chartres Cathedral.

I ask Jim if, despite Robert Owen's best efforts, there is indeed some spiritual wellspring that brings people to New Harmony. He replies, "People kept saying to me, 'I don't know why I'm here, but this place has a real spiritual draw for me.' When you start hearing it not from one, two, or three people, but from a lot of people, you start to take it seriously." Jim, for his part, attributes all this good feeling to the native burial mounds one finds throughout this part of the country. He even mentions the 1994 reburial at Mount Vernon (over archeologists' strenuous objections) of three thousand Hopewell burial relics that were recovered from the black market. If Jim's right, then maybe Robert Owen was simply no match for the mound builders, the Rappites, and Jane Owen.

Standing beside a small grove of linden trees—a grove made sacred, one might say, by its presence inside Johnson's high brick walls—I am beginning to feel a vague inner stirring myself. I tell Jim that I think I might sit for a spell on one of the stone benches beneath the trees and reflect on my day in New Harmony. We shake hands, and I thank him for being such an excellent tour guide.

"Hey, no problem. In fact, if you want to stay another night, I'll knock ten dollars off the price."

I had planned to hit the road tonight and get a jump on the long slog across Indiana, but it seems as if Jim could use the extra scratch, so I say sure.

When he leaves, I'm the only person left in the Roofless Church. I think back to what the Pleasant Hill gardener Zach Davis said about the word *paradise* deriving from the Persian word for enclosure. He said that a framed space, like his garden, gave that space a feeling of wholeness and sacredness. The first-century Roman author and architect Vitruvius, in his treatise *On Architecture*, wrote approvingly of *hypaethral* temples—ones "open to the air." Such a sentiment suggests that we should rather think of the entire world as what Henry David Thoreau called "the poem of creation." It's an idea that has always been important to Romantic poets: think of Dorothy Wordsworth telling visitors that her brother's real study was the lakes and heaths surrounding Dove Cottage; or of John Clare saying that he simply found his poems lying in the fields. Wendell Berry, a present-day poet with a deep Romantic streak, has written, "There are no unsacred spaces. / There are only sacred and desecrated spaces." That is surely an expansive view of the natural world, one that I happen to share, yet we seem to need some form of demarcation, Pleasant Hill's wooden fence or Philip Johnson's brick walls, to remind us of this idea. We are surrounded by too many desecrated places. We are surrounded by so much that we simply do not see.

I feel a deep sympathy for Philip Johnson and his Roofless Church as I sit inside it, here beneath the dome of creation. By framing the sky, these walls have the effect of calling the heavens *down* into this realm, the chthonic world of linden trees and human beings. It seems to affirm, to intensify, Thomas Merton's claim that the world is wholly transparent and the divine is shining through it at all times. If only we could see it.

However, not every visitor has been so sanguine about the Roofless Church. Take the architecture historian Charles Jencks, who wrote that after Johnson finally escaped the influence of Mies van der Rohe, the rest of his work was "entirely Camp—a demonstration of his impeccably perverse taste and motivated by historicist allusions." Jencks goes on: "Hence the entrance to the Roofless Church which recalls those of so many Nazi Villas." It's a rather startling statement, especially when you consider that those gates, which are admittedly gaudy, open onto a memorial garden for the theologian Paul Tillich, whom Hitler fired from his position at the University of Frankfurt for speaking out against the Third Reich. Tillich fled to the United States in 1933 to teach at the Union Theological Seminary—where Jane Owen was his student.

In 1963, Tillich came to New Harmony to deliver an Easter sermon at the Roofless Church. Titled "Estranged and Reunited— the New Being," Tillich's message spoke directly to Jane Owen's ecumenical belief that only the sky was wide enough to reconcile all religions. Jesus, after all, was not a "Christian"—Tillich didn't come out and say this, but he implied it—but rather a wandering Jew who experienced what Tillich called alternately a New Creation, a New Reality, a New Being. One's religion isn't important, said Tillich; what's important is to enter into that same transformative religious state in which Jesus dwelled. "The New

Creation—this is our ultimate concern," said Tillich, "this should be our infinite passion—the infinite passion of every human being." What is it, this new state? A threefold renewal of re-conciliation, re-union, re-surrection. First we must be reconciled to God and to ourselves, since at the core of our innermost self is where we find the presence of God. Next one must be reunited with oneself; that is to say, one must accept oneself wholly—one must have what Tillich called in another context "the courage to be": to be oneself. With that acceptance comes the ability to accept, find union with, others. James Baldwin wrote in *The Fire Next Time* that the reason so many white Americans hated black Americans was that, in reality, they hated themselves. And Martin Luther King, Jr., in his "Letter from Birmingham Jail," quoted Tillich's definition of sin as nothing more than separation: our separation from God and from one another. Finally, said Tillich, we must be resurrected from the Old Being of separation into the New Being of wholeness. He rejected the literal meaning of resurrection, the raising of the dead, for this psychological manifestation of a spiritual rebirth. "Where there is a New Being," Tillich concluded, "*there* is resurrection, namely, the creation into eternity out of every moment of time." Which is to say: "Resurrection happens *now*, or it does not happen at all." The kingdom of God, after all, stands right before us, made all the more obvious by its delineation inside the frame of the Roofless Church. It's somewhat stunning to think of this idea—one so important to John Dunlavy and the Shakers, and to Thomas Merton—expressed again here in the country's first secular utopia.

I walk through the objectionable gates of the Roofless Church and into the Tillich Garden, where the theologian's ashes were scattered. A short path winds through a kind of mounded labyrinth, planted only with Norwegian spruce trees. Beside the trail sits a large white stone embossed with this Tillich sentence:

MAN AND NATURE
BELONG TOGETHER
IN THEIR CREATED GLORY—

I don't know the context in which this sentence was written, but I like the sentiment, which I read to mean: We were not inexorably cast out of the original Garden, separate from nature. We can, as Tillich would say, be resurrected back into that unity with the natural world. Certainly the Enlightenment idea that man stands above nature has caused much of the environmental havoc in my home state—the blasting apart of mountains because we have figured out how to blast them apart but have not figured out a reason, perhaps even a religious reason, not to. Our tragedy, as Thomas Merton might say, is our perception that we are divided from God and nature; our salvation is the realization that we are not. That realization would constitute a New Being, a New Reality.

After dinner at the Yellow Tavern, I take a long walk beside the river, where fish are jumping near the shore and tree swallows dart out over the water, plucking insects from its surface with fantastic velocity and torque. When the river road leads me back to the Atheneum, it is dusk and Richard Meier's white porcelain building seems almost to glow in the day's last, pale blue light. I feel something, I can't say quite what, drawing me to it, and I am suddenly seized by the conviction that I must hurdle its low gates and ascend to the observation deck at the top of this alabaster beacon. In no time I sprint up three flights of stairs and am standing at the highest elevation in New Harmony. I cast my gaze over the town George Rapp laid out along a small grid two hundred years ago. Much of it is now obscured by the mature oaks and maples that line the streets. But between the town and the river, I can see the cemetery where many of the Rappites who died of mosquito-borne malaria are buried. They lie in unmarked graves, as do the indigenous people whose mounds stand close by. Off in the distance, I see the hillside where many of Robert Owen's descendants are buried, some beneath elaborate headstones. They wanted to be remembered here in New Harmony, one supposes, not for the failure of Robert Owen's utopia, but for the very attempt. For the possibility, the fortitude. If Owen's methods were misguided, his vision was not. He could see a future purged of cruelty and want. And it must be said, his influence remains scattered but sustained. Any modern form of socialism that isn't based on a centralized state apparatus owes something to the man. In the end, here in New Harmony, his vision failed him. But like the Atheneum, reaching down around me from the river to the town, from the darkling past to the unformed future, it was a beautiful failure.

A Simple Act of Moral Commerce

The next morning, I'm making good time through southern Indiana, breezing past the half-mile stock car tracks, grain silos, and a sign advertising "show pigs." The plan for today is to make it from one side of the state to the other, and into Ohio by the time the Cincinnati Reds take the field against the Pittsburgh Pirates at 7:10. When I cross the White River, I notice a flagpole flying a faded Stars and Stripes right out in the middle of the water. Then suddenly, outside the town of Shoals, a swarm of black police cars and an ambulance start hurtling past me. Before I realize what's happening, their tires squeal into a roadblock formation and the police are shouting and waving frantically for everybody to get off the road. I'm too far behind the other cars, and apparently a couple of blessed minutes too late, to see a man walk out of a gun store that he had just robbed and shoot a cop in the parking lot with one of the stolen guns. The fugitive took off through the cornfield, and if we had had a drier spring and the farmers had gotten their crop in the ground earlier, he might have gotten away. But there's no place to hide among corn that's only two feet tall, and the shooter was quickly apprehended. As the wounded officer is being loaded into the ambulance, a local guy is going from car to car, recounting the sequence of events. We sit still for an hour until the police reroute traffic through a small farm community. As our caravan crawls along, I feel my wanderlust beginning to cool. There are, after all, other men like this shooter driving these same roads, looking to do harm. I start thinking about the Terrence Malick film *Badlands*, Flannery O'Connor's short story "A Good Man Is Hard to Find," and the banality, or at least the pervasiveness, of evil. Once, while I was taking a long drive through the Adirondacks with the writer Ginger Strand, she casually stopped to mail a letter to a long-distance trucker named Adam Leroy Lane, who was doing seventy-five years for the murder of two women who had the misfortune of living, and thus dying, near truck stops. Ginger said highway killers were the subject of her next book, and in her research, she'd found this dissonant artifact: a 1958 *U.S. News & World Report* article about the *Badlands* killer, Charles Starkweather, that ran on the same page as a piece about signage for the country's new interstate highway system. An illustration of a sample sign read:

METROPOLIS

UTOPIA

2 MILES

But as Charlie Starkweather and Adam Leroy Lane have proven, the American highway, or even a long two-lane road like this one, can be a decidedly dystopic place. Speed and anonymity make it so.

For hours, this long line of traffic creeps through the cornfields of Indiana, slower than someone walking. All around me this vast monoculture reaches to the horizon. I watch a farmer drive up and down the rows, spraying chemical fertilizer from a large tank mounted on the back of his tractor. I remember what Zach Davis said back at Pleasant Hill about the eyes-to-acres ratio on the American farm. Zach had two eyes for two acres; this

Indiana farmer has two eyes for who knows how many hundreds, maybe thousands, of acres. Thomas Jefferson once envisioned the United States as an agrarian nation made up of "God's chosen people"—that is, those who worked the land. Today farmers make up about 1 percent of the U.S. population. And most of that 1 percent does very little that resembled farming in Jefferson's day, or even fifty years ago. Most spend their time like the man on this tractor: driving and spraying. Which is why there are so few farmers still around: their work has been mechanized into something that requires very few people, but hundreds of thousands of oil tankers. Careful observers have pointed out that today, in every sense except the most literal one, what we eat is mostly oil. Oil drives the heavy machinery of the modern factory farm, it is the basis for the chemical fertilizers and pesticides that this farmer is spraying, it fuels our heavily processed food, it provides the main ingredient in the packaging of that food, and of course it powers the semi-trucks that carry food farther and farther every year. Except for cars, the food system uses more fossil fuel than any other part of the modern economy. Much of the corn that surrounds me right now will be turned into, not food, but fuel. The rest will become high-fructose corn syrup or will go to feed cows, ungulates whose stomachs haven't evolved to eat corn. Which is to say, we've created, over the last fifty years, an incredibly perverse kind of farming, and farm policy, in this country. The reason we've done so is that, like almost every other part of our economy, such a system benefits the wealthy few—the big oil companies and corporations such as Cargill and Monsanto, who make all the fertilizers, the pesticides, and the patented seeds that resist those pesticides.

In fact, the very same volatile compound being used to blow apart the mountains of central Appalachia for coal—that is, ammonium nitrate—is the same chemical fertilizer that the Indiana farmer is spraying on his corn. A good portion of it will wash down the White River and contribute to a dead zone in the Gulf of Mexico that is now the size of Connecticut. The reason these farmers use such fertilizer to begin with is because there was so much of it left over from bomb material after World War II. Also, it was cheaper and easier than fertilizing the natural way, with animal waste from the farm. So the animals were moved off the farm and warehoused in enormous feedlots, where their waste, once a free fertilizer, has become a real health concern for both the animals and the communities living around the feedlots, which the EPA calls concentrated animal feeding operations, or CAFOs. Each cow in a CAFO requires six barrels of oil to keep it in corn when it should be feeding on grass and fertilizing the farm as it ranges.

The chemical fertilizers and pesticides that drove the so-called Green Revolution that began in the 1960s were supposed to raise yields and feed the world; fifty years later, there are far more hungry people in the world (eight hundred million), and farmers have to spray more and more fertilizer because the ammonium nitrate itself has depleted the soil of natural nutrients, just as it has increased erosion by destroying microorganisms and breaking down the fundamental structure of the soil. What's more, the Green Revolution, financed by the World Bank and the World Trade Organization, pushed small farmers off their land the world over and forced poorer countries to grow export crops, such as fruit and cotton, for the richer countries and to import from the richer countries the food they used to grow themselves.

The defense for such a counterintuitive way to meet our most basic needs has always been that bigger farms produce larger yields. But according to the 1992 U.S. Census of Agriculture report, smaller farms are actually two to ten times more productive per unit acre than larger ones. And as this country's foremost agricultural researcher, David Pimentel, points out, smaller, organic farms "not only use an average of 30% less fossil energy but also conserve more water in the soil, induce less erosion, maintain soil quality, and conserve more biological resources than conventional farming does." Of course, such farms are not growing huge monocultures of commodity crops; they're usually growing a diverse range of animals and plants—ones that people can actually eat.

I think about the Indiana farmer disappearing into the distance on his tractor, putting himself at risk of non-Hodgkin's lymphoma because of the chemicals he sprays, and I think about Zach Davis, back at Pleasant Hill, methodically picking potato beetles off his plants. To farm Davis's way, David Pimentel's way, Thomas Jefferson's way, will obviously require a lot more eyes on the acres. It will require us to think about agriculture as not just a biological and economic act, but also a cultural and political act, perhaps even a spiritual act. For Jefferson, being a good farmer made one a good neighbor and a good, freethinking citizen. "Corruption of morals in the mass of cultivators," he wrote, "is a phenomenon of which no age nor nation has furnished an example." Jefferson's farmer was resourceful and independent. He wouldn't bend to a foreman on a factory floor. To support farmers such as Zach would make us good neighbors as well, neighbors who maintained an independent local economy and at the same time did our part to keep soil in place, keep toxins out of the water, and cut the distance of supply lines. Does that sound too utopian? Maybe. But right now farmers' markets are the fastest-growing part of the food economy in this country. And to ensure that we produce fewer drive-and-spray farmers and more like Zach Davis, we have to do only one profoundly simple thing: buy what they grow. In the presence of increasingly undeniable climate change, there is no way we can continue eating oil. We cannot eat in the next fifty years the way we did during the last fifty. We'll have to convert to sun and soil, grass and natural fertilizers. We'll once again have to make nature the measure of our most basic human and animal act: eating.

As it turns out, because of a lone gunman and the bottleneck he created, I don't make it to the Reds game until the middle of the third inning. This means, at least, I can easily find a scalper willing to unload an excellent ticket behind home plate for only twenty bucks. Now that the day's heat has dissipated, it's a perfect night for baseball. As I settle into my seat with two bratwursts and a ten-dollar beer, an orange sunset spreads out across the Ohio River behind right field. When I was a kid, the slick new Riverfront Stadium, with its gleaming white façade and unnaturally green Astroturf, *was* my definition of utopia. In 1975, the year of the Big Red Machine, I kept a daily scrapbook of the season. And though I was a catcher on my Little League team, it wasn't Johnny Bench but rather the Reds' third baseman, Pete Rose, who was my guy. Even today, when I see old footage of the now-disgraced Rose tearing around the bases, turning singles into doubles with a kind of animal ferocity, my heart races a little. I feel like I'm watching an artist. In 1978, Rose strung together a forty-four-game hitting streak. Once it became clear that he was on a streak, and that he might break Joe DiMaggio's 1941 record, my stepfather and I watched every one of those games together on the TV in our basement family room. On July 19, facing the Phillies, Rose had gone 0 for 4, and it didn't look like he would bat again. But the Reds rallied in the ninth to get Rose to the plate. And when, to everyone's surprise, he laid a bunt down the third base line and beat it out, my stepfather and I leapt into an embrace with the kind of pure, unself-conscious joy we seldom displayed around each other.

In the previous two seasons, the Reds had won consecutive World Series against the Red Sox and Yankees. Soon, free agency would fritter away the team, but baseball writers still talk about the '76 Reds in the same breath as the '55 Dodgers and the '27 Yankees—the best teams of all time. In 1984, Rose ignominiously returned to manage the Reds, and bet on the team. In 1989, Commissioner Bart Giamatti banned him from baseball, for life. Tonight, outside the new ballpark, one vendor sells a shirt that reads I'M WITH PETE . . . GIVE ME TWO HUNDRED ON THE REDS. Off the field, Rose turned out to be a real piece of work. The stories about his public boorishness abound. A friend of mine once served him and two much younger women drinks all day at Turfway racetrack, but on a three-hundred-dollar bar tab, Rose left no tip. This year, he and his new, highly augmented wife had a short-lived reality show in which Rose came off as vaguely racist and unvaguely dumb. And while I've never believed one can derive great life lessons from the world of sports, I still puzzle over how Pete Rose could be so beautiful on the diamond and such a disappointment beyond its baselines.

Over the years, the Astroturf faded so badly at Riverfront that you could hardly make out the ball coming off the bat, and in 2002 the city demolished the stadium to build its new boutique ballpark. I could do without the ersatz steamboat stacks (the "PNC Power Stacks") that shoot off fireworks after a Reds home run, but I like the natural grass and narrow foul lines that let you sit closer to the action. Tonight the Jumbotron camera sweeps over the crowd, and whom does it stop on but—Pete Rose? Here he is, still banned from baseball but not, apparently, from sitting in the stands, taking in a game. The crowd gives him a standing ovation, and the Jumbotron declares, "4,246 hits—greatest of all time!" (When Mickey Mantle heard Rose had broken the hit record, he supposedly said, "If I hit that many singles, I would have had to wear a dress.") Rose looks to be aging badly, but I still feel nostalgic for what he used to be, for what the team he captained once meant to me.

Awash in such memories, it finally occurs to me that I forgot yesterday was Father's Day. Or maybe I didn't really forget. The last time we were together, my stepfather and I got into an argument in a restaurant over, of all things, Cincinnati's Creation Museum, which maintains that the world is only 6,006 years old. My stepfather had just visited it with some of his church friends and had become convinced that the earth was indeed very young. With my wife punching my leg under the table, I raised my voice about the fossil record and said some uncharitable things that I now regret.

Now I dial my stepfather's number on my cell phone, and when he answers, I lamely suggest that, on the road, one loses track of what day it is.

"Where are you?"

"I'm at a Reds game," I say, hoping that this one constant in our lives will assuage hurt feelings.

"Hey, I can hear it! What's the score?"

"Nothing to nothing," I say, and just then, the Reds shortstop Zack Cozart uncorks a home run to left field, and the applause drowns out our voices.

The next morning, I leave my motel early and walk a few blocks past some well-preserved art deco architecture to the corner of Fifth and Elm. This is where I stood thirty-seven years ago to watch the parade for the returning World Series champs. And this is where, 150 years before that, a veteran of New Harmony, a man named Josiah Warren, started the county's first cooperative store.

All of the reformers I have written about up to this point are the subjects of numerous biographies, and the communities they founded, such as Pleasant Hill and New Harmony, still stand as monuments to a more idealistic age. Then there's Josiah Warren. Though he is generally regarded as this country's first anarchist and the founder of the country's first successful anarchist villages, no historical sites honor his memory, and the only biography, William Bailie's short monograph, is long out of print. Yet, in an age defined by financial graft and economic inequality, Josiah Warren remains curiously relevant in a way other nineteenth-century utopianists do not.

Of course today, when we think of anarchists, we usually conjure images of white kids with pierced faces and unconvincing dreadlocks: unemployed potheads with only a sketchy understanding of why they want to overthrow Wall Street. Warren was none of these things. He possessed a mild disposition and shrank from public debate. Nor was there anything very physically remarkable or imposing about him. He was short and thickset, with a prominent forehead, long sideburns, and close-cropped wiry hair. He was an industrious family man (that is to say, he was a man with a family) who spent much of his life inventing printing presses, a new form of musical notation meant to democratize that art form, and this country's cooperative movement, which began on this street corner.

Yet, before all that, Josiah Warren was simply one of many New Englanders who in the early 1800s followed the frontier spirit down the Ohio River. Born in Brighton, Massachusetts, in 1798, Warren may have been a descendant of Richard Warren, who arrived in Massachusetts on the *Mayflower*, and he may have been related to Joseph Warren, the Revolutionary War hero killed by the British at Bunker Hill. In his book *People and Places*, the Harvard philosopher George Santayana describes the "Brighton Warrens" as a "dissentient family." Yet an extensive family geneal-ogy makes no mention of a "Josiah," who by 1825 had migrated downstream to Cincinnati, where he was making ends meet as a music teacher. His singular achievement up to that point was the invention of a lard lamp, which burned more cheaply than lamps using tallow or oil. He had just begun manufacturing the popular lamp in 1826 when he attended a lecture Robert Owen gave in Cincinnati about the "new moral order" he had just founded in southern Indiana. Warren, his mind suddenly fired by Owen's utopian vision, sold the lamp factory and packed his wife, Caroline, farther down the Ohio, then up the Wabash to New Harmony. There he took up the role of bandleader and music teacher, "the community's only two successful institutions," according to Kenneth Rexroth's study *Communalism: From Its Origins to the Twentieth Century*. In 1927, when Owen blamed New Harmony's collapse on Americans' lack of forbearance and charity, Warren reached a different conclusion: the fault was not with American individualism as such, but rather with Owen's well-intended but ultimately misguided notions about human improvement. No matter how glorious one's vision of the brotherhood of man, no matter how intricately that vision has been translated into a system of social engineering, *people don't like to be told what to do*. They will ultimately chafe at the rules of the most benevolent monarch, and the operations of paradise soon become compul-sive drudgery. What's more, Warren suspected that New Harmony failed because communal socialism suppressed individuality, and in doing so, it robbed the individual of both initiative and responsibility. Finally, Owen treated diversity at New Harmony the wrong way: as something to be behaviorally modified rather than simply accepted.

These conclusions rattled Warren, who had badly wanted to believe in the possibility of Owen's utopia. Still, he resolved to determine for himself how society should begin yet anew. The key, he decided, was that a "successful society must be the natural growth of the interest that each one feels in it from the benefits of enjoyments derived from it." The whole must first serve the individual parts. The community must begin with individuality and diversity, not the suppression of the individual to a common cause.

Slowly, in response to Owen, Warren began to formulate his own brand of social reformation. It combined two basic ideas: the first, sovereignty of the individual, said that every person is a law unto him- or herself, and a person's rights are primary to those of any other institution, including the state; the second, voluntary cooperation, said all social undertakings should be conducted in the mutual interest of all parties involved. To prevent the abuse of the first principle and to ensure the consanguinity of the second, Warren proposed that they be held together by a single economic mandate that he called "equitable commerce." Its simple premise predates Marx and is far more radical: *cost should be the limit of price.* Robert Owen and Constantine Rafinesque had suggested this in their own writing, but little had come of it, and neither extrapolated out the theory as Warren would. In his own economic manifesto, *Equitable Commerce,* Warren stipulated that price should not be determined by the value of something to a buyer, but rather by the cost of producing it, measured in time, exertion, and materials. A man dying of thirst, after all, will give everything he owns for a glass of water—that is its *value* to him at the moment—but only a scoundrel would charge or accept such a price. Yet this logic that value should determine price is, to varying degrees, the basis of modern capitalism. What's more, if life's basic necessities become too plentiful for the capitalist to make a profit, he can destroy tons of grain and corn simply to drive the price back up. "The most successful speculator," wrote Warren, "is he who can create the most want in a community, and exert the most from it. This is civilized cannibalism." Such a system made both goods and money artificially scarce, and in so doing ensconced the rich in their wealth and kept the poor in a state of servitude. Warren wasn't necessarily proposing an anticapitalist system; he was simply taking the profit motive, and thus the abuse motive, out of the game. Everyone had a right to his own property and pursuit of happiness—Warren took the Declaration of Independence very seriously—but no one had the right to manipulate and abuse a currency to keep someone else poor.

Warren concluded that the central injustice out of which all other social injustices multiplied involved the question of labor and the historical mistreatment of laborers by the moneyed and propertied classes. "It is now evident to all eyes," he wrote, "that labor does not obtain its legitimate reward; but on the contrary, that those who work the hardest fare the worst." For Warren, to resolve the injustices of labor would mean finally to set society on a truly egalitarian footing—everything else would follow.

To right the labor problem, along with the everlasting problems of greed and inequality, Warren determined that society needed a new form of currency that he called the labor note. Had the combined wisdom of any country ever equaled that of a pumpkin vine, Warren claimed, it would have figured out a way to bring supply in line with demand. Yet this could never happen as long as financiers upset that ratio by treating money itself as a commodity to be traded, manipulated, and abused. Money, Warren insisted, should have one function: "that of standing in the place of the thing represented." It should be only a symbol of real wealth, human and natural capital, not an embodiment of wealth itself. Warren's scheme, therefore, was to substitute his labor note for federal currency, and in so doing to "abolish all systems of finance." The labor note would be nothing more than a calculation of the amount of time and effort that went into producing a particular good or performing a particular service. In its simplest form, if you spent three hours building me a bookshelf, I would give you a three-hour labor note for some service I might render in return, such as tutoring your children. And if there was nothing you needed from me, then you could exchange the labor note with someone else. The beauty of this new currency was that it could not be abused by speculators or manipulated by unscrupulous bankers, and the absolute fairness of this system thrilled Warren.

If followed out to its logical conclusions, he reasoned, the labor note would abolish the distinctions between the rich and the poor because everyone would be engaged in an equal exchange of labor. Wealth would constitute only what a man or woman could offer others in the form of skill or labor. In fact, the most disagreeable work (say, collecting the garbage) would be the most lucrative because so few would want to do it. *The entire class system would be reversed.* To combine labor notes with the principle that cost is the limit of price was, in Warren's fine phrase, "a simple act of moral commerce." Its repercussions, however, would be revolutionary. It would, Warren maintained, "strike at the root of all political, commercial, and financial corruption, and contribute largely to establish equity, security, liberty, equality, peace and abundance, wherever it shall be introduced." The problems of society would be solved.

Yet was this right? Decades later, writing in the third person, Warren recalled, "Day after day he retired into the woods outside [New Harmony] to ponder and to detect if possible some lurking error in his reasoning: but the closer he criticized, the more he was confirmed." Warren resolved, therefore, to return to Cincinnati and put his theories to the test. He would open a general store, called the Equity Store, that would operate exclusively on the principle of labor for labor, my time for your time. If this venture proved successful, he would take his theory of equitable commerce to the next stage and start an "equity village" where, he hoped, "the new ideas could be applied to the affairs of social life."

So, in 1827, Josiah and Caroline Warren departed New Harmony and took a steamboat back up the Ohio River. Presumably with the profits from selling his lamp factory two years earlier, Warren took out a ninety-nine-year lease on eight blocks of prime real estate in the heart of Cincinnati. His Cincinnati friends were skeptical of his plan and often reminded him of the recent failures at New Harmony. Society, it seemed, was less enthralled with its reformers than the reformers were with society. Yet Warren maintained that he was simply taking on the role of an ordinary storekeeper, except that he was "going to set and regulate his prices by an equitable principle instead of having no principle." Eventually, Warren tired of trying to justify his new venture, realizing that "as old words will not explain new things, new things must explain themselves." So, on May 18 of that year, here at the corner of Fifth and Elm, he opened the doors of the country's first business based entirely on the principle of equal exchange of labor. According to *A Documentary History of Industrial Society*, Warren's Equity Store was "the first scientific experiment in cooperative economy in modern history." Today, more than thirty thousand co-ops of one form or another exist in the United States. Warren's was the first.

He convinced a wholesale grocer to take a chance on his venture by positing that his store would provide an answer to the great failure of New Harmony. The wholesaler agreed that Warren could take what he wanted for inventory and pay for it when the goods were sold. Warren priced the groceries and some dry goods at the cost he had paid for them, plus a small fee for heating and lighting his store. Instead of factoring into the price a profit for himself, as any other merchant would have done, Warren mounted on one wall a clock that he reset whenever he began helping a customer. However long that took was the cost the customer owed Warren in exchange for some reciprocal labor. The actual goods were paid for in cash, but Warren's time was compensated with a labor note so as to "emancipate our supplies as well as ourselves from the tyranny of common money." A labor note might read something to the effect of DUE TO JOSIAH WARREN—THIRTY MINUTES OF CARPENTER'S WORK, OR FIVE POUNDS OF CORN. That is to say, the notes were backed not by gold or any federal currency but, rather, by something almost everyone needed and everyone in the Midwest could grow: corn. Warren printed up the labor notes himself on onionskin paper, and they evolved over the decades into handsomely engraved artifacts. The earliest notes were the size of a dollar bill. On the left side stood a crude image of blindfolded Justice holding her scales below the motto COST THE LIMIT OF PRICE. Down the right margin of the bill ran the words LABOR FOR LABOR. Years later, Warren added this statement to the note: THE MOST DISAGREEABLE LABOR IS ENTITLED TO THE HIGHEST COMPENSATION—assuming all laborers involved agreed on what that compensation was—and in the upper-right corner of an 1871 labor note, the image of a pocket watch rests under the words TIME IS WEALTH. If it turned out that the customer could provide no service Warren needed, the shopkeeper would set a labor price on some staple, such as coffee, and the customer would buy that product from Warren and then give it back to him for resale. Warren, in return, would give the customer, say, an hour of labor for the pound of coffee.

Because of the prominently displayed clock with which Warren measured his own labor, the new enterprise quickly became known around Cincinnati as "the Time Store." After a few months of modest business, Warren began buying more goods at auction, and soon added some medications, carbonated soda, and tartaric acids to his stock. An elderly seamstress bought the medicine she needed from Warren, who later boasted, "The medicines, bought in the common way, would have cost her sixty-eight cents; they now cost here seventeen cents and five minutes of her needle work, given her note for the work. She saved the wages of about two days labor in this little transaction of about five minutes." In return, the seamstress made cloth bags for the store in exchange for two hours of Warren's labor notes.

Hundreds of other similar reciprocal transactions took place at Fifth and Elm. For the next two years, the Time Store succeeded precisely according to the principles that Warren had conceived in the woods outside New Harmony. One day, Warren loaned thirteen dollars to a man about to be turned out of his house because he couldn't pay the rent. When the man came back two weeks later to pay his debt, he told Warren, "Your loan saved my family from so much distress that I will gladly pay you any premium you choose to ask." Warren replied, "You are a stranger to the principles upon which business is done here." The man insisted that his gratitude knew no bounds, but Warren would accept only a small pittance for the time it took him to draw up the original loan. This tenet that profit should come only from one's labor extended to land speculation. A few years later, after Warren had deemed the Equity Store a success and was ready to move on with his more ambitious communal experiments, he simply returned his eight blocks of real estate to an understandably shocked Nicholas Longworth, from whom he had leased them. By then, the land was worth considerably more than he had leased it for, but Warren refused to accept a profit when the price of the land had appreciated, as he saw it, through no effort of his own.

In doing so, Warren rejected hundreds of years of financial practice and returned to the unequivocal ban on usury that lies at the heart of Judaism, Christianity, and Islam. From the Latin *usuria*, meaning "demanding in return more than was originally loaned," usury is assailed in all canonical scriptures far more often than, say, homosexuality. Yet right around the time Adam Smith was writing *The Wealth of Nations*, the Catholic Church was quietly abandoning Pope Benedict XIV's doctrine "On Usury and Other Dishonest Profit." Never a religious man, Warren agreed absolutely with Aristotle: "The trade of the petty usurer is hated with most reason: it makes a profit from currency itself, instead of making it from the process which currency was meant to serve."

Over the years, however, Warren's rigorous monetary principles gradually exasperated his wife, Caroline. Thirty years later, when the two were living apart—she back in New Harmony and he in Boston—Warren wrote to ask her thoughts on a new publication he wished to start. "Your proposal," Caroline replied, "meets with my—objections, as usual. *You* are not *made* of the right material, to even *make* it pay cost, *it* that is, a paper of any kind, or book either, with you is an *out*lay, not an *in*come." But back in Cincinnati in the late 1820s, the couple's son, George, had just been born, and Caroline still seemed to share her husband's dream of social transformation. Back then, perhaps the greatest indication that Warren's first experiment in equitable commerce had been a success came from a remark made by a Cincinnati steamboat captain, Richard Fogler, who once told the members of his church, "Well, brethren, people have been disputing for eighteen hundred years about what is the true Christianity. Now if you will go down to the corner of Fifth and Elm Streets, you will see it in operation for the first time in the world." Even the Shakers, after all, sold their goods for a profit.

Today, where Warren's modest Time Store once stood there now looms a stone edifice crowned with a glass pyramid: the Duke Energy Convention Center. My feelings about this are complex and perhaps at times irrational because my feelings about James Buchanan Duke, and the university he founded, are of the same nature. In 1890, James Duke of Durham, North Carolina, formed the American Tobacco Company, a monopoly that drove so low the price paid to tobacco farmers that many in my home state of Kentucky, a state heavily dependent on its tobacco crop, never rose out of poverty. The writer and tobacco farmer Wendell Berry once told me that his grandfather used to say, "All James B. Duke ever gave us was six cents for our tobacco, foreclosure, and not enough of anything but fear." After the Department of Justice indicted American Tobacco under the Sherman Antitrust Act and forced it to dissolve, James Duke got into the energy business. In 1970, deep miners in Harlan County, Kentucky, went on strike because Duke Energy refused to pay health benefits to miners dying from black lung. The strike stretched on for months and wasn't resolved until a gun thug hired by Duke killed a striking miner named Lawrence Jones.

Now Duke Energy generates 58,200 megawatts at its mostly coal-fired and nuclear power plants. But shortly after its founding, in 1924, James Duke's power and tobacco money endowed the founding of Duke University. Seventy-eight years later, the Duke men's basketball team beat my team, the University of Kentucky, in an overtime game in the East Regional finals of the NCAA Tournament. In what is now universally known as "the greatest college basketball game of all time," Christian Laettner, with no time left on the clock, hit a turnaround jumper at the top of the key to win 104–103. But here's the thing: earlier in the game, Laettner, whose own teammates couldn't stand him and who made jejune coeds carry his books to class, knocked the spindly UK center Aminu Timberlake to the floor and then stomped on his chest. Unbelievably—*unconscionably* would not be too strong a word—Laettner was not ejected from the game, and as a result, UK suffered (*I* suffered) a loss that took years to get over, if in fact that is the case.

Such are my feelings about James Buchanan Duke as I stand at the corner of Fifth and Elm. One of the country's most progressive enterprises, Josiah Warren's co-op, run with labor notes, has been replaced by a convention center financed by one of the country's most regressive sources of both money and energy—one that is, what's more, party to the most coddled, petulant, and self-satisfied college basketball team in the country.

Back at my hotel, I pack up and hit the road, heading east along the Ohio River. Rusting barges line the opposite bank of the river. Newer ones struggle upstream with their mountainous loads of coal. The day is overcast, and an early morning mist mingles with the emissions from the smokestacks of the coal-fired power plants that line the Ohio and have helped make it the most polluted river in the country. I think of the line from the poet Richard Hugo, "A town needs a river to forgive the town." Or maybe what a river really needs is a city to act on that absolution and find another way to light its buildings and fire its boilers.

While I don't mean to belabor my grievances with the Duke family, the fact remains that Duke Energy is one of the main reasons the Ohio is so polluted. Consider the W. H. Zimmer Power Station, where I pull over to take a picture of the sign that says taking pictures here is prohibited. This plant alone dumps 270 pounds of mercury into the air each year and, consequently, into the Ohio River. Because of such dumping nationwide, the National Academy of Sciences reports that more than sixty thousand babies are exposed to enough mercury in utero to cause permanent brain damage. That is to say, eating fish caught in the Ohio River is probably the worst thing a pregnant woman from Cincinnati could do. What's more, the nonprofit Clean Air Task Force attributes twenty-one deaths and thirty-two heart attacks each year to the fine particle pollution (soot, heavy metals, and sulfur dioxide) that spews from the Zimmer plant.

On up the road, I stop for coffee in New Richmond, a town once vital to the Underground Railroad and the place where James G. Birney founded one of the country's most important abolitionist newspapers, *The Philanthropist*. Just as I'm about to walk into Peacock Pastry, as if on cue, I hear an arresting, anguished squawk coming from behind the building.

"Did I just hear a peacock?" I ask the woman behind the counter.

"You did. His name is Jacob. We named him after the founder of New Richmond, Jacob Light."

"Where exactly is he? I mean the peacock."

"Oh, he just wanders around town. People feed him."

Sure enough, back outside with my coffee and donut, I spot Jacob the peacock strutting past, sweeping up the street with his long, bejeweled tail. Like some kind of town crier, he issues harsh, unsolicited edicts as he passes by.

I drive on. Today the river is brown and sluggish. At its confluence with Indian Creek, I reach the tiny town of Point Pleasant, which turns out to be the birthplace of Hiram Ulysses Grant, whose name later became Ulysses Simpson Grant due to a mix-up with paperwork at West Point. Grant was born in a two-room clapboard house that now stands just off the road. Back in Kentucky, you can't drive within a fifty-mile radius of Abraham

Lincoln's birthplace without seeing signs to that effect. But where is the love for Grant, the man who won the war for Lincoln? I find the answer in an odd bit of symbolism beside the road. Below the blue U.S. Grant Memorial Highway sign is another that reads:

REPORT DRUNK DRIVERS
1-800-GRAB-DUI

That seems to be the one thing Americans know about Grant: that he was a drunk. And it's true, the man could certainly tie one on. But he also fought the Ku Klux Klan while president, tried to reverse Andrew Jackson's virulent policies toward Native Americans, and wrote, at Mark Twain's urging, what may be the greatest war memoir since Caesar's. His letters to his wife and children are beautiful and filled with nuance. To paraphrase Lincoln when his other generals complained about Grant's boozing, give me what he's having.

Farther on, old Federalist-style homes occupy higher ground on the left side of the road, while down on the right, the river is lined with campgrounds filled with large campers but no cars. Many of the campers have wooden porches and metal awnings built onto them so they function as weekend places for Ohioans who then return to their jobs during the week. Out in a field, a heron stands motionless near a native burial mound, conical like the ones back in Indiana, but much taller. A few miles later, I see the small green sign that reads UTOPIA.

Here, on this stretch of bottomland, Josiah Warren built his first equity village—the only utopian community in this country that was actually called, at least by some, Utopia. However, all I see today is the Village Market, a little mom-and-pop store with two gas pumps and living quarters built onto the back. There's a small FOR SALE sign stuck in the grass.

I fill up and then go inside, where a lean, older man makes me a ridiculously large ham and cheese sandwich for $2.50.

"So this is Utopia?" I say.

"Yep," he replies, grinning.

"But you're moving," I reply, gesturing to the sign outside the door.

"Doesn't look like it. Nobody's buying."

"So you're tired of Utopia?"

"Oh, it's all right," he says with a slight cackle. "I've been here thirty years."

"Where did the name come from?" I ask.

"I don't know. Something about the nineteenth century."

When his wife appears from the back of the store to take my money, I ask her about the name.

"Been here so long I can't remember," she tells me.

In fact, a historic marker stands right across Route 52; you can see it from where we're standing. Yet even had they read it, the marker makes no mention of Josiah Warren. Instead, it credits "followers of Charles Fourier" with founding this particular utopia. Most of the sign describes a flood that killed a group of spiritualists on December 13, 1847. (Today the only website for Utopia, Ohio, is StrangeUSA.com, which is devoted to its supposed status as a "ghost town," haunted by the dead spiritualists; the website rates the scariness of Utopia with seven human skulls out of a possible ten.) The historic marker concludes: THUS THE IDEA OF THE PERFECT SOCIETY, OR UTOPIA, DIED. In fact, 1847 was the year Josiah Warren *arrived*.

The sign is right about one thing: the American utopian movement spawned by the French writer Charles Fourier got here first. In his *History of American Socialisms*, John Humphrey Noyes divided out the prime movers of the American communitarian impulse into "revivalism" and "socialism." The Shakers and Rappites were evidence of the former; the Owenites of the latter. "The Revivalists have for their great idea the regeneration of the soul," Noyes contended. "The great idea of the Socialists was the regeneration of society, which is the soul's environment." Each in the end failed, said Noyes, because the Revivalists ignored the larger society and the Socialists ignored the higher callings of the heart.

Into this breach stepped a self-educated French shop clerk who claimed he could regenerate the soul and society at the same time. Charles Fourier agreed with the pre-Socratic philosopher Heraclitus, who said men talk about the world without actually taking the time to look at what they are talking about. Consequently, said Fourier, all Western philosophy was rubbish because it ran counter to human nature by trying to make us into something other than who we naturally are. Happiness was the point of life, wrote Fourier, not virtue, or goodness, or truth. In pursuit of virtue, we too often repress the natural instincts, which then reappear perversely as malevolence. Far better, said Fourier, to work with, rather than against, the instincts, and to organize communities in such a way that individual desires serve the general good.

In 1832, a well-heeled twenty-three-year-old New Yorker named Albert Brisbane was in the middle of a six-year educational sojourn through Europe when he came across one of Fourier's self-published volumes. Brisbane had already met Goethe, Felix Mendelssohn, Franz Liszt, and Heinrich Heine, but it was the obscure Frenchman who transformed his thinking and gave the American his life's work. Brisbane tracked down the ailing, nearly destitute Fourier and asked to be schooled in his theories. He then returned to New York two years later with the "sole thought to transmit the thought of Charles Fourier to my countrymen." There Brisbane published *Social Destiny of Man; or, Association and Reorganization of Industry*. It was both the first American translation of Fourier's writings and the first extrapolation of how those theories might be brought to life in the New World. When the *New-York Tribune* editor Horace Greeley read *Social Destiny of Man*, he offered Brisbane a front-page column in his popular newspaper with the sole purpose of disseminating the gospel of Fourierism. The column dramatically increased the *Tribune*'s readership. Fourierist societies, whose members called themselves associationists, spread from New York to Iowa. Land and cotton speculation had brought about the bank Panic of 1837, which plunged the country into a prolonged economic depression. There was a better path forward, Brisbane argued, and thanks to an obscure French visionary, he knew the way.

The depression, along with the revival spirit that was still a force in the country, had made many Americans quite amenable to the gospel that Brisbane was preaching. Unlike today, the power of the banks and the ideology of commercialism did not seem completely inevitable. In the 1840s it did not seem too late to turn the ship around, to replace inequality and individualism with fairness and cooperation. The utopia of solidarity still seemed a real possibility, and Charles Fourier had provided the operating manual.

In 1843 a Fourier Association formed in Cincinnati, with visions of soon breaking ground on its own Ohioan phalanx about thirty miles upriver, in Clermont County. Josiah Warren himself addressed the group in 1844 and warned them that a joint-stock commune based on shared property would collapse under all its high-minded constitutions, just as New Harmony had. "I know that a large portion of my hearers are engaged in an enterprise with the best possible motives and the highest hopes," Warren told them, "but you cannot succeed; you will fail within three years." At that point, Warren asked the group to remember his warning and then consider his alternate plan of equitable commerce. In May 1844 the Scottish journalist/archivist A. J. Macdonald accompanied by steamer 130 associationists to the site of their soon-to-be-realized phalanx, a site that Macdonald observed did indeed possess "all that could be desired, hill and plain, rich soil, fine scenery, plenty of first-rate timber, a maple-sugar camp, a good commercial situation, convenient to the best market in the West." But in July 1847, word trickled back to Warren that his prognostications had come to pass: victims of floods, debt, and internecine lawsuits, the Clermont Fourierists were calling it quits. Warren took a trip upriver to have a look for himself. "I had not been landed from the steam boat thirty minutes," he recalled twenty-five years later, "when Mr. Daniel Prescott (a stranger to me) approached and said, 'Well, we failed, just as you said we should—it worked just as you said it would. Now I am ready for your movement.' "

Since he closed the doors of the Cincinnati Time Store in 1829, Warren had been trying to find some small body of believers with which to plot a larger utopian scheme. Back then, though, he could persuade few of his customers to take the great leap with him: to leave Cincinnati and build a New Jerusalem in the northern part of Ohio, where land was cheap. For all his insights into what truly motivates *Homo economicus*, Warren lacked the charisma characteristic of most social visionaries. "He had no magnetic qualities so needful in persuasion or gaining converts," remembered one of his later converts. "Also he was a timid man and hated to wrangle." Still, as cities such as Cincinnati moved toward rapid industrialization and a specialized factory system, Warren was teaching himself the generalist skills he would need to build his first equity village—skills such as house framing, ironworking, and carpentry. He even devised an ingenious method for making cheaper bricks out of sun-dried mortar. Yet his most important apprenticeship, the one that would preoccupy him all his life, came in printing.

Warren was convinced that egalitarian media were the greatest handmaid to radical social change, especially since the mainstream papers of the day would give no credence to his anarchist philosophy of cooperative individualism. "It was evident," he surmised, "that any new truths which tended to break up the present suicidal and desolating habits of business must have a printing power of their own." And the contributions Warren made to the history of printing are quite extraordinary. He began by building what was probably the country's first continuous-feed rotary press, an innovation so obvious in his eyes that "it was simply given to the public" without a patent. This self-inking "speed press" could generate sixty copies a minute as opposed to the five copies produced by the standard press. He exhibited his invention in New York in 1932, and a few years later, Hoe and Company was reaping large sums of money marketing an identical press, one that would revolutionize printing toward the end of the nineteenth century. In 1930, Warren was also inventing a rubber type plate, made out of shellac, tar, and beeswax, that was a cheaper substitute for metal type and far quicker to manufacture and set. A letter still on file at the New Harmony Working Men's Institute from Warren's son, George, reads, "Well I remembered in 1830, when I was a little chap. I watched my father making type at the same fireplace at which my mother cooked the meals." The impetus behind all Warren's printing innovations was to put the media in the hands of the masses. To that end, he sought to "combine all the implements of printing into a single piece of household furniture to stand in the next room to the piano." In 1851 the Smithsonian Institution, perhaps at Robert Dale Owen's urging, used Warren's rubber type to print its first book catalog. That same year, the Boston publisher John P. Jewett hired Warren to set up and supply rubber type for his new press. Crispin Sartwell, in his valuable anthology of Warren's writing, *The Practical Anarchist*, points out that a year later, Jewett published the first edition of Harriet Beecher Stowe's *Uncle Tom's Cabin*, which, as Sartwell writes, "raises the possibility that this epochal work was first printed using Warren's apparatus."

In 1832 a cholera epidemic broke out in Cincinnati. On his new rotary press, Warren printed thousands of leaflets containing medical guidance for warding off the disease. His young son helped distribute the leaflets and, years later, recalled that the city issued a resolution of public thanks for his father. The following year, Warren turned the efforts of his press from public health to public agitation. In January 1833 he published the country's first anarchist newspaper, the *Peaceful Revolutionist*, a four-page weekly wherein Warren inveighed against the corruption of cities, the critics of his Time Store, and public education—diatribes he interspersed with home remedies such as his cure for malaria (black pepper mixed with molasses). His overriding concern, however, was with the way governments hid behind the guise of law to exert state power over the liberties of individuals.

Warren had recently come under the influence of the philosopher Alexander Bryan Johnson. In fact, Johnson's *Treatise on Language* is one of the few books we actually know Warren read, since rarely in his writing did Warren lean on earlier thinkers, or at least profess to. Johnson's particular philosophy of language was as radical as Warren's philosophy of labor, and it reached many of the same conclusions as the American pragmatists would one hundred years later. Johnson argued that words are blunt and inadequate instruments for representing reality. Whereas nature always shows itself in an infinite display of particularity, words always rise to the level of the general, so that a rose is a rose is a rose. Not only was language only fossilized poetry, as Emerson asserted, but its fossil became outdated and unreliable as soon as it hardened into words. Thus, because language could not be trusted to be a mirror of nature, it had to be judged, as the pragmatists would later argue, by the actions it inspired. The word *God*, for instance, is particularly vacuous unless the belief in that word makes a difference in our lives and the lives of others. Warren transposed Johnson's theories into an attack on the whole enterprise of government, an institution based, after all, on an abstract language of laws that could never be brought in line with the complexities of human reality.

The particular word fossils that Warren could not abide were the ones first set down in the U.S. Constitution and later used by the federal government to justify civil war. Southern slavery was obviously a grotesque violation of Warren's "sovereignty of the individual," but he also had nothing but contempt for the North's argument for "union," a word so vague and empty of meaning that it could be used only in an act of brutal state coercion (as when Lincoln hanged deserters of the Union army after making them sit on their caskets all day). There was a time when the word *union* held legitimacy because it could be tied to a particular reality—the fellow feeling that brought on the American Revolution. For Warren, "This union existed independent of words: it was the necessary and unavoidable effect of the circumstances of that time." Yet that action of union soon ossified into a proscriptive social contract that betrayed the heart of Jefferson's original justification for independence. Sixty years later, the United States government was insisting, in Warren's words, that "the laws shall be obeyed, and that the union must be preserved. But these words *must* and *shall* rouse the ghost of murdered liberty to resistance." They murdered Warren's most fundamental human right, individual sovereignty, in the name of a verbal abstraction. In that respect, the only legal union Warren cared for was one that protected every individual's "liberty to differ from others."

The same year Warren started the *Peaceful Revolutionist*, his and six other families bought a four-hundred-acre tract of land in Tuscarawas, Ohio, where they set out to build a small village based on labor notes and labor exchange. The historian James J. Martin called Tuscarawas "the site of the first anarchist community in America, years before anything similar was attempted in Europe." Warren never actually referred to himself as an anarchist; historians and political theorists would affix that title later. Certainly Warren's version of anarchism was distinctly American. He never sought to overthrow any government, like his European and Russian counterparts, but rather to undermine the state through the success of his experiments in noncoercive, cooperative living. He would live and work in the gaps left open by the state, and in doing so, show its cumbersome apparatus of law and power to be unnecessary, irrelevant. Government would then simply decay out of disuse.

Tuscarawas, however, never had a chance to succeed; malaria and influenza leveled the community within a few years. (Apparently Warren's antidote of black pepper and molasses wasn't as effective as he thought.) Soon after, the Panic of 1837 caused Warren again to suspend his ambitions for reform. So while the depression lingered into the 1840s, Warren retreated with his family to New Harmony, where he set up another Time Store and devised a new method for musical notation, one that completely did away with the treble and bass clef, sharps, flats, and the need to transpose different musical keys. Warren's impulse to simplify sheet music was the same that lay behind his printing inventions: he wanted to break what he considered the monopoly of music publishers and make learning music more accessible, more likely "to elevate, refine, and harmonize and humanize a people." Yet he could find no publisher willing to jeopardize the entire industry, along with a six-hundred-year-old tradition of writing and transposing music. Warren again castigated the publishers for possessing "the one great, all-absorbing object of money making," and then turned his efforts to another radical form of writing: the political manifesto.

Warren wrote and set in his new rubber type the country's first overtly anarchist document, *Equitable Commerce*. There Warren distilled twenty years of notes into a document that made his case against the state and for the founding of a radically new form of community. He contended that the only historical justification for government was the "interchange of mutual assistance" and "security of person or property." In both cases, every government known to man had failed, turning the guise of armed protection into conscription, coercion, and the general abuse of power. It was, said Warren, Robespierre's insistence that the "people" must be molded into one will that betrayed the French Revolution and led to the guillotine. We can simply look to the biological diversity all around us, he argued, to see that individuality, particularity, is the first law of nature. "Individuality thus rising above all prescriptions—all authority—every one, by the very necessities of nature, is raised above, instead of being under, institutions based on language," he wrote. Musical harmony was a perfect embodiment of how different notes sounding together forge something beautiful: "the most humanizing art." Compulsion would never lead to social harmony. The state cannot make a person act responsibly; responsibility can be truly assumed only by the individual acting on conscience. It can come only from below. Only by "raising every individual above the state," wrote Warren, will "society take the first successful step toward its harmonious adjustment." In Warren's perfect world, the individual actually *becomes* his or her own state. Warren published *Equitable Commerce* at New Harmony in 1846. It was physically a small book, issued in a limited edition, but James J. Martin called it "the first important publication of anarchistic doctrine in America." Twenty-seven years later, John Stuart Mill, in his *Autobiography*, wrote of "a remarkable American, Josiah Warren, who had framed a System of Society, on the foundation of 'the Sovereignty of the Individual,'" a concept Mill credited for inspiring his own seismic book-length essay *On Liberty*.

Yet in *Equitable Commerce*, Warren went beyond Mill's argument by maintaining that the individual could not achieve true liberty as long as the question of labor went unanswered. The entire subject of fair and just remuneration for work had to be revised: money had to be replaced with the labor note. In the final section of his manifesto, called "The Application," Warren sketched out exactly how one of his equity villages would commence. Because language could not be trusted to build consensus among men and women, Warren called for no constitution or set of bylaws. Instead, members of the community could form voluntary alliances to get their houses built and their needs met without ever compromising the rights and liberty of each sovereign self. To begin, a group of like-minded people would come together and, on a ledger, list everything they could individually supply in one column, and every good or service they desired in another. "These," said Warren, "become the fundamental data for operations." Unlike New Harmony, where Robert Owen's benefaction encouraged sloth, Warren's communities would bustle with work and the vigorous exchange of labor. "Let no one move to an equity village," he warned, "till he has thoroughly consulted the demand for his labor, and satisfied himself individually that he can maintain himself individually." When Warren said "labor for labor," he meant it. The New Harmony drinkers wouldn't have lasted a week in Warren's equity village.

The price of goods would be self-regulating because, after all, no one would pay fifty hours of labor notes for a pair of shoes when another cobbler in the village could supply shoes of equal value for thirty hours of notes. Thus Warren's communities would operate according to the supposed efficiencies of capitalism without the motive of avarice. Quality would regulate demand. Also, because there would exist no profit motive, no one would be hocking shoddy goods to cut costs. Meanwhile, the cobbler who couldn't make a good pair of shoes in thirty hours would simply be encouraged to quickly apprentice himself or herself to another occupation. Such was Warren's simple blueprint for his own new moral order, one that would reach Robert Owen's ends by radically divergent means.

Finally, in 1847, in the ruins with the Clermont Phalanx, Warren got his chance. Only six families that Warren described as "almost destitute" remained by the time he arrived. That was fine; equitable commerce was a political philosophy explicitly designed for the poor, the homeless, those who had little more than their own willingness to exchange labor for labor. Warren convinced a local landowner to lease him twenty acres of land, with the promise of not raising its price for three years. Warren divided the land into eighty quarter-acre lots, which sold for fifteen dollars each, and the families set to work. This was in July. By December, four of the six families had homes that were paid for or nearly paid for. The resettlers laid out roads and alleys. Daniel Prescott set up a brick kiln, a sawmill, and a gristmill. A few years later, the village had grown to over two dozen families who had erected twenty-six buildings among them, including, of course, a Time Store. The sawmill functioned as an exemplar of Warren's principles: a man could work in the mill, and then pay for his quarter-acre lot with labor notes to another man who needed lumber from the mill, which he paid for with the labor notes he accrued from the man who bought his land. Warren crowed, "The cooperation was as perfect as cooperation could be, yet everyone was entirely free from all trammels of organization, constitutions, pledges, and every thing of the kind." A certain villager named Mr. Cubberley explained to a local paper how labor notes made the whole experiment succeed:

These put us into a reciprocating society. The result was, in two years twelve families found themselves with homes who never owned them before. Labor capital did it. I built a brick cottage one and a half stories high, and all the money I paid out was

$9.81. All the rest was effected by exchanging labor for labor. Money prices, with no principle to guide, have always deceived us.

The inhabitants alternatively called the new village Utopia or, more cautiously, Trialville. Moreover, it was a trial they wanted to conduct away from the public eye. "It has been thought important from the beginning," Cubberley reported, "not to make the place notorious, as it would cause great inconvenience to the residents, there being no public house for the entertainment of visitors." Beyond that, if the trial didn't work, none of the Warrenites, least of all Warren himself, wanted to suffer the public shaming that befell New Harmony. Still, by 1854 the tentative experiment seemed to be working. More than one hundred people had arrived to be part of it, though the ever-restless Warren had moved to New York City in 1850 to conduct "parlor conversations" in the hope of starting an even larger equity village somewhere in the Northeast. As with the Time Store, he left Utopia as soon as he judged it a success. The small town, in his mind, had completely repudiated Owen's and Fourier's socialist utopias, and it had proven that men and women could form a society without a state—a realm of voluntary cooperation that required no compromise of liberty on the part of the individual.

That's about all we know of the original anarchist village of Utopia. Surrounding land speculation soon created a stranglehold that prevented it from growing beyond those original eighty lots. As a result, many of the original founders moved en masse to Minnesota, where land was abundant and cheap. Today, the town that bears the name Utopia consists of two roads and about twenty homes, mostly double-wides. At the end of one road sits the weather-worn Nuts N Boats Campground. It's empty since this is a weekday. The gate is locked, and a menacing German shepherd barks at the end of a short chain. Today Utopia feels, frankly, a little sad.

How Should People Live?

I drop down into West Virginia at Huntington, and then, for most of the day, follow narrow roads along streams and rivers that thread through small valley towns. Tributaries tumble down from these steep slopes to become Coal River. Mobile homes line the banks, punctuated by churches and abandoned mechanic shops. The packed parking lot at the Eden Baptist Church suggests that a revival is in progress. Almost every yard has a garden of corn and tomatoes, a "right smart," as people used to say throughout Appalachia. There are signs in the yards professing a love for either Jesus or coal, or both.

Large coal tipples spring up periodically on both sides of the road, depositing huge mounds of the bituminous ore for trucks to haul away. These drivers brush inches from my rearview mirror all day. There is no place in the eastern United States that produces more coal than these southern West Virginia counties. And everyone around here pays a price in terms of the water they drink, the air they breathe, the floods created by strip-mined land, the house foundations shaken and cracked by all the blasting, the family members killed by the speeding coal trucks. When I reach the town of Whitesville, I pass a long granite wall covered with the black silhouettes of miners; it stretches out beside the road as a monument to twenty-nine men who, in 2010, paid the highest price.

On April 5 of that year, a methane fireball ripped through underground shafts at the Upper Big Branch mine in Montcoal, West Virginia, killing the twenty-nine miners. It was the country's worst mining disaster in over forty years. When I heard the news on the radio that morning, my first thought was "I bet it's a Massey mine." And it was. Under the ruthless leadership of CEO Don Blankenship, Massey Energy unapologetically accumulated one of the worst safety records of any coal company in the United States.

From January 2009 up to the day of the explosion, the U.S. Mine Safety and Health Administration (MSHA) cited the Upper Big Branch mine for 639 violations, 68 of which involved "high negligence." Over the last decade, fifty-four miners have been killed in Massey mines. Jeff Harris, a former Massey employee who quit to work for a union mine, told a Senate committee on April 27 that the company routinely put production over safety. "As soon as the inspector leaves the property," Harris said of Upper Big Branch, "they take all the ventilation back down and start mining coal." Unfortunately, as a Labor Department investigation later revealed, it was the ventilation system that would have prevented the buildup of the methane that ignited the explosion on April 5.

Pondering all those violations and the deaths that followed, I found a single question forming over and over in my mind: What if the workers themselves had owned those mines? Unionized mines do a better job of maintaining worker safety than nonunion ones; would a worker-owned mine be better still? Would the ventilation curtains have remained in place even after the inspectors left? If the miners themselves had owned the mine, would they still be alive?

I began doing some research to see if any such mines exist throughout the coalfields of Appalachia, but I could find none.

For a brief decade, from 1917 to 1927, a cooperative mining town called Himlerville did operate in Martin County, Kentucky, right across the Tug River from notorious Bloody Mingo County, West Virginia. The Himler Coal Company was founded by a Hungarian coal miner and newspaper editor named Henrich Himler on the premise that the workers would be the stockholders and the stockholders would be the workers. Each year the company's profits were distributed as dividends, and every miner, no matter his position, shared equally in stock bonuses. At first Himlerville flourished, boasting handsome cottages, gardens, and indoor plumbing. There was a library, an auditorium, a school, and a bake shop. There was no typhoid, as in the company towns across the river in Mingo County; nor were there gun thugs patrolling the grounds to intimidate miners and thwart collective bargaining. By 1922 the Himler Coal Company had raised its base capital from $500,000 to $2 million, and decided to open two new mines. Then coal prices plunged, and the railroads brought in competition from larger corporations. "In 1927, the company was sold at auction to private capitalists," wrote the Appalachian scholar Ronald Eller, "and the only effort at cooperative mining in the southern mountains came to an end." The brief utopian age of American coal mining was over.

I did not think I would be following the dystopic legacy of the Industrial Revolution when I left home six days ago; I thought I was searching for utopia. Yet I suppose it was inevitable, since our country's most persistent utopian myths of comfort and accumulation are powered by the coal that heats and cools the buildings where we live and work, drives manufacturing, and as billboards throughout this state insist, KEEPS THE LIGHTS ON (as if there were no other way). I feel a kind of relief when I finally leave coal country behind and cross over into Virginia. There, in the New River Valley, low clouds cast long shadows into the folds of the mountain spurs. Unlike the Appalachians, the Blue Ridge Mountains have the look of gentle, not crashing, waves, and the Blue Ridge Parkway, a two-lane that circumnavigates wide, beautiful valleys, has got to be one of the best excuses for the automobile in America. I have been driving it all my life, and today, with the windows down and a late sun slanting across the valley farms below, I feel a low-key excitement to be moving again along these flanks and through these mountain passes. A few box turtles are making their ponderous way across the road. A wild turkey struts around at the edge of the forest. Mountain laurel is blooming at the highest elevations.

I stop to eat a sandwich beside the remnants of an old narrow gauge line, a kind of temporary railroad that transported more than one hundred million board feet of timber out of these mountains in the 1920s. About fifty feet away, a doe and her fawn jump timidly across the tracks and back into the forest understory. Off in the distance, across the wide Shenandoah Valley, the mountains seem to recline in a painterly repose. I'd like to stay and watch the sun set behind them, but I've got to get to Louisa, Virginia, tonight, where a room is waiting for me at an intentional community called Twin Oaks. After finding no evidence of Josiah Warren's legacy back in Ohio, I'm ready to see what an actual, working utopia looks like.

Last month, when I told a colleague at a dinner party about my summer travel plans, he replied, "Utopian communities? Are there any still around?"

Actually, there are, though these days they prefer to call themselves egalitarian or intended communities. The Fellowship for Intentional Community (FIC) lists more than three hundred such examples of communal living in the United States and thousands worldwide. Only seven of those American sites qualify for recognition by the Federation of Egalitarian Communities (FEC). To achieve that rarefied status, a commune must hold land, labor, and income in common, advocate nonviolence and ecological sustainability, and practice some form of direct decision making. Of the FEC's seven community members, three reside in Louisa County, Virginia. The reason for their choosing that county is simple: lax zoning laws and modest real estate prices. If one hundred counterculture types want to plop down on some cheap farmland and not get harassed by the locals, Louisa has historically been the place.

I cut over the Blue Ridge Mountains at Franconia Notch and make the quick descent to Charlottesville, passing below the white dome of Thomas Jefferson's Monticello. It's another half hour to Louisa County, where at dusk I travel back roads through farmland and woodlots until I pull up to the oldest egalitarian community in the country, Twin Oaks. Swallowtails flutter around the tall zinnias at the entrance. Behind them, a farm stretches from the road to a cluster of residences covered in gray barn wood. I follow a gravel road up to plain but handsomely aging buildings encircling a main courtyard and connected by narrow brick paths. One of the paths leads to an English garden, where herbs and perennials mingle. Beyond those beds, long rows of vegetables stretch down to a cornfield. Farther off, an orchard surrounds a pasture for the Twin Oaks milking herd and a large chicken pen. The henhouse is built on the back of a long two-wheel trailer. A low array of solar panels runs across the middle of the farm.

Adder, a pale young man with long blond hair, meets me in the garden. He is the designated host for my visit to Twin Oaks. He apologizes for having child-care responsibilities tonight, but promises to show me around in the morning. For now, Adder, shoeless in a woman's thin skirt, points me to a small guesthouse, where I find my name on a card taped to the door of one of four rooms. Each room, like each of the buildings at Twin Oaks, is named after a former utopian community. My door reads WALDEN TWO.

The sparsely furnished room, like the food I will eat at Twin Oaks, is free—I have been asked only to do a little work during my stay as recompense for the hospitality. There's a set of bunk beds, a small table, and a chest of drawers in the room. I settle into the lower bunk and pull from my suitcase a copy of B. F. Skinner's utopia novel, *Walden Two*. In 1967—the year of the Summer of Love, and my birth—eight friends, mostly graduate students, read this book by the founder of behavioral psychology and decided to bring

160

that fiction to life. Altogether, their assets added up to two thousand dollars; they had a benefactor who was willing to lease them 123 acres of farm and forest land in Louisa and a parent willing to float them a loan for the mortgage. The small group moved into the only structure on the place, a small farmhouse, and began planting a garden. "Some of us were happy," one of them, Kat Kinkade, remembered twenty-six years later in her history of Twin Oaks, *Is It Utopia Yet?* "Central to my own happiness was my conviction that there was no task on earth more important, or certainly more interesting, than the building of an egalitarian community." While Kinkade left Twin Oaks at times to visit or help create other intentional communities, she always returned to the region, and after succumbing to bone cancer in 2008, she was buried in the small Twin Oaks cemetery beneath a simple circle of quartz stones.

Before coming to Twin Oaks, I made a determined effort to read *Walden Two*. Utopian novels, by their nature, tend to be clunky and formulaic. There is little character development, and the plot, what there is of it, is usually driven by whatever ideological crochets induced the author to take up a pen in the first place. Unending monologues about the failures of Western culture are issued by some wise patriarch from the future, and in the end, everyone agrees that something must be done, so they do it. Still, there are pleasures to be taken in the pastoral fantasies of William Morris's *News from Nowhere* or in the quaint Bostonian love story in Edward Bellamy's *Looking Backward*. There is, however, no pleasure to be taken in the leaden prose and tireless sermonizing in *Walden Two*. The book is so damn dull I abandoned it halfway through. I try now to give *Walden Two* another chance, since it is my room's namesake, but it's no use. I toss it aside after ten pages and pick up instead Kinkade's *Is It Utopia Yet?* Apparently, the founders of Twin Oaks abandoned Skinner's behaviorist ideas pretty quickly. "Walden Two idealism is nothing now but a quaint and somewhat embarrassing part of our history," wrote Kinkade. Most of the founding grad students quickly departed Twin Oaks, and there weren't a lot of other B. F. Skinner followers ready to scrape by on a marginal farm and in even more marginal accommodations. Still, a whole other group of people was: hippies. As it happened, a dotted white line soon led some of them right from Woodstock, New York, to Louisa, Virginia. The hippies shared the utopian dreams of *Walden Two*, the vision of a culture that abandoned the ideologies of consumerism and the military-industrial complex; they just didn't share Skinner's belief that behavior modification through positive reinforcement was the way to get there. "Our members are practically always doing what they want to do, what they 'choose' to do," claims T. E. Frazier, the fictional founder of Skinner's Walden Two; "—but we see to it that they will want to do precisely the things which are best for themselves and the community. Their behavior is determined, yet they're free." No self-respecting hippy would have swallowed that line of talk. A former Twin Oaks member who calls himself (or herself?) Nexus put it this way in an article on the Twin Oaks website: "In *Walden Two*, Frazier says, 'Give me the specifications, and I'll give you the man!' while hippies would counter, 'Just be yourself and don't put your trips on other people, man.' It is not surprising that Walden Two was left behind when hippies became the majority at Twin Oaks."

Last week, when I was back among the Shaker ghosts, I wondered: If by some happenstance Pleasant Hill suddenly reverted back to an intentional, egalitarian community, could I live there? Let's even get rid of the celibacy requirement and the religious framework. Let's say one hundred men and women converged at Pleasant Hill to reprise the Shaker story, but this time they could have sex, and talk while they worked, and cultivate a sense of conviviality the Shakers seemed to lack. Could I be one of them? Could I live in such close quarters, sharing almost everything, especially work and wages? There was one place to find out. And here I am.

In the morning, Adder knocks on my door and shows me to the dining hall, called Zhankoye (or just ZK), after a Jewish farming collective started in Crimea in the 1930s. The members of Twin Oaks scare up their own breakfast, usually something light prepared in their own residence kitchens. Lunch and dinner are prepared here in ZK, which also functions as the main clearinghouse for communication among members. I pour delicious cream from the Twin Oaks dairy over some granola and follow Adder to a message board where small notes are stuck into one hundred small pouches. "It's our e-mail system," he explains. Another board announces any events or invitations to gather for that evening. (Tonight one member is throwing a birthday party for herself; another is starting a coffee klatch.) Yet the main source of written interaction occupies one wall in the main dining room. Here, about thirty clipboards hang from individual hooks, and all are bulging with paper. This is the Opinions and Ideas (O&I) board, the source of most change, or resistance to change, at Twin Oaks. Anyone with an idea for how things should be done differently— someone wants the whole community to go vegan, for instance— can start a new clipboard. One idea currently collecting a lively set of responses is a proposal to change the reduction of work for older members. Right now, beginning at age sixty, a member's workload is reduced by two hours a year. The new proposal is to begin the reduction at age fifty, but reduce it by only one hour per year. Opinions on this are mixed.

"Members read the O&I the way many people outside of Community read the daily newspaper," wrote Kat Kinkade, "though in our case the 'newspaper' is mostly one big editorial page, with many editors." Members attach their comments to each clipboard. Once everyone has had his or her say about a proposal, the motion, as it were, goes to a council of three people called the planners.

The one thing Twin Oaks has retained from *Walden Two* is what the novel calls a planner-manager form of governing. The three planners serve a limited term and are responsible for the community's long-range decision making. The managers are those in charge of specific areas of work, from the farm to the kitchen to the various manufacturing operations at Twin Oaks. The managers oversee all daily decisions, and the planners are responsible for decisions that affect the whole community. To an outsider, it might seem that the planners wield considerable power in a community that espouses complete egalitarianism. The reality, says Adder, a planner himself right now, is that most members take on the role rather reluctantly. (In fact, there are currently only two planners because no one has come forward to be the third.) Something like Plato's reluctant philosopher-kings, the planners don't really want power—there is, after all, really nothing to be gained from it at Twin Oaks—and are serving only at the request of the community. Once a planner is nominated, members offer input about the candidate for ten days, and then a "Veto Box" is set out. If less than 20 percent of the community votes no (which I sense is almost always the case), a new planner is elected. The main job of the planner is to respond to the O&I board, and act on the wishes of the majority. As it turned out, much to the vegans' frustration, there was too much community resistance to giving up meat and dairy. The motion failed. "You don't want to trample over the minority," Adder says over tea—the community has determined that coffee is too expensive—in the main dining room. "At the same time, if the minority can stop the majority from doing what they want, there's a similar power imbalance. More than anything, my job is to figure out what other people want." The planner-manager system has been working for forty-six years in part because almost everyone is a manager of some aspect of the community, so individuals are constantly rotating in and out of various work teams. If there arise any grievances with the managers or planners, then a Council of Intermediaries steps in to allay the community's concerns.

Twin Oaks hardly ever dips below or swells above one hundred members: right now there are ninety-three adults and seven children. Each permanent member is voted in after a six-month trial period. With community feedback, a Membership Team (three men and three women) makes the final decision for acceptance. Everyone works forty-two hours a week, doing pretty much whatever work they choose. Each Sunday, the communitarians fill out a labor sheet declaring where and when they want to work;

then labor assigners do their best to pair desired labor with seasonally crucial labor: woodcutting in the winter, harvesting vegetables in the summer. Two and a half hours are credited to each member each week, which adds up to two and a half weeks of annual vacation. Anyone can pile up overtime and bank it toward more vacation days. As in Josiah Warren's Utopia, all work is valued equally: one hour of work is one hour of work. Twin Oaks is small enough to ensure accountability: no one can cheat on his hours for long and have it go unnoticed. Yet Twin Oaks doesn't tend to attract people who would want to game the system. "The work gets done not because people need labor hours," Adder explains. "There are people who have vacation balances of thousands of hours that they are never going to spend. And they do the work because this is their home and this is the work that needs to get done."

There is no money at Twin Oaks. After your forty-two hours of work, all life's essentials (food, housing, health care) are free. "I never have to worry about paying rent or having enough to eat," Adder tells me. However, each member is paid a fluctuating monthly stipend, based on community profits—right now it is at a record-high ninety dollars—for the things one can't find at Twin Oaks: coffee, for example. I ask Adder what most people spend their stipend on, and he says, "Treats and vices." Besides the coffee, it's mostly things such as beer, juice, cigarettes, a movie ticket.

"Last month," Adder says, "I bought a yo-yo."

Twin Oaks tries to maintain as much wage egalitarianism as possible within its boundaries. Members are, however, allowed to accept gifts from friends and family, and they are allowed to have family members pay for their vacations outside Twin Oaks.

Adder and I walk down toward the main courtyard, past a crew working and joking in the vegetable garden, and up to the second floor of the residence called Harmony. Everyone at Twin Oaks can own as much as each individual can fit in his or her private room. Everything else is communal.

"This is what we call the Commie Closet," Adder says of a room devoted to hanging racks packed with clothes. "I come over here every morning and pick out something to wear." Today, like yesterday, that means a woman's long-sleeve blouse and another skirt.

"It's liberating," he says—not of the skirt, I think, though it could be of that as well, but of the independence from owning clothes in particular and things in general. "I get a personal kick out of not having a lot of stuff." That's not to say people don't get attached to, say, a comfortable shirt they don't want to donate to the community clothes bank. Yet the overall mood of the place follows John Dewey's seven-word injunction, "Hunger not to have, but to be."

"It's nice to not have to worry about carrying my wallet around," Adder says. "I think of this entire community as my house. I can go leave my laptop somewhere, and it's not going to get stolen. It's the same as leaving it in my living room. It's knowing your property is safe, but also not having to be attached to personal property."

Though Adder is earning labor credits for showing me around, he also has to get to one of his other jobs. So he passes me off to Keenan, a married father of two who has lived at Twin Oaks since 1983. In fact, Keenan and his sons, Rowan and Arlo, just finished building a ground-level residence for hospice members of Twin Oaks. Keenan and I walk along the gravel road that winds under mature beech and oak trees, toward Tupelo Ridge, the manufacturing side of Twin Oaks, where one ton of tofu is produced each day of operation, and seven thousand hammocks a year get woven into existence.

Keenan is, at the moment, incensed about something he recently read: a passage from Ayn Rand's book *Philosophy: Who Needs It?*, in which Rand takes Twin Oaks to task for squelching individual ambition and competition. (It particularly seemed to bother Rand that at Twin Oaks skinny-dipping had replaced competitive swimming as a form of leisure.)

"The original idea of Adam Smith–style capitalism made sense," Keenan allows. "But that idea has been totally twisted by corporate America to say that if you limit the pay a CEO receives, then you are totally undermining human motivation. Twin Oaks is an experiment in human motivation because there is zero motivation here to work hard, to perform well, or to be innovative or creative. We do away with any motivation. Not on purpose; that's just the side effect of equality. And that is why Ayn Rand hated Twin Oaks. Yet individuals here maintain their motivation to make art, to engage in personal growth, to create new businesses and make them run in the teeth of a scheme that provides no personal motivation. Here the motivation is intrinsic." Yet, it might be argued that intrinsic motivation seems to come from the traces of B. F. Skinner's philosophy that haven't entirely disappeared from Twin Oaks. "Environment affects people's behavior," Keenan admits. "If you put people in a positive, healthy environment, you are going to get positive, healthy people." In other words, behaviorism.

As an example, Keenan points to his son Arlo, who after spending a year away from the farm, on a Twin Oaks version of the Amish Rumspringa, has decided to return and join the community as an adult member. Keenan's road to Twin Oaks was much longer. His father, Ralph W. McGehee, was a CIA agent who ended his career by writing a recriminatory memoir, *Deadly Deceits: My 25 Years in the CIA*. "My father was extremely bitter about the experience," Keenan says. "He never knew what motives he was supporting. The decisions were made far from him, and it was always very murky." Then he laughs and says, "The thing about Twin Oaks is it is all very clear what's happening. It may be stupid or inefficient, but it is absolutely transparent who is making decisions and who benefits."

When Keenan went off to George Mason University to major in business, he found himself in the library most evenings reading utopian literature. At some point it dawned on him that the question he was trying to answer for himself was the question that lies behind all utopias: How should people live? One day, as he was thumbing through the card catalog—remember the card catalog?—he found right behind the citation for Skinner's *Walden Two* the listing for Kat Kinkade's first book, *The Walden Two Experiment*. He drove down to visit Twin Oaks and soon decided that perhaps this place held the answer to his question. Still, he was only two classes shy of a degree, and Kinkade herself urged Keenan to go back to school.

"It was the very opposite of the 'Come join us' cult experience," Keenan says. "Kat told me, 'Twin Oaks will be here when you're finished with school.'" But Keenan had already resolved to stay. He began teaching himself carpentry and soon set about building a visitor's cottage. And here arises one of Ayn Rand's other criticisms of communities such as Twin Oaks: that people with real expertise will leave to be better compensated in the capitalist economy, and only amateurs will remain. That is precisely what happened with Keenan. A highly skilled carpenter named Will, who had been at Twin Oaks for ten years and acted as project manager for the construction of Zhankoye, openly mocked Keenan's abilities as a builder. He turned much of the community against the project as well, and ultimately he made it known that if the cottage project continued, he and his family would leave Twin Oaks. Kinkade and the other planners at the time had to make a decision: acquiesce to what Kinkade called Will's "proud professionalism" or stick up for "ordinary communitarians." They did the latter, and Will and his family moved away. Kinkade justified the planners' choice by arguing, "Amateurism is, I believe, at the core of what Twin Oaks is . . . Those of us who remain for many years do become professional in certain areas, but they are not areas that exercise sweeping control over the Community's direction. Will longed for what could not be had." There certainly are experts at Twin Oaks, such as Pam Dawling, who oversees the vast garden and is the author of *Sustainable Market Farming*, but for the overall labor economy of Twin Oaks to work, being a generalist is the name of the game. Will was going to remain only if he were tacitly put in charge of planning all Twin Oaks' infrastructure. It was too much *Atlas Shrugged* for a community based on complete egalitarianism. To Ayn Rand, Will's departure proved her theory that Twin Oaks was doomed to fail. She wrote her attack on the community a year after Keenan arrived. Yet thirty years later, both Keenan and Twin Oaks are still here, and his latest project, the hospice residence, is a handsome monument to a Jeffersonian, Josiah Warren brand of self-taught generalism.

That is something Keenan wants to pass on to Arlo and Rowan, which is why carpentry became a crucial part of their education. Keenan and his wife, Kristen, are one of five married couples now living at Twin Oaks. Together, they have seven children. The original Twin Oaks plan, based on *Walden Two*, was for all children to be educated together in the behaviorist ways that B. F. Skinner, and Robert Owen before him, urged. The Twin Oaks pioneers even built a small school for that purpose. Yet, over the years, parents couldn't agree on one teaching philosophy or a standard curriculum, and gradually each family decided on its own version of homeschooling.

Anyone outside the family receives labor credits for helping school or care for the children at Twin Oaks. The main difference, Keenan says, in terms of raising children, is this: "In the mainstream, children are taught to obey, and here at Twin Oaks, children are taught to negotiate. Kids are taught early on that they are empowered." Keenan even theorizes that at Twin Oaks, "kids learn to speak early because they see that talking can get them things." On the flip side: "Adults speak to children with respect. Even if they're throwing a tantrum, adults say, 'It looks like you're really having a hard time,' rather than 'There's no reason to be upset.' That's when the parents end up yelling as much as the kids." And that, Keenan says, doesn't happen at Twin Oaks.

Married couples tend to stay here longer, but they also tend to keep more to themselves—the principal reason the Shakers and Robert Owen wanted nothing to do with marriage. In the evenings, for instance, Keenan's family will often stream a movie on Rowan's TV, a luxury he bought by doing carpentry work outside Twin Oaks. The community's economic egalitarianism doesn't apply to the children of Twin Oaks: that is, anyone under age eighteen. They, after all, didn't choose to live this way.

We walk past Modern Times, the mechanic shop named after

Josiah Warren's final experiment in equitable commerce out on Long Island. Inside, two bearded men are working on a busted fuel pump, and another is repairing a bicycle derailer. Parked outside the shop is a small fleet of cars and a couple of trucks, all with individualized license plates that read TO, followed by a number. Keenan points to the rusted-out fenders on an aging Corolla. Then he utters again the word I hear a lot at Twin Oaks when members are speaking about the world beyond its 465 acres: *mainstream.*

"People in the mainstream are proud of their clean house and new car," Keenan begins. "Here it's a mode of transportation. And our cars are grubby. The dirtiest car in any Charlottesville parking lot is a Twin Oaks car, and that's because nobody has any sense of identity tied up in the car. It's not who I am. The building where I live is not who I am. It's not like, I have a job and I bought all this stuff. So I save a bunch of money, because if you're trying to project a certain image, you spend a lot of money on that image. One of the hardest things about making the decision to live at Twin Oaks is you no longer have a very clear identity. In mainstream culture, people have an identity: this is my wife, this is my job, this is where I live. And it's easy to invite people into that and say, 'This is who I am.' Coming to Twin Oaks, you have to let go of all that. There's not a career you do in particular. I think that's really hard for a lot of people. A lot of people just can't make that leap to telling their friends and family, 'I'm living in a commune, and that's who I am.' When you take the leap to live at Twin Oaks, your personal identity is adrift, and I think for a lot of people that's very painful." In a sense, it sounds like the shedding of masks that Thomas Merton experienced when he became a monk at Gethsemani. Yet, there, the point was, and is, to lose one's ego-driven identity so as to find oneself in God. Here at Twin Oaks, even that is not an option, or at least not part of the official charter.

Black chickens are pecking through the leaf litter of Twin Oaks' sizeable woodlot as we approach two large warehouses. Industrial sounds and a pungent, almost sickly smell emanates from one building, while the other softly hums with the sound of a mechanical loom that spins string into rope. Herein lies the answer to what has made Twin Oaks profitable for almost half a century: tofu and hammocks. As Twin Oaks' founding members quickly departed, much of the community's early theorizing fell to Kat Kinkade. She convinced the newcomers that they needed one successful cottage industry that would support the rest of their subsistence living. The early hippies of Twin Oaks decided to make hammocks. And they made very good ones. In the late 1970s and early '80s, Twin Oaks secured a contract with the retail giant Pier One to make fifteen thousand hammocks a year. It's one of the common inconsistencies of almost every American utopia, past and present: that its internal politics (anarchism, communism, millennialism, or whatever it may be) is always subsidized in some way by the capitalist Leviathan that surrounds it. When Pier One decided to stop selling hammocks, orders obviously dropped, so Twin Oaks went into the tofu business.

I take a quick peek inside the noisy tofu plant, where workers are pouring soy curd into a large processing machine. Over at the hammock shop, one young man is running wooden frames through a band saw and then cutting the rope holes on a drill press. A Top 40 radio station is playing in the background. When the guy sees us, he sheepishly turns down the music, as if he just got caught consorting with the mainstream. The hit parade aside, Twin Oaks really does look like Marx's socialist ideal, where a man hunts in the morning, fishes in the afternoon, and rears cattle in the evening. It is a place where everyone seems busy and productive, where obnoxious foremen don't exist, and where all workers share equally in both the ownership and the profits from their labor.

Back outside, I ask Keenan how far up he thinks such a model could be scaled. "I'd say it can't go beyond a thousand people," he replies. "After that, they would take advantage of the system." Labor sheets could be fabricated or ignored. Both labor and social capital would be harder to maintain. Reciprocity might break down. So, rather than growing beyond its one hundred members, Twin Oaks' solution, its counterforce to the problems of an outsize and abusive economy, is to encourage and even subsidize new egalitarian communities. One such place, called Acorn, lies just seven miles down the South Anna River.

In the afternoon, I make the short drive over to Acorn. I cross the muddy South Anna on a narrow bridge and pass through a wide swath of woods that separates this much smaller egalitarian community from neighboring farms. The woodland buffer, as it turns out, provides good cover. When I climb the narrow stairs of Acorn's main building to look for a guy named Thomas, I find him sitting across from a pretty young woman wearing a dark sarong tied at her waist and nothing else. A month earlier, when I contacted Thomas about a possible visit, he sent me the *Acorn User Guide* and suggested I read it before arriving. The "Nudity Norms" section of the primer alerts visitors that "during the summer it is a common occurrence for people of both genders to garden or do outside work topless or naked." So I coolly pretend that there is nothing odd about a girl sitting topless at a computer. And of course there isn't. When you live in paradise, you get to act like it.

The *User Guide* also instructs newcomers to "think of visiting Acorn as visiting a foreign country." The boundaries of that country were created in the early 1990s, when the Twin Oaks waiting list grew so long that its members decided to form an auxiliary community on this seventy-two-acre farm. Twin Oaks bought the farm—it still holds the title—and in 1993, Acorn tenuously took root. In this foreign country there live thirty citizens, along with an ever-changing cast of guests, interns, and applicants making trial visits. When the population reaches forty, Acorn has to close its borders. But in lean years, the numbers have dropped to *Robinson Crusoe* levels, making the term *community* almost meaningless.

Like Twin Oaks, Acorn worked to establish a cottage industry of its own. Yet the efforts were so negligible that one member, a guy named Cricket, took on an outside job to help pay Acorn's bills. He went to work for the Southern Exposure Seed Exchange, a small business that the University of Virginia biologist Jeff McCormick ran out of his house. The idea was to collect and disseminate as many varieties of heirloom seeds as McCormick could find. The business grew quickly, and eventually McCormick found he was spending all his spare time just filling orders. In 1999 he asked Cricket if Acorn's members might be interested in buying the seed exchange. They were, they did, and buying Southern Exposure turned out to be, as Thomas later tells me, "the best decision Acorn ever made." Today Southern Exposure does a million-dollar annual business, almost all of it over the Internet.

Here in Acorn's main office, the walls are covered with seed posters, and orders seem to be piling up on every available flat surface. Thomas, fully clothed, has a brown beard and shoulder-length hair. He shakes my hand, and we walk back outside, where a naked young woman greets the postman, who, unfazed, hands her three packages.

"You didn't catch me on a great day," Thomas warns. "Today I've just about had it with Acorn."

I'm not at all prepared for this kind of opening remark; I was saving my tougher questions for later.

"What's going on?" I ask lamely.

We set off walking through an herb garden, toward an old farmhouse. "I came to Acorn from Twin Oaks five years ago because I wanted to be in a looser, more flexible community," Thomas says. "Twin Oaks budgets all its labor and all its money to the penny. But now it's like, be careful what you wish for, because we all have different ideas of what freedom means, and we all have different ideas of how much of other people's freedom we can tolerate. And I've noticed that I've hit my wall of how much of other people's freedom I can tolerate."

We haven't walked fifty yards and here we are, already at the nub of the whole utopia problem: What do you do when someone else's idea of paradise conflicts with your own? What do you do when, as I infer to be the case with Thomas, someone else makes you work harder for your idea because he or she isn't working at all?

When we reach what Thomas calls a "terribly built classic southern farmhouse, with further commune-style jury-rigging," he quickly returns to the role of tour guide. "When we opened up some of the walls," he tells me, "we found newspapers from 1908." Presumably they once acted as insulation. The place does look hard-worn, with doorjambs far out of plumb and mattresses filling most available floor space. "Community abhors a vacuum," Thomas jokes by way of explanation. In fact, Acorn is operating beyond capacity right now, so a few of the newer members are sleeping in tents in the woods.

He and his partner share a room upstairs, where they are currently trying to conceive. Right now there is only one child at Acorn, an infant, along with a woman who is very pregnant. Five years ago, Acorn put a moratorium on families, by which it really meant children. An era of what Thomas calls polyamory began. "I think a lot of people move to Acorn"—move here from the American mainstream, that is—"because they think they'll have more sexual freedom," Thomas says. And, he adds, they're probably right. "The sexual politics here are mostly a free-for-all. Other than sex with minors, we don't really impose anything on sexuality." I am almost certainly the only person on these seventy-two acres wearing a wedding ring today. Yet now, Thomas tells me, the idea of family is creeping back into the picture, and polyamory is giving way to monogamy with some of the older members.

If Acorn hasn't completely absolved itself of bourgeois cultural mores, it also, like Twin Oaks, has not completely cut economic ties with the world beyond these seventy-two acres. "In terms of economic self-sufficiency," Thomas says, "we're perfectly self-sufficient. We grow and sell things and make a profit. We're not on food stamps or welfare. We are basically internally anarcho-communist, and we are externally a capitalist organization." Does such a seeming contradiction compromise Acorn's experiment in social engineering? In truth, all American utopian communities, even the staunchly independent Shakers, maintained some economic connection to the unenlightened world around them. The Shakers packaged (for the first time) what we now call heirloom seeds, just as Acorn does. In that sense, one might argue, Acorn's idealism (in the form of nongenetically modified seeds, small symbols of self-sufficiency) reverberates out into the larger culture. But perhaps that begs a larger question: What exactly is Acorn's philosophical and political stance vis-à-vis the consumer culture that surrounds it? Is this a utopia of reconstruction or a utopia of escape? The answer, I think, is that it's both and neither. It is a mistake, I now realize, to overlay the millennial ambitions and expectations of the nineteenth-century utopianists onto these twenty-first-century communities. Are Twin Oaks and Acorn out to change the world? Not really. Or, if they are, they realize that first they must change *themselves*. It's a stance Henry David Thoreau would have readily endorsed. Seek reform in your heart before you seek it in others, he chided his liberal neighbors. "The reform which you talk about can be undertaken any morning before unbarring the door," he wrote. "We need not call any convention." Though the current egalitarian communities do hold an annual convention, their purpose seems more about honing the blueprint for cooperative, nonexploitive living, not taking down the system they have fled.

When I ask if there is an element of escapism involved in making the decision to join a community like Acorn, Thomas laughs and says, "Oh yeah! But there's escapism in suburbia, too. I think living in communities is actually really hard. The hardest thing I've ever experienced is being in a relationship with someone in the community and breaking up with her. In the city, you say, 'Okay, I'll see you twice a year.' And here you're seeing her every day."

Several goats wander across the road where Thomas and I are walking. Though the dietary fare at Acorn is generally vegetarian, Thomas says these billies will eventually end up on dinner plates or in some stew. A temporary fence surrounds an orchard where chickens take dust baths in the shade of the pear trees. Two ancient camper trailers, the kind my dad used to hitch behind our family station wagon, have been converted into henhouses. Thomas describes the food politics at Acorn as local omnivore. "We say we only buy groovy meat," he explains. "Groovy" means anything either local or organic, or both.

Thomas leads me past what he calls "Acorn's greatest Dumpster dive ever." It's a makeshift workshop made out of steel beams that members of Acorn salvaged from an old warehouse they were paid to dismantle about ten years ago. In a way, it represents what I'm beginning to think of as the dual nature of the Acorn landscape. On the one hand, you have to applaud the ingenious, improvised element of the workshop, or the camper–chicken coops, or the hot tub down by the pond that has been fashioned from the kind of old propane tank my grandmother used to have flanged to her house. Acorn has the feel of the 1960s "drop cities," communes built out of the detritus of the American consumer dream. Everything is DIY, and all this resourcefulness is admirable. Yet the overall effect is one of disarray, even dinginess. Perhaps it's just the heat of the day, but the whole place seems to have a *sag* to it. A mailbox rusts incongruously beside a fire pit in the courtyard, and I get the feeling that it has been sitting there for years.

The one structure at Acorn that does impress is the new office for the seed business that is currently taking shape behind the other buildings. Using traditional timber framing techniques and local timber, the Acorn communards have set in place the two-story skeleton that will eventually house Southern Exposure. Today a local contractor is operating a crane as a guy in sandals, purple shorts, and a Chinese straw hat guides one of the higher beams into place. Both men and women are at work on the site, clothed and unclothed.

Thomas and I walk past the "smoke shack," where two heavily pierced and tattooed anarchists seem to be shirking their duties of the day—though, for all I know, they have just shucked twenty pounds of beans for the community's lunch and are taking a well-deserved smoke break. Thomas's mood suggests otherwise, and they seem to be the source of his displeasure this morning. For one thing, if you smoke at Acorn, you cannot do much of the garden work, because you might pass on the tobacco mosaic virus to the plants from which seeds are saved. You also cannot work in the seed-packing department. In other words, you get out of a lot of work simply by taking a smoke break. Ironically, the success of the seed business might be contributing to community indolence. "If we're kind of lazy and inefficient," Thomas tells me, "we'll still have enough money to survive." The result is what he calls a two-vision community. Thomas's vision involves "a high level of communication, a vision of growing the business as an engine for creating new communities." The other vision involves a definition of anarchy—not Thomas's definition, he insists—whereby anyone who wants to live at Acorn can, and anyone should be allowed to work or not work as he or she sees fit. It seems more of a high-school-kid-who-just-discovered-the-Sex-Pistols kind of anarchy than the kind Josiah Warren introduced to this country almost two hundred years ago. In Warren's version, the first principle of liberty had to be counterbalanced by personal responsibility. Being shiftless back in Utopia, Ohio, meant you would soon starve.

"The big thing that's coming up now is accountability for labor," Thomas says. "We need some system to make sure everyone is pulling their fair share." At Twin Oaks, of course, labor sheets ensure such accountability, and if you don't perform your forty-two hours of work each week, you will eventually be asked to leave. But, as Thomas said, Acorn rejected such formal regimentation long ago. The reason is that, unlike Twin Oaks' planner-manager form of government, Acorn operates on a model of consensus. That means everyone has to agree on every change made in the community; if someone doesn't agree, he or she must at least consent to stand aside and not block the new proposal. To reach such consensus on labor sheets, Thomas suggested, would be highly unlikely in the current climate. That gives him only two options, really: bottle his current frustrations or leave.

Earlier this morning, in the Twin Oaks mechanic shop, a guy named Puck, who was repairing a bike, dismissed the Acorn consensus model as "totalitarian" for precisely that reason: it's a way of ensuring that no change, even needed change, take place. As a result, Acorn has gone through some severe boom-and-bust cycles in its twenty years, where the only way to bring about change in the community is for it to nearly fall apart and for those responsible for the failure to leave. Then new people join. But because Acorn doesn't, in Thomas's view, have a very specific mission, other than the key principles of egalitarianism, division arises and the cycle starts all over again.

"I want something more from my life other than someplace where we just work and hang out and smoke pot," Thomas says as we pass out of earshot of the smokers. He envisions starting new communities with profits from Southern Exposure, or perhaps even starting a worker-owned co-op built around a similar business, one that would propel Acorn into a more sustainable future. "Hammocks are good business," Thomas allows, "but no one ever moved to a commune to weave a hammock." I see his point; as a vision for melding one's actual labor with a progressive worldview, seed saving seems much cooler than hammocks or, for that matter, tofu made from monoculture soybeans. I think for a minute that the ideal egalitarian community would combine the organization of Twin Oaks with the seed-saving business of Acorn. But that's missing the point, I realize. The key to these communities is decentralization, not consolidation. Their adherents want to create *more* places that follow the egalitarian model, not fewer.

We are heading down a dirt road that leads past the four acres Acorn has put under cultivation. A man and a woman are staking tomatoes as we pass. When I first contacted Acorn, it was Thomas alone who returned my e-mails. I knew that neither he nor anyone else at Acorn held an official title. So what is his role, I wonder, and is there some kind of unspoken hierarchy in the community?

"We had a woman here a year ago who was having a psychotic break," Thomas says. "She kept talking about needing to see the king of Acorn. I said to her, 'Am I the king?' And she said, 'No, you're just the administrator.'" Thomas laughs. He looks a little too laid-back to be a king, but he obviously possesses the administrative skills to help run a one-million-dollar business.

Actually, Thomas's background is in poetry; he earned an MFA from Columbia, where he studied with John Ashbery and

Kenneth Koch. "That really prepares you for living in a commune," he jokes. After his parents divorced, Thomas says, "I came up with this notion that a more flexible, self-created family was more reliable." So after graduate school, he began visiting intentional communities and eventually landed at Twin Oaks, and then Acorn. Now, after five years, he obviously wields a certain degree of influence. "The idea is to not be hierarchical, but hierarchies inevitably come into play," he says. "There's the hierarchy of who's the most persuasive in meetings, or who's been here the longest, who has the most cultural knowledge, who works the most in a particular area. There are spheres of influence."

As we pass a few more gardeners on their way back for lunch, I notice that people make very little casual eye contact here or at Twin Oaks. It's the dynamic of a large family who sees so much of one another, at such close proximity, that everyone dispenses with the usual social pleasantries. Perhaps here, affection can be taken for granted.

Thomas excuses himself to take care of some office business, and I take a seat at one of the picnic tables in the courtyard. The community as a whole seems quite a bit younger than that at Twin Oaks. Anarchy, at least this version of it, looks like a young person's game. Ingrid, a young woman I meet over a bowl of bean salad, has just graduated from Bennington and was working as a roofer when a friend suggested she check out Acorn.

"I was not aware that places with this amount of sharing existed," she tells me. Slim with short brown hair, Ingrid wears a tattered plaid shirt. At first, the word *sharing* strikes me as almost quaint—something we instruct children to do, but that they soon realize has little application in the world their parents inhabit. Yet that is really Acorn's fundamental task, according to Ingrid. It is what called the community into existence in the first place, and it is in some ways the most important critique that egalitarian communities offer the larger culture. "Why do we need fifty vacuum cleaners in fifty apartments," Thomas had earlier asked rhetorically, "and fifty dishwashers and fifty cars when we can probably get by with five?"

At Acorn, a critique that begins with American hyperindividualism soon moves on to the corporate culture that has centralized so much wealth and power. "In my wacky narrative about human life," Ingrid begins, "there's the trajectory toward dependency on huge organizations who roll forward with motivations of making sure this imaginary number"—the bottom line—"continues to grow, and that's their goal. But there's this other emerging trajectory of independence, on learning to care for yourself and care for the larger community. And I would like to facilitate that." The way she's decided to do that is through another fundamental human act: saving seeds. As of this year, Southern Exposure saves and disseminates more than seven hundred varieties of organic seeds free of genetic modification. Some of those seeds come from other farms, including Twin Oaks—the Edisto 47 muskmelon seed is a favorite—and the Berea College Farm, down the road from where I live in Kentucky. From January to April the Acorn workers do most of their retail business; from March to August they tend to the gardens; from August to October they harvest, clean, and test their seeds; in the fall, they ship ginseng and goldenseal around the world; and at the end of the year, they print up the new catalog and start all over again. Southern Exposure specializes in heirloom and open-pollinated varieties of vegetables, herbs, and flowers.

Open pollination is simply, as Ingrid says, "the default nature of plants." Rather than cross-breeding two compatible types of plants to form a hybrid or, worse, genetically altering a plant in a lab, open pollination depends on wind and insects. Indeed, as we're talking, a fat bumblebee works a bouquet of bee balm that fills a mason jar on the picnic table where we sit. Seeds from a hybrid plant, say, a Better Boy tomato, won't replicate that same tomato in the next growing season because they will revert back to the qualities of one of their parent plants. Open-pollinated seeds, by contrast, are stabler and will reproduce plants just like their parents. If a seed from an open-pollinated plant dates back beyond 1950, when hybridization began in earnest, it's considered an heirloom seed—one that has been passed down from grower to grower for at least sixty-five years.

"If we sell you our seeds," says Ingrid, "you can keep them and you can save seeds from those tomatoes and they will come true to type, true to the variety. For me, it's about individual food sovereignty." That's a far different form of individualism than the consumer and antigovernment varieties that occupy so much bandwidth in this country. But it seems to me a truer form of individualism in that it involves an ethic of responsibility at the most elemental level of sustenance, an ethic that seems missing in the rights-based demand for more guns and less health care.

Food sovereignty has been on Ingrid's mind lately, ever since Southern Exposure joined a lawsuit against the biotech giant Monsanto. For many in the sustainable agriculture movement, Monsanto is publicly traded enemy number one. Nothing seems as repulsive to these growers as the notion that something living—a seed, for instance—can be made the subject of a human patent. Yet Monsanto doesn't stop there. Once it has patented genetically modified seeds, seeds that are resistant to its own Roundup herbicide, Monsanto sues farmers (to the tune of over $15 million) for patent infringement. If pollen from a Monsanto crop has blown over to a neighboring farmer's field, that farmer can be sued for growing Monsanto seed. The farmers surrounding the Acorn land grow genetically modified corn and soybeans. If, Ingrid says, Monsanto sued Acorn because some of that pollen blew across the South Anna River, "we would be economically devastated."

So, two years ago, to preempt such legal action, Southern Exposure joined the Organic Seed Growers and Trade Association, along with eighty other plaintiffs, in a lawsuit asking that organic farmers not be held liable if their plants are contaminated with Monsanto's genetically modified genes. The organic farmers also asked that the courts declare GMO patents invalid because they violate—well, they violate the laws of nature. On the first matter, the plaintiff's lawyer, Dan Ravicher, argued, "It seems quite perverse that an organic farmer contaminated by transgenic seed could be accused of patent infringement, but Monsanto has made such accusations before and is notorious for having sued hundreds of farmers for patent infringement, so we had to act to protect the interests of our clients." What's more perverse, says Ingrid, "is the absurd concept that the wind and bees could be controlled. In my mind, we should switch this thing around and say, it's the responsibility of farmers using genetically modified crops to stop them at the edge of their property. Which, of course, would be economically impossible."

Still, to almost no one's surprise, the judge ruled against the organic farmers. "My major memory of it," says Ingrid, "was 'Man, these Monsanto lawyers really have nice suits and they have really nice shoes; I think we're sunk. This is the nice-suits game, and I think they won.'" But not before Monsanto made binding assurances that it would not "take legal action against growers whose crops might inadvertently contain traces of Monsanto biotech genes (because, for example, some transgenic seed or pollen blew onto the grower's land)."

It was a small victory in a much larger fight to preserve biological diversity in the food system. While we're talking, a woman named Ira, the unofficial CEO of Southern Exposure, joins us. She is the only African American member of Acorn and, in her sixties, the oldest by decades. In fact, Ira was one of the founding twelve members and has lived at Acorn or Twin Oaks for forty-six years. By the time she was twenty, all of Ira's family had passed away. "So," she says, "the community became that for me."

Yet Ira bristles when I suggest that she might be the matriarch of Acorn. "Nobody here ever tells anybody else what to do," she says. "So I feel all that comes with more age and knowledge is more responsibility."

Ingrid, who has been at Acorn for two years, agrees, but says, "There are people who have taken responsibility for so much that they're constantly trying to make sure things don't fall apart." Ira and Thomas seem to be two such people, though Ira doesn't acknowledge as much.

Ingrid, for her part, has taken on what she calls "the heroically disgusting experience" of taking the trash to the dump each day. "I think we have a serious clutter problem," she says, as if reading my own earlier thoughts, "so I enjoy removing things."

I asked Ira and Ingrid about the hardest part of living in an egalitarian community. Ira is succinct: "You can't always get what you want." That, in seven words, is the downside of consensus-style radical democracy. But perhaps it is also an articulation of how mature people act when they acknowledge that in a community, a city, or even a country, their own rights and desires are not the only consideration when it comes to the health of the whole.

"For me," says Ingrid, "the hardest thing at Acorn is balancing what you do in service to the community and putting energy into things you dream about learning and doing for yourself." And for the recent architecture student, that tension can manifest in both spatial and symbolic ways. "When I lived in an apartment, I would rearrange the whole place to throw a dinner party," she says. "You know, create a particular kind of environment. So I do scrape my fingernails on the sense of control over space that I don't have here. I have this one box where I can do whatever. But here," she says, gesturing to the communal space all around her, "it's like: this is all our world all the time. So I do feel like, in my own utopia, maybe I would have a living room."

One of Acorn's problems, it appears to an outsider, is indeed space: there doesn't appear to be enough of it, at least not enough under one roof. Thirty people eat, sleep, and hang out in only two buildings, the farmhouse and Heartwood, the rammed-earth structure that functions as kitchen, cafeteria, office, living space, and dormitory. When Ira and Ingrid move on to their next tasks, I linger awhile in the community room inside Heartwood. A group of women are cleaning up, and a young man is standing over a large bread machine, mixing ingredients for the evening meal. Multiple strips of yellow flypaper hang from the ceiling, and the only light in the house comes from outside. Gillian Welch's CD *Soul Journey* plays in the kitchen, and two of the women sing along as they clean.

Several of the conversations I overhear are about leaving Acorn. One young man tells a woman, "Why don't you just take a vacation?"

"I haven't been keeping track of my labor," she says, "so I don't know if I've logged enough time for a vacation."

The problem is that if anyone leaves, that person has to give up his or her room, so that when they return—and it sounds as if many do return—they may well be back in a tent in the woods.

As I listen to this talk of taking leave, I realize that perhaps I've been thinking about utopia as too static an entity, a place like Pleasant Hill, where time stood still because the Shakers were already living in the fullness of time, the millennial ever-present. They, after all, had nowhere to go until the resurrection. But here at Acorn, in the twenty-first century, things are more fluid: people come and go and come back again. They might move to Twin Oaks; they might, as Ingrid did, take a six-month bike ride across the country. Acorn is obviously important—its principles and people are important—but it certainly isn't the only future that these mostly young people can imagine.

Thomas told me the longest most people stay at Acorn is five years. Maybe, except for Ira, that's the life cycle of such intense, close communal living. "I've been here five years," Thomas said earlier, "and I'm thinking of leaving."

Still, when I catch up with him later, down by the swimming hole, he seems a little more sanguine about the place he has called home for half a decade. What would make him stay? I ask. It's simple, he replies: this is a community of people who want and need each other's company and cooperation. What's more, Acorn demonstrates that the human race can lower its consumption and create the conditions for economic justice. "This is how human beings were meant to be organized," Thomas says; "small groups of people sharing at a low subsistence but stable level."

According to the pioneering work of the American ecological philosopher Paul Shepard, Thomas is right. Shepard argued that because *Homo sapiens* evolved into a species during the Pleistocene era, our entire genome is encoded with a Paleolithic need for small communities and a closeness to the natural world. Hunter-gatherer groups were, Shepard reminds us, egalitarian, leisurely, humble before the mysteries of the cosmos and the natural world. They emphasized sharing over hoarding. They owned very few things, but those objects, such as a knife with a finely engraved bone handle, tended to be extremely well made. They welcomed outsiders and understood land ownership only in a collective way. Perhaps as a result of that, they made no instruments of war. We moderns, on the other hand, invented history and progress and angry sky gods; we shed our genetic predispositions in the name of superficial change and novelty. We want to be something that we are not, something godlike and alienated from the most fundamental processes of life. We want others to kill our food and build our shelters and even tell our stories. So, argues Shepard, we suffer all manner of psychological maladies and social violence. "We are free to create culture as we will," Shepard writes, "but the prototype to which the genome is accustomed is Pleistocene society." And we can return to it, he says, because we never really left; it is encoded in our every cell.

Shepard might disapprove of the domesticated plants and animals at Acorn, and he himself could certainly be accused of romanticizing our ancestral past. Yet, as Thomas suggests, this small community does represent many of the Pleistocene virtues of our genome-bearing ancestors. Shepard would have approved of its size and that it has placed, in the middle of its courtyard, what Shepard calls the "greatest innovation of humankind": a fire circle. In the conclusion of his last book, *Coming Home to the Pleistocene*, Shepard wrote, "Socially the fire circle is typically composed of about twenty-four persons or a twelve-adult council of the whole. This group size is magic for our species. It is deeply embedded in the human unconscious, the perfect number to deal with a problem, visit and dance, mourn and celebrate, tell a story, plan for tomorrow, hold a council, or eat a bison." While I doubt the young anarchists at Acorn eat (or kill) much bison, they do hold councils and deal with problems through consensus building. They make music and dance and, when it isn't the middle of summer, presumably tell stories around the fire. In their own singular manner, they do seem to be cutting a narrow path back to the Pleistocene.

I make it back to Twin Oaks in time for dinner, served buffet style and eaten mainly, since the weather is nice, at picnic tables outside ZK. I pile my plate with cucumber salad, lentils, cornbread pancakes, and a sort of goulash labeled "Dumpstered beef," which is exactly what it sounds like. Members from both Acorn and Twin Oaks routinely rifle through the Dumpsters behind supermarkets for meat they regard as gratuitously discarded and perfectly edible. I'm not exactly sure what kind of beef I am eating—the sauce is quite heavy—but it isn't bad. Back at Acorn, Thomas told me the Dumpster diving was "more of a political thing than a necessity thing." Political, I surmise, because the Dempster-Dumpster has become perhaps the most profligate symbol of the American culture of disposability and waste. According to Reuters, Americans throw away $165 billion in food annually, about half of what actually gets cooked or grown. I had a student once who made a short documentary film that showed him furnishing an entire student apartment from the Dumpsters behind a local strip mall. Apparently, many of the larger chain stores simply discard anything returned to the store. So my student found sheets, curtains, blankets, towels, and all manner of cleaning supplies. It's as if these Dumpsters represent the guilty conscience of capitalism—condensed, chaotic versions of the big-box stores themselves, the source of an alternative economy wherein waste equals sustenance. One part of the country shops through the front of the mall; another scavenges in the back.

One table inside ZK is designated the "fun table." Work cannot be discussed there, which is, I surmise, a testament to how seriously Twin Oakers take work: they have to find a designated place *not* to talk about it. Outside, I join a circle of a dozen men and women eating on homemade wooden benches, along with a dancing little girl who is determined, as she whirls, to be shed of her dress.

In my short time at Twin Oaks, I've noticed that a meta-commentary often runs throughout casual conversations about the very *idea* of Twin Oaks.

"Can you pass me the salt?" someone says.

And the salt passer replies, "Of course. That would be an excellent way to practice community building."

When Twin Oaks sponsored its own six-word story contest last year, one entry (my favorite) read, "We share everything. Hey, that's mine!" The fact that these one hundred people are here means that they take the principles of Twin Oaks very seriously, so they're free not to take themselves too seriously, free to poke fun at their own noble aspirations.

Soon the group is swapping stories about "trippers"—members who drive to Charlottesville to buy things for other members, using their monthly pay. Apparently trippers are known for misinterpreting their shopping lists, and hilarity often ensues. As it turns out, there's more than one way to gloss the phrase "six Magic Hats." One tripper went to a costume store and bought six felt top hats when, in fact, what was wanted was a six-pack of the craft beer called Magic Hat.

Before coming to Twin Oaks, I had expected, and slightly dreaded, some great community-building activity after dinner: a large drum circle, an epic game of ultimate Frisbee, or raucous skinny-dipping. But most people simply wander off in small groups to do their own thing. A klezmer trio practices outside ZK, some couples go for walks, and other people just hang out with their housemates. I walk down to the river and watch a member of the Twin Oaks dairy team—a man who appears to be the most amiable prototype one might imagine of the Jeffersonian farmer—singing to six Holsteins as he urges his herd out of the pasture, across the road, and back into the barn for milking.

I settle into a hammock chair that hangs from—what else?—an oak tree near the main courtyard, and take out my copy of the novel that set this whole movement in motion—Thomas More's *Utopia*. In 2016, the slim volume will be five hundred years old. Nearly two thousand years separated it from Plato's *Republic*, two millennia during which utopian thinking practically disappeared from Western literature and philosophy. Christianity, as interpreted by the Apostle Paul, had hung the kingdom of God in the heavens, and it wasn't until the decline of the Middle Ages that adventurous thinkers began again searching *this* world for a utopian order. The invention of the magnetic compass, no doubt, had much to do with that. It fired the imaginations of mental travelers like More, who began to conceive of some terra incognita where life seemed more civilized than sixteenth-century Europe.

The narrator of *Utopia* is a seafaring wanderer named Raphael Hythloday, and his critique of medieval Europe bears an uncanny resemblance to presidential candidate Bernie Sanders's take on present-day America. All social systems, charges Raphael, are "conspiracies of the rich to advance their own interests under the pretext of organizing society." Pride and vanity have made men greedy, and created an unnatural condition of vast inequality. For the proud, prosperity isn't measured by "what you've got yourself, but what others haven't got." Thus the wealthy enclose the commons, driving the poor to starvation and theft. "You create thieves," Raphael says incredulously, "then punish them for stealing!" He certainly would have something to say about this country's epidemic of incarceration. As for the financial system (then as now), Raphael observes, "People like aristocrats, goldsmiths, or money-lenders, who either do no work at all, or do work that's really not essential, are rewarded for their laziness or their unnecessary activities by a splendid life of luxury." The inhabitants of Utopia, where Raphael sojourned for five years, solved all of these problems by simply eliminating money and ensuring an equal distribution of goods, just as Plato recommended in his *Republic*.

However, if *Utopia* still stands as a useful critique of modern capitalism, it falters badly as a model of reform. Today, More's Utopia looks much like a parody of, or a prequel to, Soviet-style communism. Utopia's fifty-four towns all look exactly the same, the houses look the same, and the Utopians all wear the same drab clothing. There is no private property and, as Raphael reports, "everything's under state control." Mayors, elected by the people, pretty much run the show. The culture is thoroughly patriarchal, so much so that on feast days, wives kneel before their husbands and ask forgiveness for whatever perceived sins they might have committed. Anyone who indulges in premarital sex is severely punished because, reason the Utopians, very few people would want to get married if they knew how much more fun it is to have multiple sexual partners (prospective brides and grooms are, however, allowed to see their partner naked before deciding on marriage because, reason the Utopians, you wouldn't buy a horse before removing the harness and saddle for a full examination). Those caught in adultery are often made slaves—*Utopia* is a very Catholic book—who then perform all the unpleasant work of the country.

But those who haven't fallen into iniquity enjoy an admirable kind of happiness that seems to draw from the rival classic philosophies of the Stoics and Epicureans. Happiness is, as Raphael says, "the *summum bonum* towards which we're naturally impelled by virtue—which in their definition means following one's natural impulses, as God meant us to do." Like Epicureans, the Utopians (modestly) enjoy sex, food, exercise, music. Like the Stoics, they believe in a supreme being, "quite beyond the grasp of the human mind," who is identical with nature. Thus "they can please God merely by studying the natural world, and praising Him for it." When Raphael tells the Utopians about Jesus, they immediately convert to Christianity since, as the Shakers believed, "Christ prescribed of His own disciples a communist way of life." Yet the Utopians revere religious tolerance above all else, and they devise a powerful deterrent to fundamentalism: anyone who becomes too zealous in proselytizing for Christianity, or any other religious creed, is either exiled or made a slave. This is in keeping with the sentiments of their founder, Utopos, who "considered it possible that God made different people believe different things, because He wanted to be worshipped in many different ways."

As I read *Utopia* here in the context of Twin Oaks, I imagine myself as a modern Raphael, portaged by automobile instead of ship to this relatively unknown island of equality, religious freedom, and homogeneous architecture. Like the Utopians, the members of Twin Oaks have essentially abolished money and all the ills that accompany it. Certainly they would agree with Raphael when he says, "With the simultaneous abolition of money and the passion for money, how many other social problems have been solved, how many crimes eradicated. For obviously the end of money means the end of all those types of criminal behavior which daily punishments are powerless to check: fraud, theft, burglary, brawls, riots, disputes, rebellion, murder, treason, and black magic." None of that goes on here, which makes me think, as I close the book, that perhaps this place really does deserve to be called— utopia.

The next morning, I wake with the roosters to meet the garden crew. Since I've maintained backyard vegetable beds for most of my adult life, I figure I can make myself most useful among the long furrows of Twin Oaks. Six of us are gathered around the tool-shed next to the original farmhouse, which now functions as the main office. Hoes, rakes, and shovels hang in neat rows inside the small wooden shed. Our work team's "honcho" (the Twin Oaks term for supervisor) is a young woman named Rayne, and she has a long list of what we need to accomplish in four hours. Tomatoes, cucumbers, chard, and watermelons need harvesting. Potatoes need to be mulched. Harvested beds need to be turned, scuffled, and replanted. We divvy up the work, some volunteering for certain tasks. When one aspiring member named John says he'd like to help harvest watermelons, Rayne replies that only full members are permitted to work among the melons.

"So much for doing away with hierarchies," I say by way of a joke, but no one laughs. Instead, John and I are relegated to pulling, clipping, and washing carrots. As we toss their green heads into a plastic bucket to be composted, I ask John what brought him to Twin Oaks. He says that after college he ended up in a soul-sucking job with the Norfolk, Virginia, Chamber of Commerce. My own family is from the Hampton Rhodes area of Virginia, and I can readily attest that having to live in Norfolk *and* work for the Chamber of Commerce sounds like its own circle of hell.

"I just wanted to do something completely different with my life," John says.

"Looks like you came to the right place."

He gives a quick grin and says, "Yeah, this feels right to me."

Before the Great Recession of 2008, most people came to Twin Oaks because they had some tangential experience with it, or they had a passion for organic gardening, worker ownership, sustainability politics—something like that. But in the last five years, there are more applicants like John: individuals dissatisfied with their place in the larger culture and looking to make a decisive break. Yesterday I met a young man who was a loan originator before the housing bubble burst. "It was such dishonest work," he told me. "I just couldn't live with myself any longer." So he chucked it all, sold his car and condo, and came to Twin Oaks.

When we're done with the carrots, John and I grab two shovels and rakes and head back to turn and prep the now-empty bed. Since John is working shoeless, I do the shoveling and he rakes behind me. Then we lay in four rows of beans. The soil here is incredibly rich and loamy. I love the smell of it in the cool morning air.

With that task done, John heads off to pick chard; I report back to Rayne and offer to harvest cucumbers.

"Do you know how to pick cucumbers?" she asks.

The answer seems so obvious that I think it's a trick question. "Uh, yeah, I think I do," I reply hesitantly.

"We don't pick them if they still have three sides," she explains. "Only if they're round on the sides."

Though I've been growing my own cucumbers for twenty years, I'd never even thought of cucumbers as *having* sides. "I think I see what you mean," I say and grab a basket.

"I'll come with you," Rayne says, and I suspect her of doubting my judgment when it comes to cucumbers. (*Cucumis sativus* is, after all, in the same botanical family as the melons that newcomers are forbidden to harvest.) As we work, Rayne, who is on a long hiatus from graduate studies in Massachusetts, asks what I'm writing about. I briefly explain my project and how Twin Oaks fits into and extends the utopian tradition.

"When I came to Twin Oaks," she says, "I was ecstatic to be

living around such cool people and in such a cool place. I used to go on and on about it. But now I realize that a lot of my friends here are just as depressed as my friends back in graduate school." She is quiet for a minute, and then says, "I think maybe we as humans don't really evolve to be happy."

Looking up, I realize that I am suddenly confounded by Rayne's remark. Happiness, after all, is the bedrock of secular utopianism; at least it has been since Robert Owen and Charles Fourier. And why would Twin Oaks have adopted B. F. Skinner's belief that environments can be manipulated to change a person's behavior if the ultimate goal wasn't to become happier people? Skinner even claimed that human environments could be changed to short-circuit evolution and *make* people happier. Wasn't that the point of Twin Oaks? Create a community where sociability and sharing are the norms, and the unexploited social animals will be happy, or at least happier. Then again, I suppose the real shortcoming of behaviorism is that we are made up of more than just our actions and reactions. If one is given to depression due to family history or some chemical imbalance in the brain, moving to Twin Oaks isn't going to solve much. I keep all these thoughts to myself, and we work our way down the row.

"You really do know what you're doing," Rayne finally allows as I finish my row with a full basket of perfectly plump cucumbers, no flat sides to be seen. "There are a lot of people who've been here for two years and still don't know one vegetable from the other."

"Well, I guess there's always the tofu factory," I say as we load our harvest into a two-wheeled handcart beside baskets of chard, tomatoes, and beans.

"Can you take these up to the kitchen?" Rayne asks. "It'll be time for lunch by then."

As it turns out, there is a planners' meeting at two this afternoon in the science fiction library of the Oneida building, and Adder tells me I'm welcome to sit in on it. He and Twin Oaks' only other planner, a young woman named Sapphire, perch cross-legged on old couches and talk over open binders in which they make notes in longhand. Here in the science fiction library there are no signs of any innovation after . . . well, after the three-ring binder.

Much of the planners' decision making for today involves the mundane stuff of community, such as whether to take any punitive action against a member who has defaulted on a three-hundred-dollar loan he took out to buy a dog. Other decisions, though, are of deathly import. Last year, an eighty-nine-year-old member decided that she wanted to stop eating and drinking. She was in considerable pain and ready for death to take its course. Adder and Sapphire consulted lawyers, psychologists, and physicians. It turned out that as long as no family member objected, the woman's decision was legal and, they decided, ethical. So, with the blessing of the planners, the woman began to act on her final decision. Yet other community members were alarmed, both about the act itself and about the bad publicity it could bring if word got out that Twin Oaks was assisting a suicide. Still, the planners Adder and Sapphire, both in their twenties, had weighed all the evidence and made a decision; the community had to respect that. Then a week into the hunger strike, the woman's son contacted the police, who arrived at Twin Oaks and took the woman to UVA Hospital for a psychiatric evaluation. The son's intervention was the one thing the planners couldn't control; nor did they want to. They were simply acting on the woman's plea for a dignified end. After the son entered the picture, the woman could return to Twin Oaks only if she agreed not to act on her death wish again. She consented. Still, Adder and Sapphire's original decision seems to me like a heavy weight for such young people to bear. But that is the planner-manager system. If a manager doesn't have jurisdiction—that is, if the issue doesn't concern his or her work group—then the planners act as the Supreme Court of Twin Oaks. They hear the arguments of the community, expressed through the Opinions and Ideas board, and then they rule.

———

It's late afternoon when I catch up with Valerie, a middle-aged yoga instructor—at least, that's one of her many jobs—who arrived at Twin Oaks in 1992. When I ask about her background, Valerie simply says that she didn't want her parents' suburban life. Today, she is Twin Oaks' communications director, its liaison to the outside world. In that capacity, she has thought long and deeply about why this community outlived all the other communes and drop cities that sprang up in the 1960s.

"We're still here because of our incredible structure," she tells me as we walk down to the main courtyard on this cloudless day. I mention that when I was at Acorn yesterday, I saw very little of anything resembling structure.

"Well, if you have too much structure, you're rigid," Valerie explains, "and if you have too much flexibility, you're unstable. Twin Oaks edges toward one side of that spectrum, and Acorn edges toward the other." Acorn's consensus model of governance can work there, she explains, because it's a smaller group of people. It's easier to get everyone together and easier to get them all on the same page, however grudgingly. Twin Oaks is more sprawling, with many more moving parts, so decision making flows through the Opinions and Ideas board, then the planners and managers, and finally back into the larger community.

We sit down at a round wooden table at the center of the courtyard. A steady stream of what Valerie calls "Twin Oakers" pass us on their way from one task to another. A father and daughter roll around in the grass while, nearby, two bearded men in their forties work across from one another weaving a hammock.

"The most important thing we're trying to do here," Valerie begins, "is create a life where we can live in accordance with our values. That's our raison d'être, the big reason we live so differently from"—and I already know what word is coming next—"the mainstream." Valerie speaks quickly and intensely, never losing eye contact. Her tone is one of a teacher patiently explaining a complicated piece of calculus to a tenth-grader. She is, I'm beginning to sense, the anti–Ayn Rand of Twin Oaks. "If you look at people's life cycles," she continues, "they're born in a hospital that someone else owns, they go to a school that someone else runs, they work for a company that someone else owns. All of those things that happen are owned and controlled by somebody else. Regardless of your own values and how you would like to manifest them in the world, you have to fit yourself into those organizations' and institutions' values, which are often not at all what your own values are. What we're doing is birthing our babies at home; schooling our children at home; working in our own worker-owned business; and when we die, we are buried on our own land with no chemicals. Marx talks about owning the means of production. I think we take it a step further and own every aspect of our lives, and we can therefore do them in a way that manifests our values."

Like the earlier Shakers, the Twin Oaks communitarians have withdrawn from the larger culture in an effort to realize those values. And like the Shakers, they have created a largely self-contained garden paradise where exploitation and alienation, those great Marxist hobgobblins, do not exist. Perhaps there is a kind of millennialism involved here as well: the secular Twin Oaks crowd isn't replicating the kingdom of God, but they have invented a model for how we might live when and if the consumer culture collapses under the weight of its own appetites.

"For people who want to change the world, there are two streams," Valerie maintains. "You can be an activist, which is great; I'm glad those people are out there. But that's an *against* energy. What I see us doing is the other stream: creating an alternative. If we resist and are successful, but have no structures to replace the existing structures that we think don't make sense, that's not helpful, either. We're building alternative cultural structures. Our perspective is not that we want a bigger piece of the pie; it's that we want a different pie." In that sense, Twin Oaks could be thought of as the flip side to the Occupy Wall Street phenomenon. Were the 99 percent ever able to topple the 1 percent who rule the financial markets, Twin Oaks would represent an alternate economy to the Wall Street paradigm.

Of course economists aren't flocking to Twin Oaks to study

the new decentralized paradigm. And the members of Twin Oaks aren't screaming to be heard. Unlike Occupy, this is a decidedly low-key kind of radicalism. Obviously everyone at Twin Oaks would *like* to change the current political and economic system; they wouldn't be here otherwise. But that change may take a very long time, and obviously the fight can be frustrating. At Twin Oaks, one can step into a socialist utopia overnight. It's already here, hidden away in Louisa County.

I float past Valerie my theory about the four kinds of utopias (solitude and solidarity, escape and reconstruction), and then I posit that of those four, each must be either a model or a critique. She gazes skyward to consider this, and then says, "I think Twin Oaks is a silent, elegant critique in its model-ness."

Valerie reminds me that the four pillars of wisdom at Twin Oaks are egalitarianism (land, labor, and income are held in common), income sharing (see *egalitarianism*), nonviolence (there's no domestic abuse here), and cooperation. On a day-to-day level, that last one is often the hardest to maintain.

"We're trying to cooperate around everything: food, kids, our businesses," Valerie says. "And we live so close to each other that we have to have far better social skills than most people living in the mainstream. To a certain extent here, you can run your own show." One longtime resident, for instance, has started his own line of rustic furniture. "But it has to fit in with all the other shows. You have to merge what's important to you with what the group is clearly telling you is important to the group." What Twin Oaks loses in individualism it gains through collectivism. When, for instance, ten people are cooking dinner for the whole group, instead of one hundred people fending for themselves, a lot of time and labor gets saved. When cars and washing machines and vacuum cleaners are shared, a lot of money gets saved. When twenty people live in one house instead of four, a lot of energy and natural resources are conserved. The upshot, says Valerie, "means we have a bunch of labor left over and we can do whatever we want with it."

That means work that doesn't usually get monetized in this

country—domestic work, child care, cooking, cutting a friend's hair—does receive labor credit at Twin Oaks. And the fact that so much of this work is traditionally done by women means that, in many ways, Twin Oaks represents a belated manifestation of Robert Owen's postpatriarchal utopia. If Twin Oaks hasn't completely done away with marriage, it has certainly dismantled an economic system that favored the husband over the wife, the property-holding male over the suffragette.

What's more, the work that women and men choose to do is completely up to the individual. In Ayn Rand's utopia, only the powerful and the wealthy enjoy real economic freedom; at Twin Oaks, such work and wealth are distributed with absolute equality *and* absolute autonomy. "At almost any minute you can be doing exactly the work you want to be doing and not any other work," Valerie says. She sits with her legs crossed as if preparing for meditation. My back aches slightly from the morning's gardening.

Aside from her work as community liaison and yoga instructor, Valerie manages the wood-splitting crew (no small feat in a community that heats almost entirely with wood), works in the pillow shop (for the hammocks), and acts as the Twin Oaks delegate to the Federation of Egalitarian Communities. "The backbone of Twin Oaks is our labor system," she explains. "That's our religion. We have these high priestesses and priests who are the labor assigners. We fetishize the labor sheet. People here derive a lot of their identity from their work areas."

Listening to Valerie, I try to think of a metaphor for Twin Oaks, and then it comes to me: the self-organizing nucleated cell. Twin Oaks is incredibly self-organized and yet no one seems to be—no one is—"in charge."

What has changed in the twenty-two years Valerie has lived at Twin Oaks? She nods toward the two men weaving a hammock together. "We specifically redesigned our hammock jigs"—a jig is a wooden contraption set up on saw horses with a line of clothespins running down each side—"so that two people could use them at the same time, and we did this so that people would be able to talk and hang out while working." During the Pier

One years, Twin Oaks needed to make a hell of a lot of hammocks (fifteen thousand a year), so everybody spent some time in
the hammock shop. But when Pier One discontinued its outdoor
line of furniture, hammock demand at Twin Oaks was cut in half.
The unintended consequence, says Valerie, is that you no longer
find yourself standing across the hammock jig from someone you
don't know very well, or at all. After the Pier One contract expired,
Twin Oakers retreated a bit into what Valerie calls their natural
social groupings. "It's not a problem," she says, "but from my perspective, it's weakened the social fabric slightly."

The other change has been the introduction to Twin Oaks of
personal media consumption. When Valerie and Keenan came to
Twin Oaks, there was one TV in the whole place. "Now everyone
has their own laptops and devices," she says. "It means that there's
more people in boxes watching boxes, which didn't used to happen.
It's changed the flow of social energy: more personal entertainment
instead of looking to the larger group for your engagement."

I tell her I was surprised yesterday when Keenan said he
spends many nights watching movies with his family on his son's
TV. That's pretty much what my wife and I do at home, where we
make no claims to upending mainstream culture.

Valerie nods and says, "That would have been blasphemy when
Keenan and I moved here." But even an agrarian utopia such
as Twin Oaks is not immune to a digital snake in the grass. Even at
Twin Oaks, authentic, unalienated experience at times succumbs
to screens large and small; though it must be said that during my
visit no one makes a cell phone call in a public space, and one
woman sharply reprimands her partner for looking at his phone
during today's lunch.

A few weeks before coming to Twin Oaks, I was sitting at a
bar alongside three friends. They were staring into the small light
of their phones while I pretended to be interested in the game on
the TV above the bar. My friend sitting next to me looked up and
said, unironically, "What did we do before cell phones?"

I shrugged and said, "We talked to each other."

"That's so funny!" she said, though I'm not exactly sure what she meant. At least in their public spaces, the Twin Oakers have managed to keep the genie contained and keep some semblance of the oral tradition alive.

I tell Valerie what Rayne said this morning in the cucumber patch about happiness, and I ask her if, as with so many of the nineteenth-century utopias, happiness is even one of the aspirations at Twin Oaks.

"It's definitely *not* one of our stated goals," she says, "and it's a toss-up about whether it's even one of our unstated goals." She motions again to the two men weaving the hammock. "I'm not an expert on behaviorism," she says, "but as I would describe it, the main thrust is that one sets up a situation such that it results in a desired outcome by the use of positive reinforcement." And, indeed, the weavers are laughing and having a good time as they work and talk. "Clearly the idea of personal contentment was built into the idea of our hammock jig. So one can *assume* that happiness is a generally desired outcome." What's more, Valerie says, Twin Oaks strongly emphasizes a pleasant work environment over efficiency: "So, again, as a community we are placing a value on our members being happy while they work, even at a real financial cost to the community. And giving workers complete freedom of employment choice would theoretically imply that we value maximum satisfaction at least in the work realm."

Beyond the sphere of labor, Valerie goes on, no one at Twin Oaks has to worry about rent or food, car payments or debt; there's no pressure to keep up with the elusive Joneses. "Someone even does our taxes!" she exults. "But life here is very stressful in its own way, largely around issues of sharing so much. We have stress about trying to balance out meeting everyone's preferences, wants, and needs, none of which are small things, at least from an internal, emotional perspective. So maybe at Twin Oaks we just find other things to get stressed about."

Or maybe it's really a question of absolute versus relative happiness. "I truly do believe that if you asked Twin Oakers if they were happy in the context of actively comparing their lives to what they'd be like if they weren't living here, you would get a *very high* percentage of people pretty unequivocally stating that they are happier here," Valerie says. "But if the question was asked in terms of whether they are happy in relation to how happy they *could* be in their ideal world, or compared to someone else, you'd get much different answers." We do, many of us, carry wherever we go the principal source of our troubles: ourselves. Behaviorism can do nothing to fix that.

All this leads me back to my original question upon arriving at Twin Oaks: Could I (or would I want to) live here? I have certainly never visited any place where people truly did, as Valerie said, live their values as honestly and unhypocritically as the communitarians of Louisa County, Virginia. At Twin Oaks and Acorn, there really is no exploitation, no violence, no economic or political inequality. Here members collectively own their labor, their labor's product, and their means of production. It would be hard to imagine a more emancipatory work environment than one in which you choose *when* to work, *what kind* of work you do, and *with whom* you do it. And in a community of generalists such as Twin Oaks, drudgery in the workplace does seem rare.

I come back to what Keenan said about identity—that at Twin Oaks you must create a new identity outside the one most of us build through the things we buy: cars, houses, clothes, speedboats. His point, as I take it, is that at Twin Oaks, identity is harder to come by, but ultimately more authentic. It must come from within and can be judged only by one's actions. At Twin Oaks, you are what you do—not what you wear or drive, not the teams you follow, not the church you attend, not the country club you belong to. It is a rigorous, more honest conception of identity, one to which I feel a strong sympathy. But could I actually adopt it? I think about all of my own worldly possessions and try to imagine what I could live without.

My wardrobe is already pretty bare-bones, small enough to fit in a modest chest of drawers. If I resided at Twin Oaks, I wouldn't need my truck to take me to my teaching job or to retrieve loads of compost for my raised vegetable beds back at home. I obviously would no longer own my house; or, rather, I wouldn't be beholden to the bank that owns most of it. All the furniture, then, would have to go, which I think I could live with. Thanks to the capitalists at Spotify, I could replace my vast collection of vinyl records with a ten-ounce mobile device. That leaves my sprawling library, which would have to be distilled to its most essential elements. Difficult but by no means impossible—I'm not, after all, ever planning to read *Gravity's Rainbow* again.

The Shakers of Pleasant Hill slept six to a room and owned almost no personal possessions. That sounds to me like the opposite of heaven on earth. But at Twin Oaks and Acorn, there is private accommodation that can be filled and configured in whatever ways one is inclined. I try to imagine what my own room at Twin Oaks might look like. There would be a twin bed, a chest of drawers, a reading chair, and a writing desk. Bookshelves would be affixed to the walls.

What would I miss? The flat-screen TV on which I watch UK basketball and Cincinnati Reds games. The small collection of art my wife and I have accumulated. And, of course, my wife. As a thought experiment, I have been acting as if I were single, but I wouldn't come to Twin Oaks without Melissa, and there's no way she would stay for more than a visit. Keenan's point that one's house, how one furnishes and decorates it, should have nothing to do with one's identity would make absolutely no sense to Melissa. Our house *is* a manifestation of her good taste and aesthetic judgments, and she likes it that way. I do, too, if I'm being completely honest.

Before I set off on my utopian travels, Melissa repeatedly voiced half-serious concern that I would not return, that I would find a group of like-minded people and disappear into my own world-mending reveries. But there was really never any chance of that. Thoreau said, quoting Diogenes, I think, that a man who owns a lion is in fact owned by the lion. I suspect I could be shed of my symbolic lions (my truck payment, my mortgage), but I realize in my short time at Twin Oaks and Acorn that I could never live these collectivist dreams. I'm too tight-assed to become a nudist. I'm too much of an introvert, too ill-suited for the relentless socialness of these admirable communities. I want to be left alone to read and write and to wander the woods around my house. I belong too much to my own utopia of solitude that consists of me, my wife, my dogs, and a few dependable neighbors. Here in the utopia of solidarity, I fear I would yearn for that isolation.

What's more, I suspect I am too much one of the restless Americans whom Alexis de Tocqueville first observed. I don't know that I would be content to settle down on this farm for years and years. I would miss the speed of driving back roads in the summer with the windows rolled down and the radio blasting. I would miss knowing that if I wanted to get up and go, my keys would be by the door. Such impulses, I know, are inconsistent with my higher values that say, "Leave a smaller carbon footprint, be part of something larger than yourself." But I can't help it. The one hundred courageous souls at Twin Oaks live out my values far better than I do. Sure, I garden, raise chickens, and cut my own firewood, but they are the ones who have undertaken the messy day-to-day job of living the unexploited and unexploiting life.

I tell Valerie as much, and she sweetly, mercifully lets me off the hook. "This way of life isn't for everyone," she says. "It's actually for the very, very few."

Reluctantly, I agree. In the morning, I have to be out of my Walden Two room so another guest can move in. In truth, I'll be ready to go.

A Clearinghouse for Dreams

I wake again with the roosters, but today I quickly pack my truck and put the community of Twin Oaks in my rearview mirror. I'm cruising along the incredibly straight Zachary Taylor Highway, while to both my right and my left white sails swell with a morning breeze as small boats skim lightly across the beautiful Lake Anna. My spirits are slightly buoyant as well, as they always are when I find myself alone, especially alone and driving, after a few intense days of community. For now, my utopia of solitude is this pickup truck with the wind whipping through the cab. By the time I reach Manassas, I've decided to abandon for one day my interstate prohibition. I've decided it's time to cover some ground by shooting up the Northeast Corridor along I-95. But when I reach the stalled traffic on the D.C. Beltway, where nobody is driving in the Ride Share lane because everyone, including me, is driving alone, I'm met once more with the redundancy of it all. It's as if ghost cars from Twin Oaks and Acorn are zooming along the Ride Share lane like our collective guilty conscience (or, at least, mine), and I remember one of the bumper stickers on a car in Modern Times, the Twin Oaks auto shop. It read MY OTHER CAR ISN'T MINE EITHER.

Actually, the utopian community of Modern Times, forty miles outside New York City, on Long Island, is where I'm soon headed. But for now I can't shake the problematic nature of my trip, the irreconcilable dilemma that I'm burning a lot of fossil fuel so I can visit this country's most stable sustainable communities. There's a good reason the naturalist Donald Culross Peattie called Americans "speed-drunk monkeys." Today I'm certainly one of them, so to drown out such thoughts of my hypocrisy, I pop in the "Utopia Mix Tape" I made prior to departure. My only real criterion for the tape was that it bear no evidence of John Lennon's saccharine and overexposed "Imagine." Beyond that, a general sense that the world could be a better place determined my choices. Once I hit on Sam Cooke's "A Change Is Gonna Come," everything else followed from there, into this:

"A Change Is Gonna Come," Sam Cooke
"Blake's Jerusalem," Paul K.
"Saturn," Stevie Wonder
"People Have the Power," Patti Smith
"The World Is Turning," Toots and the Maytals
"After the Gold Rush," Neil Young
"One," Mary J. Blige and U2
"Road to Nowhere," Talking Heads
"Move On Fast," Yoko Ono
"Zimbabwe," Bob Marley and the Wailers
"Tir Na Nog," Van Morrison
"Tree of Life," Nadirah Shakoor
"Maundering," Bonnie Prince Billy
"I'd Love to Change the World," Ten Years After
"First We Take Manhattan," Leonard Cohen (with ghost
    track "Democracy")
"The World Turned Upside Down," Billy Bragg

That last song marked another early directive that would eventually point the way toward my utopian drive. A couple of years before I bought George Lockwood's book *The New Harmony Movement*, I discovered Billy Bragg's album *Life's a Riot*. It's just Bragg singing over a blustery electric guitar that he plays as if he were sharpening a knife. But it was that one song, "The World Turned Upside Down," a utopian anthem about a seventeenth-century attempt to reclaim the English commons, that I listened to over and over. A British folk singer named Leon Rosselson actually wrote "The World Turned Upside Down" in 1974, but his acoustic version lacks the urgency, the three-chords-and-the-truth vitality, that Bragg eventually brought to the song. In 1985, I was working nights as a short-order cook, and after work I'd go back to my room in my parents' basement and listen to the Clash and Bob Marley and Billy Bragg. That music filled me with vague socialist aspirations and attitude. It made me feel suddenly, undeservedly superior to the suburbs where I grew up, and still lived. That music signaled some form of escape, I thought, from a complacent life of false consciousness, though in the end all I did was go to college on my parents' dime. But I still had "The World Turned Upside Down" stuck in my head, Bragg wailing, "This earth divided / We will make whole / So it will be / A common treasury for all." Only, by then, I had tracked down the Christopher Hill book that gave the song its title, and in the stacks of my university's cramped library, I found an ancient copy of *The Complete Works of Gerrard Winstanley*. It was Winstanley who first compelled a band of fifteen starving men, later to become known as the Diggers, to plant parsnips, carrots, and beans on a barren slope in Surrey known as St. George's Hill. In 1649, with the English Civil War finally over, the New Model Army executed Charles I, and Oliver Cromwell proclaimed a republic in England. But Cromwell's new government did little more than distribute royalists' land among men of property. Meanwhile, the price of bread doubled, and one bad harvest followed another. For the poor of England, who had fought alongside the gentry, the spoils of war were famine. Yet half the country remained uncultivated land. On April 1, the Diggers, who called themselves the True Levellers, set out, as the song says, "to work the land in common / And to make the waste land grow." Winstanley himself had herded cattle as a hired laborer until he fell into a trance one day and saw a vision of an earth shared by all men and women. An otherworldly voice spoke to him, commanding, "Work together, eat bread together." The same week that the poor men began planting on St. George's Hill, Winstanley published their manifesto, *The True Levellers Standard Advanced.* There Winstanley advanced the position that, in the beginning, God instilled in every man and woman "the same spirit that made the globe," and therefore everyone was a "ruler within himself." Only after the Fall did men set up other men to rule over them and to divide the earth's common wealth into enclosures. "From the beginning it was not so," wrote Winstanley.

If the Shakers and Rappites sought to hurry along the millennium, the Diggers meant to restore the divine law of the First Garden. For Winstanley, the law of the heart was the law of God, and the law of God was the law of nature. The law of man was the law of property. Yet how, asked Winstanley, can a man own what he did not create? It's the question that lurks behind any utopian economics.

After several weeks on St. George's Hill, the number of Diggers doubled. Freeholders, whose property surrounded the commons, feared the beginning of a movement. The men of property called on the Council of State to disband the squatters by force. On April 20 two Diggers, Winstanley and William Everard, were summoned to appear before General Thomas Fairfax, commander in chief of the New Model Army. Refusing to remove their hats, the Diggers defended their actions to the general. "If," Winstanley argued, "the local manor lords can prove that the earth was made by Almighty God peculiarly for them, and not for others equal with them, then we have trespassed in digging upon their rights; but the earth was made as free for us as for them; therefore they have trespassed against us as fellow creatures in troubling us with their tyrannical arrest, and hindering us from our righteous labour." This notion seemed to amuse General Fairfax, who found Winstanley and Everard harmless enough. He even visited St. George's Hill in May to secure Winstanley's assurance that the Diggers had no designs on violence. While there, he noticed some barley beginning to sprout.

Until the crops were ready to harvest, the Diggers resolved to cut timber on the commons in exchange for food. They promised to make known to the public how much they received for the wood and how much food it bought. They found, however, that the lords from surrounding manors were already felling trees from the commons for profit. The Diggers asked if the propertied classes could not cut trees from their own land and leave the commons to the propertyless poor, who, after all, paid taxes and had helped topple Charles I. The freeholders responded by bringing a charge of trespassing against the Diggers in the court at Kingston. Winstanley told the jury, "In that we do dig upon the hill, we do not thereby take away other men's rights, neither do we demand of this court or from the Parliament what is theirs and not ours." Nevertheless, ten landowners convicted the Diggers and fined them thirty pounds. Because the Diggers had no money, Kingston bailiffs confiscated four cows that a friend had loaned Winstanley for milk and cheese. Winstanley went before the bailiffs and pleaded that they could take his property, which amounted to a few tools, but the cows did not belong to him. When he finally recovered the animals, he discovered that they had been beaten with clubs, and their heads were swollen. "It grieved tender hearts to see," wrote Winstanley, "and yet those cows never were upon George Hill, nor never digged upon that ground, and yet the poor beasts must suffer because they gave milk to feed me." When he returned to St. George's Hill, Winstanley found that all the Diggers' tools had been taken and their makeshift homes leveled. They planted one last crop of rye, and with no money to build proper shelter out of wattle and daub, the Diggers waited out the winter under tiny hutches.

In the spring, the Diggers abandoned St. George's Hill and

resettled a mile away, on Cobham Heath. There they built huts and planted eleven acres in corn and wheat. Winstanley implored the surrounding manor lords to "lie still and cherish the Diggers, for they love you." He added, "If you have much money, give it not away to destroy men, but give it to some poor or other to be a stock, and bid them go and plant the common; this will be your honor, and your comfort." That sounded pretty much like a famous sermon delivered in Palestine nineteen hundred years earlier, but the local Christian gentry was not moved to charity. Led by Parson John Platt, the minister of Horsley and also a wealthy landowner, the propertied men turned their cattle out onto the commons and let them trample the Diggers' grain. When they still refused to leave, men dressed in women's clothing went rampaging through the cornfield, destroying all the Diggers' crops. Though the Diggers did not fight back, the manor lords beat them so badly that some had to be carried home on a cart.

Finally, Parson Platt convinced General Fairfax that the Diggers were not only thieves, but heretics who "held women in common." At last, Fairfax sent a group of soldiers to drive the renegades from Cobham Heath, though he instructed the troops not to inflict harm. A few days after the soldiers left the heath, Parson Platt returned to the commons with hired men, who tore down the Diggers' homes and kicked a lingering Digger's pregnant wife so hard she miscarried.

Winstanley went to Parson Platt directly and tried to reason with him: Did the minister not see, based on scripture, that a poor man had as much right to the earth's bounty as a rich man? Parson Platt told Winstanley that if he could prove his claims by scripture, then he would let the Diggers alone. On the Monday of Easter week, Winstanley presented to Platt his treatise, *An Humble Request to the Ministers of Both Universities and to All Lawyers in Every Inns-a-Court*. It read, in part:

When Mankind lives in the unity of the one Spirit of Righteousness, he lives in the light, and the light lives in him . . . But when Mankind lives in division, contention, and covetousness, one part of Mankind hedging themselves into the earth by force and sword, they hereby shut out another part of Mankind, making them slaves. This was man's fall. Jer. 45.5 The Scriptures declare the resurrection of the spirit of freedom within mankind. This spirit of Love, Patience, Humility, and Righteousness, is called the light of the world, and the salt of the earth. It is the restoring spirit, teaching all men to do as they would be done by. He that hath this spirit will never strive to be a Lord of Manor or divider of land; for he will quietly suffer everyone to enjoy the freedom of his creation.

The Diggers returned to Cobham Heath to wait for an answer from Parson Platt. On Good Friday, it came. Leading fifty men on horseback, all bearing torches, Parson Platt set fire to every shelter the Diggers had built and to all their tools. The Diggers' scheme to reverse the Fall of Man was over. Parson Platt hired guards bearing swords to patrol Cobham Heath day and night like the cherubs who kept Adam and Eve out of Eden.

Three hundred sixty years later, we're still trying to reclaim the commons from the modern manor lords, only now the commons are controlled by all the corporate Bigs: Big Oil, Big Coal, Big Agra, Big Pharma. Eight months from now, in North Carolina, a Duke Energy coal ash waste pond will collapse and dump eighty-two thousand tons of toxic waste into the Dan River—this after the state repeatedly ignored citizen complaints about leaking ponds. The state will fine Duke Energy a pittance, and business will go on as usual: the commons, in the form of mountains, will be blown apart, and the by-product of that mining will get dumped back into the commons in the form of polluted rivers. What should be a shared natural inheritance (rivers, mountains, air) gets polluted by so-called corporate citizens who privatize enormous wealth—that's the "enclosure" part—and then socialize what John Ruskin called the "illth." Put another way, corporate vandals take what isn't theirs and then pollute the commons with waste that should not be ours. There's a phrase for this: the tragedy of the commons. Garrett Hardin, the economist who coined the term, thought that it would be Winstanley's lower classes who overused the commons, but as it turned out, it was the privatizers of the extractive industry who largely caused the deracination.

The problem with this, of course, is that the modern utopia we call the free market can succeed only by continuing to plunder the commons. And as we are now finding, that commons— even the commons of the atmosphere—is finite. In 2005 the United Nations' Millennium Ecosystem Assessment found that 60 percent of the ecosystems that support life on earth are being overused. There is only so much you can extract and so much air or water in which to dump the by-products before trouble, illth, ensues. Which means that we can't go on like this. Capitalism, once the brilliant solution to scarcity, is now making scarce the elements of survival.

The good news is that there are a lot of smart people thinking about how to wrestle the commons away from corporate privatizers and manage them sustainably. One of the smartest is Peter Barnes, a former journalist and founder of the progressive long-distance company Working Assets. Barnes, sounding a bit like a latter-day Robert Owen, claims that modern capitalism leads to three pathologies: the destruction of the natural world, widening inequality, and a "failure to promote happiness despite the pretense of doing so." Barnes defines the commons as the stuff we share, inherit, and should pass on to future generations. The problem we run into is that the world is dominated by two entities: the corporation and the state, and as seen by the Duke Energy coal ash disaster, the latter usually does a poor job of regulating the former. Barnes's compelling solution, utopian in its scope and ambition, is to introduce a third institution: the trust. The goal of the commons and the goal of a trust, he argues, are largely the same: to preserve assets and deliver benefits to a broad class of beneficiaries. Perhaps the most successful American trust of this kind is the Alaska Permanent Fund, which takes oil revenue and pays an *equal* annual dividend to every Alaskan man, woman, and child. Such a trust could be established to protect and manage any kind of common: a river, a forest, the recording industry, even the climate.*

The rich remain rich because they control the resources of the commons; the poor remain poor for exactly the same reason. The commons trust could go a long way toward solving the problem of inequality not by *re*distributing wealth—that thing Americans can't seem to abide—but by *pre*distributing it. After all, the natural wealth of the commons should *already* belong to everyone; there can hardly be a more utopian thought than that. It's only those who can turn a profit at the expense of the commons who convince us to think otherwise. "On the one hand," said Barnes in his 2003 speech "Capitalism, the Commons, and Divine Right," "by limiting commons usage, [trustees] would diminish pollution and the destruction of nature. On the other hand, they would partially offset the maldistribution of private-property income." By providing access to the commons and equitable dividends paid for that access, we would, says Barnes, "produce the most happiness with the least destruction to nature." And so the pathologies of capitalism are cured, or at least greatly ameliorated. What's more, by inviting more citizens back into the commons, we would begin to re-create the kind of communities sought by the Diggers, the Shakers, and the anarcho-nudists of Louisa County. Those communities would be bound by a new economic arrangement that created local wealth, protected local resources, and prevented local exploitation by powerful outside interests.

* Barnes ultimately envisions a "Sky Trust" that would solve the global climate crisis by making all fossil fuel companies purchase emission permits from a trust representing every person on the planet. The trust's income would then be used to remediate damage done by climate change and to rebate individuals for higher energy bills. UN scientists would decide where to set a global cap on emissions, and then rights to the atmospheric commons would be divided in proportion to each country's population—absolute equity. Poor and populous countries with more permits than emission could sell their excess permits to richer nations. And if it all sounds too simple, it is worth noting that the Congressional Budget Office found, of all the cap-and-trade proposals put forward so far, the Sky Trust would be easiest to implement and would have the most positive effect on household incomes.

As I drive the New Jersey Turnpike, the day darkens until, as Wallace Stevens once wrote, "it was evening all afternoon." When I reach the outskirts of New York City, a dense fog is moving in over the Verrazano-Narrows Bridge. I see little but the tollbooth that charges what seems like a criminal amount of money, thirty-three dollars, to enter Staten Island. Though I pride myself at being an old-school navigator, a student of the passenger seat map, I am now helplessly at the mercy of the GPS system I borrowed from my parents before the trip. It takes me along the Hudson River and then deposits me onto the Long Island Expressway.

At the Utopia Parkway exit, I veer off—how could I not?—and drive through an older, mixed-use suburb of Flushing. The baseball field is overgrown, and some of the garage doors have been tagged with graffiti, but overall it looks like a fairly ordinary American neighborhood. People are walking home from the grocery store and hanging out at the auto glass shop. Still, no one around here would probably apply the word *utopian* to this place without some inflection of irony (see the Fountains of Wayne song "Utopia Parkway"). I pull up to the curb in front of a gray, two-and-a-half-story Dutch Colonial, the former home of the shadow box artist Joseph Cornell. One of the wonderful coincidences of modern life is that the man who is arguably this country's most utopian artist—a man who created small spaces so intensely drenched with a dream world, with the imagination's most sumptuous projections—actually lived on a fairly nondescript street called Utopia Parkway. In the basement of this, his mother's house, Joseph Cornell created a kind of art unlike any other in the twentieth century.

The twenty-five-year-old Cornell moved into this house with his mother and his younger brother, Robert, in 1926. All three of them would live here, not at all harmoniously, for the rest of their lives. Joseph's father had died of leukemia in 1917, and his mother made it clear to Joseph that it was his job to support both her and Robert, who was born with cerebral palsy. According to his biographer Deborah Solomon, Cornell never outwardly questioned this arrangement. He never went on a date, as far as anyone can tell, and he almost certainly died a virgin. He worked a job he loathed, peddling textile samples, like his father, in the manufacturing district of Lower Manhattan. Between appointments, and to avoid going home, Cornell foraged through used bookstores and junk shops, collecting all manner of discarded ephemera. To amuse Robert, he emptied out a round cardboard pillbox and placed small fragments of mirror all around the inside walls. Then he stuck pins through the bottom of the box, placed wobbling thimbles on top of the pins, and cut an eyehole in the side of the box. When Robert looked into this tiny camera obscura, he saw a vast thimble forest, and it thrilled him.

Cornell made many variations on these pillbox assemblages to amuse Robert, and in the early 1930s he began exhibiting them, along with some collages from his scavenging, at the Julien Levy Gallery off Fifty-Seventh Street at Madison Avenue. Levy called the show, a bit patronizingly, "Toys for Adults." Back at home, the overbearing Helen Cornell thought her son's new hobby foolish, and she resented that her house was becoming cluttered with Joseph's arcane miscellanea. So Cornell moved his evolving operation down to the basement, where he wouldn't be bothered. There he was free to fill up archival boxes with seashells, found love letters, clay pipes, bracelets, watch parts, cork balls, star charts. Some boxes were simply labeled FLOTSAM and JETSAM. He called the basement his "clearinghouse for dreams." If, as the German theorist Ernst Bloch says, utopianism is "a realm of conscious dreaming," Cornell was the most conscious of American dreamers. In 1936 he created his first shadow box, the art form that would make him famous. In it, a map of the moon is set against the wooden box's back wall. Pieces of glass partition off a white clay pipe from a doll's head on a small platform and a pale blue bird's egg resting inside a champagne flute. The philosopher Heraclitus said, "The most beautiful order of the world is still a random gathering of things insignificant in themselves." That was Cornell's aesthetic *exactly*. He would scour New York for its castoffs, its cultural detritus, and he would redeem those objects by placing them in a new, strange kind of harmony within his boxes. The effect was incantatory, alchemical, magic. Nearly everyone who sees Cornell's work for the first time thinks so. Despite the fact that Cornell couldn't draw, paint, or sculpt, there was still nothing quite like this in the history of art. Sure, he found a kinship with surrealism or Marcel Duchamp's ready-mades, but that work came out of a deep suspicion of art itself, a post-Freudian world of fraught sexuality and psychic darkness. All of Cornell's work is about reclaiming a sexless realm of innocence and wonder. It's a world that would have greatly appealed to the Shaker founder, Mother Ann Lee, and indeed we might think of Cornell's boxes as illustrations of the spiritualist visions that occurred during the decade known as Mother Ann's Work. Because Cornell couldn't stand the world his mother had forced him to live in, he created hundreds of boxes into which he could retreat. "Our dreams are a second life," wrote Cornell's favorite French poet, Gérard de Nerval, and the boxes were dream machines into which Cornell could finally come alive. What they reveal is that Cornell's inner life was as rich and intense as his outer life was seemingly dull and routine. The present was no place to live. *Life* was no place to live. Everything depended on the box. It was the perfect escape: a utopia.

This clearly isn't the *eutopia*, the "good place," I've been tracking for nearly fifteen hundred miles; this is the *outopia*, the "no place," that formed the foundation of utopian art and literature, from the Arcadia of Virgil and Nicolas Poussin, to Thomas More's Utopia and Tommaso Campanella's City of the Sun. It is certainly the case that most artists have always felt more comfortable creating imaginary utopias than real ones. Yet many social reformers have pointed back to those imaginary utopias as their blueprints or their inspiration. As we have seen, Walter Benjamin argued that the wish-image, the wish-landscape, of utopian art might be appropriated for socialist realities. But Cornell's work seems absolutely assimilation-proof. The world of a Cornell box combines the utopia of solitude with the utopia of escape—hardly a recipe or model for social reform. An artist such as Joseph Cornell—who cared so little for community, so little for *reality*—would have had no use whatsoever for Twin Oaks. On that farm, he would have been miserable picking cucumbers and making tofu, Moreover, he would have been unable to find the raw materials that made up his art. No, it's difficult to imagine Cornell, the solitary wanderer who reconstructed his work out of urban junk shops, existing anywhere but in the pre–Andy Warhol New York City. Yet who is to say that Cornell didn't have a richer inner life than any outward reformer? Cornell cultivated an inner utopia that the rest of us get a mere glimpse of when we stare into one of his shadow boxes.

I knock on the door at 37-08 Utopia Parkway, but no one answers. Children's bikes in the front yard and the well-maintained window boxes show that a family lives here. But, really, there is little I could gain by barging in on them. Obviously the basement is no longer full of Cornell's private curiosities; indeed, toward the end of his life, Cornell worried that the coming world of homogenous plastic might make his art impossible. So I get back in my truck and set the GPS for Brooklyn.

In Crown Heights, I pull up to a warehouse that has been converted into an artists' collective and makeshift—very makeshift— bed-and-breakfast. Images of the outsider artist Henry Darger's Vivian Girls are painted on the corrugated metal door, though these particular girls are floating in a blue sea, perhaps to conceal the fact that Darger gave them all penises. That kind of public art probably wouldn't fly even in Crown Heights. Inside the warehouse, young people are "pursuing creative agendas," just as an Internet ad said they would be. "Your chances of waking up to the filming of a Beyoncé video are as good as coming home in the evening to live music around a fire in the junkyard," it promised. Someone is indeed shooting a music video off in another room when I arrive, though I see no signs of Ms. Knowles. A young woman leads me past a metal sculptor at work and a guy barking orders into his cell phone. This, I learn, is Kellam, the owner and impresario of this modern-day version of the famous Paris Beehive, where some of the most famous early twentieth-century artists lived and painted. The central space of this beehive, a kitchen and sitting area, even looks something like a Joseph Cornell box. All matter of salvaged material is scattered about: old turntables, accordions, miscellaneous pieces of twisted neon. We ascend a spiral staircase to my room, which I booked because it was the cheapest thing I could find in New York, and which the ad described as ". . . special" (the ellipsis was part of the ad). A mattress lies on a wooden floor that looks as old as the one in the Farm Deacon's Shop back at Pleasant Hill. Paint is peeling off the walls, and one wall is actually a large green sheet, held in place by joist supports. The only piece of furniture is a side table where a carafe of water sits beside two empty glasses. There's no TV, and I didn't expect one, since the house rules read, in part: "Advertisements are like acid on the brain and are banished from this space."

The house rules—there are a lot of house rules—ask guests not to bother the working artists. But as I sip my glass of water and look out over the Myrtle Street rooftops, it occurs to me that this collective of like-minded "creatives" (their word) represents something I haven't yet seen on my trip: an urban utopia, an artist's utopia. The nineteenth-century utopias felt they had to set themselves apart from cities, and they were primarily agrarian. They had to be if the communities wanted to maintain their distance from the world of sin and corruption. That world, they felt (mostly agreeing with Thomas Jefferson), was incubated in cities. But today things look a bit different. Today those who espouse the virtues of agrarianism often do so in the name of sustainability and the need to shrink our collective carbon footprint. Arguably the most sustainable city in America, the one with the smallest carbon footprint per capita, is New York. It's easy to understand why: great mass transit, small living spaces, population density. The artists of Myrtle Street aren't growing their own food, as far as I can tell, but they have replaced that utopian dream of self-sufficiency with a very low-impact way of living in a reclaimed warehouse with one bathroom and few amenities. In the era of climate change, that looks, if not utopian, then at least very future-oriented. And if this warehouse doesn't represent a utopia of reconstruction, it is certainly a utopia of solidarity.

But perhaps that's not right, either. Perhaps, like many artists, these creatives *do* want to change the world. Consider the amazing work that came out of the Paris Beehive: painting and poetry by Marc Chagall, Amedeo Modigliani, Fernand Léger, Robert Delaunay, Guillaume Apollinaire, Blaise Cendrars. You almost can't imagine the history of modernism without those artists working in those close spaces in those first decades of the twentieth century. Certainly the work of each influenced and inspired that of the others. Great collaborations took place. On a very real level, the world *did* change. Art, we might argue, is by its very nature utopian. By its very nature, art asks us to think in a different way about the realities we take for granted every day. It is a separate world, a contained world, an intensified world. The aims of much art tend to be aspirational, even if they get filtered through a negative dialectic—the dire warnings of dystopic literature, for instance.

How would these artists have fared back at Twin Oaks? There was certainly art being made there. I saw paintings and sculpture around the grounds, heard music after dinner. But at Twin Oaks, art could be a full-time job only if it brought money back into the community—if that art in some way *supported* the community. If you made art for art's sake at Twin Oaks, you did it on your own time. Somebody had to weave the hammocks, after all, process the tofu. That may be why writers such as Emerson and Thoreau steered clear of George Ripley's Brook Farm experiment, and why Hawthorne eventually left. They didn't want to shovel manure until they were too tired to write; they didn't want to place the needs of the community above their own. I don't know how the artists of Myrtle Street support themselves, but making art is clearly the priority, and whatever community is shared here happens in the service of that art.

The next morning, I leave the Myrtle Street artists to their collective work and head out on the C train into Manhattan to search out the solitary works of Joseph Cornell. The Metropolitan

Museum of Art, the Museum of Modern Art, and the Guggenheim each owns only a few of his pieces, and though I'm a bit overwhelmed by the sheer number of people I keep bumping into on the sidewalks, I'm determined to see the boxes up close.

As with any pieces of sculpture, photographs don't do them justice. Yet a Cornell box is as much a collage, or a poem, or a still life, or an assemblage, as it is a piece of sculpture. It's hard to say exactly what a Cornell box is or where it belongs in the history of art; even the museums don't quite seem to know where to place these peculiar reliquaries. Some look as though they were designed by jewelers, particularly the earlier boxes, and some look as if they washed up on a beach. I tend to prefer the latter, with their coarsely mitered corners and thick, cracking interior paint. (Cornell baked them in his mother's oven to get this effect.) Inside those boxes are pieces of driftwood, crooked nails, scraps of wire fencing, broken wineglasses, cork balls, dead starfish, wooden birds, children's blocks. These interiors are often wallpapered with faded ads from European hotels such as the Hôtel de L'Étoile or the Hôtel Eden, fragments of star charts with their astrological symbols, and old chocolate bar wrappers.

It all suggests something crucial about the artist's concept of time. It was important that almost everything in a Cornell box appear old because, like Walter Benjamin's "Angel of History," Cornell was salvaging detritus from the scrap pile of history, and redeeming it inside the intensifying space of his boxes. He was rescuing the sacred from the profane; or perhaps more important, he was *elevating* the profane into the realm of the sacred— the realm of art. He imbued the seemingly trivial with an aura, with significance. Cornell wrote of the "past transmuting the present" through his art. He wanted his boxes to be portals out of our linear sense of history, into a place where time is brought to a halt: the ultimate utopia of escape. Cornell's boxes *are* transporting— that's part of their secret. One of his more famous boxes, *Toward the Blue Peninsula*, shows an empty white interior wrapped in a white cage. A blue piece of sky is glued to the back wall, and there, at that window, the cage has been cut open. The prisoner (the artist,

Cornell, or each of us looking at the box) has escaped to the time-less, mythic place, the Blue Peninsula. Walter Benjamin believed that the utopian wish-image could become what he called a politi-cally potent dialectical image—something so shocking and inspir-ing that it would release us into the open of Marx's socialist utopia. Yet Cornell never elevated the wish-image to its dialec-tical counterpart. There was absolutely nothing political about Cornell. His Angel of History wanted to stop time, or go back in time, but not redeem it. His waking dreams were wholly aesthetic and psychological. Given a choice of someplace he might escape to in the actual world, Cornell invariably chose the ballet—that most utopian, most unreal of art forms. The ballet set his boxes, his frozen dreams, in motion. It gave them a narrative and unlocked their secrets.

At MoMA there is a jewelry box that Cornell made as an homage to the Swedish ballerina Maria Taglioni. Inside the box, Cornell placed twelve glass ice cubes in a velvet setting as an allusion to the story that the famous ballerina once stopped her carriage late at night and danced on the ice for a gang of Russian highwaymen. Cornell's admiration for Maria Taglioni extended to other women. Because he was so painfully shy and introverted, some of the boxes became shrines where he could idealize women, such as Lauren Bacall and Susan Sontag, without ever risking re-jection or entering into anything as messy as an actual romantic relationship. However much we might want to blame Cornell's mother for infantilizing and browbeating him, he was, in the end, a deeply solipsistic man who didn't seem to want a wife and certainly wouldn't have known what to do with one. He was not unlike the narrator of John Fowles's novel *The Collector*, a man who kidnaps a woman he is in love with and locks her in his basement because he knows he couldn't have her otherwise. Cornell locked women in his boxes.

Still, I would argue the *hommages aux femmes* were relatively early, minor works. Here is what a more typical Cornell box looks like: I'm standing in the Surrealism room of MoMA (in his sprawl-ing journal, Cornell wrote, "I don't dig Surrealism in the manifesto sense") before *Hotel Beau-Sejour*. This box is completely papered with hotel ads or fragments of articles from European newspapers. A white wooden parakeet is perched below a single silver ring, as if the bird might swing from it, and above a cork ball on which the bird might perform some balancing trick. A small fragment of mirror is glued to the right side of the box, across from the parakeet (this is a hotel, after all). A quarter-round piece of driftwood offers another perch in the right-hand corner of the box. At the bottom of the box is a narrow drawer into which a viewer might place— what? A prayer, a poem, a thank-you note, a payment for staying at the Hotel Beau-Sejour? Cornell tended to work in series, and this box conflates two of his favorite motifs: birds and grand hotels. Both are utopian themes. The bird, particularly the tropical bird, symbolizes flight from this world to something exotic, equatorial, prelapsarian: the Blue Peninsula. The grand hotel is a place of ultimate luxury, service, and accommodation. Everything one could possibly need resides somewhere in a grand hotel. Cornell dreamed of such places constantly, even though he never left—seemed psychologically incapable of leaving—New York City. The box was a kind of three-dimensional postage stamp that the artist sent out into the world. Yet Cornell also traveled through his boxes. What's more, as the painter Fairfield Porter once noted, Cornell traveled *in* his boxes. They were each, Porter wrote, a ship cabin that "brings the suggestion that the room is on a journey." Thus the constellations that Cornell often papered onto his walls were also portholes of a ship, views of the night sky at sea. And his boxes were microcosms of the larger cosmos reflected in the repeated imagery of the constellations.

Space Object Box: "Little Bear, etc." motif, at the Guggenheim, is one such box. A star chart with the constellations Ursa Minor and Draco has been papered against the back of the box. A child's wooden block is fixed to the bottom of the box and painted with a crude horse, perhaps Pegasus. A single ring hangs from two parallel metal bars, which hold aloft a blue ball of cork. The ball can roll back and forth along the bars, like a moon or planet in a fixed orbit. Often, though not in this box, Cornell placed a clay soap bubble pipe at the bottom of his astronomical boxes, as if to suggest that the cork ball and the silver ring are the soap bubbles that have been blown from the pipe. The pipe, a most unlikely godhead, becomes the source of those spheres, those images of wholeness and perfection. Our own round world, after all, was *breathed* into being by the divine *pneuma* of the Judeo-Christian god.

Each Cornell box becomes a kind of constellation, its few elements held together by nothing more than the assembler's intuition that these salvaged artifacts belong together. In *Space Object Box*, the map of the constellations is fragmentary—the torso of Orion is cut off—but lines radiate out from it toward the walls of the box. "Infinity," observed Fairfield Porter, "is not a matter of physical size." It can be captured in an eighteen-by-eleven-inch wooden box. Using discarded materials, Joseph Cornell was re-creating the universe, over and over. Yet he chose his materials as carefully as the God that he, a devout Christian Scientist, believed in. Everything depended on the exactness of that composition, the symbolic poetic resonance with which each object spoke to the other, the unified theory (known only to Cornell) that held this constellation together.

How can such simple objects make such a—I'll just say it—cosmic statement? That is to say, how can something so small cast such light? That's always the question that hovers around a Cornell box. One answer is: in a world of talk that grows more and more abstract, we have forgotten the pure power of the image. Sure, we can say that the objects in a Cornell box are symbols: that the cork ball is the sun or moon, that the clay pipe is the artist's Dutch ancestry, and so on. But the image doesn't need to be a symbol of anything other than itself. There is extraordinary power in the image. Because of the personal associations we as viewers bring to it, the image can bear incredible psychic freight. Without our even knowing it, the image can rise to the level of a collective archetype. And because Cornell so often chose his images from our collective childhoods, they ramify even more deeply and unconsciously. Mark Rothko hoped that his massive color-field abstractions would capture some pure emotional state and bring his viewers to tears, but a diminutive Cornell box can do exactly the same thing.

It is a world so different from ours and yet instantly recognizable. We know what all the objects are, and yet we never would have thought to place them together in this arrangement. Cornell made the familiar strange; he gave a newfound intensity to the ordinary. It's what we all want: to see our normal lives suddenly drenched with significance, with texture, with newness. To move that experience *out* of the box and into our lives would be the trick, the transformation, that Walter Benjamin so badly sought. Cornell was incapable of such a move from art to experience, and the gallery owner David Mann remembered Cornell saying to him, "You don't know how terrible it is to be locked into boxes all your life, you have no idea what a terrible thing it is." Perhaps, in the end, Cornell could see how his boxes were indeed grand hotels: amazing places to visit, but you couldn't make a life there.

After the museums close, I take the train back to Brooklyn and meet a friend for dinner. When I tell her I'm staying in a warehouse on Myrtle Street, she says brightly, "Oh, we call that Murder Street." Back in my room, I collapse onto my mattress, exhausted from all the day's walking. It's then that I notice two metal rings fastened to the wall where a headboard would normally be. For a moment I think of all the rings in Cornell's boxes, but then I see a leather whip hanging just above one of the rings. I've always considered myself a kind of connoisseur of funky accommodation, but I have never stayed in a place that actually encouraged bondage. I think for a minute that I'll call my wife so we can have phone bondage, but then I realize I don't actually know what that would entail, and anyway, one of my walls is a sheet. A leather whip—Joseph Cornell wouldn't have known what to do with it, either. Although he might have liked my sparely furnished room with its peeling paint and the maps on the walls, he would have had no use for such an object from the fallen world. It would have violated the innocence, the poetry, the psychic purity that stood at the core of his art.

The Pine Barrens Anarchists

With my bag packed in the early morning, I weave between a few couches where sleeping artists lay curled, and head off along the rather dreary Robert Moses Causeway and Sagtikos Parkway to what once was a small utopian hamlet called Modern Times. In 1850, Josiah Warren first rode the recently completed Long Island Railroad out to these pine barrens. He was accompanied by the flamboyant New Orleans lawyer Stephen Pearl Andrews, who two years earlier had heard one of Warren's "parlor talks," given on Sundays in the progressive drawing rooms of Boston. Andrews was many things: an abolitionist mobbed and driven out of Houston for trying to abolish slavery in Texas, a spiritualist, an advocate of women's rights, and a linguist who purported to know thirty-two languages. He also invented one, called Alwato, which he claimed would unite mankind under his philosophy of universology, itself a grand theory of everything that affirmed the most microcosmic earthly correspondences to the macrocosmic spheres. In Boston, Andrews had been instantly converted to Warren's more pragmatic philosophy of equitable commerce, and soon the charismatic Andrews was preaching Warren's philosophy far more effectively than its founder ever had. Beyond their agreement on equitable commerce, the two men were in every way a study in contrasts: the introvert and the extrovert, the tongue-tied inventor and the silver-tongued assimilator.

Nevertheless, the two men convinced each other that, while much of the country was migrating west, their utopian prospects lay east on Long Island, where land speculators would be slow to follow. Much of the island's pines had already been clear-cut for cordwood, and then abandoned by developers. Knowing that many of their recruits wouldn't have much capital to invest in new homes, Warren and Andrews financed 750 acres halfway between the Long Island Sound and the Atlantic with little money down and a five-year bond on the balance. When they rode out to survey their acquisition, Warren recalled, "There was not, at that time, even a cow path in sight, among the scrub oaks that were everywhere breast high." Warren and Andrews set 90 acres of the 750 aside for the town they would call Modern Times, a sobriquet that suggested that a new, less gilded age was dawning. Seven streets ran north and south, while seven avenues ran east and west. Within this grid sat forty-nine blocks, each divided into four lots so each family would have a corner lot with room for a truck garden. Each parcel would, of course, be sold to settlers at cost: twenty dollars. Warren eventually hoped for a diverse population of one thousand people—enough to supply all the labor and services the community would need and could trade for with labor notes.

Modern Times never came close to that number, but today the town, renamed Brentwood, has swollen to sixty thousand residents. And judging from the number of bodegas that line the main road into town, many of them came here, if not with utopian aspirations, then at least harboring some version of the American Dream, a better life than the one south of the border. Towering pines line the streets, and the scent of their resin drifts through my windows—"Asthma finds great relief in our piney air," wrote one early settler—as I drive through neighborhoods where a couple of El Salvadoran flags hang from the houses.

At the Brentwood Public Library, I sit down at a computer and bring up a forum page for the website City-Data.com. There someone asked innocuously, "How is Brentwood, New York these days?" Many of the responses sounded like this one: "If you consider 20 Central Americans living in a house that was a three bedroom house that they turned into an eight bedroom house good, than I guess things are good." One of the website's pie charts confirms that in 2013, the Brentwood population was 68 percent Hispanic. Most of the website posters seemed to agree that Brentwood was a great place to live in the 1960s and '70s. Then, they say, the schools deteriorated and developers threw up a lot of cheap housing. "I'm not sure what happened," wrote someone with the moniker Crookhaven, "but they should change it back to Modern Times."

Beyond the shadowy anonymity of the Internet, however, things don't look so bad. Here at the library, English- and Spanish-speaking children play together as their parents check out books and sit at computers. I'm here to track down the first written history of Modern Times, composed by the village's oldest-surviving member, Charles A. Codman. A librarian leads me to the archive room, where she searches through several filing cabinets. She tells me that many of Brentwood's Latino residents arrived in the 1970s to work at Pilgrim State, the largest psychiatric hospital in the country, a place where at one time two thousand lobotomies were performed each day. When she finally locates Codman's "Brief History of the City of Modern Times," she hands me the loose-leaf typescript with corrections done by hand. It appears to be the original copy. Though there's no date on the yellowed pages, Codman wrote in his introduction that "it is more than half a century that I look back upon." Since Codman moved to Modern Times in 1857, his manuscript must be about a hundred years old. The librarian leaves me at a long table to study the brittle document.

In 1852, at the Musical Hall of Boston, Codman first heard Stephen Pearl Andrews lecture on Warren's principles of equitable commerce, and he "felt convinced that the solution of the Social problem had been found." Five years later, he bought two lots on Second and Third Avenues, built a house on the labor-exchange system, and set himself up as a sign painter. He arrived with a small coterie of skilled workingmen and -women who became known as the "Boston group." To begin his brief history of the people who first made their grubstake in these pine barrens, Codman wrote that he was "glad to give my testimony to the motives of the Pioneers and to rescue their reputations from any imputations put fourth [sic] by those who had no just conception of their motives and aspirations." Indeed, it appears that Modern Times was misunderstood and misrepresented almost from the start. Such calumny would prove to be the greatest frustration of Josiah Warren's life.

In the spring of 1851, Warren built the first permanent house at Modern Times, making bricks out of Long Island gravel and lime, and then drying them in the sun. He quickly sold the home at cost (one hundred twenty dollars) and built a larger, two-story structure that housed a Time Store, a print shop, and a "Mechanical College," where Warren taught the new settlers the arts of brickmaking, carpentry, letterpress stereotyping, and music. He loathed the apprentice system that spent five years teaching a man something that, according to Warren, he could pick up in five days. Warren was a generalist of the Jeffersonian stripe: he believed that to preach a doctrine of radical individualism, one must practice the arts of radical self-sufficiency. One state away, a loner named Henry David Thoreau was living alone beside a small pond and writing a book to that effect, though he and Warren seemed completely (and oddly) unaware of each other. For his part, Warren wrote, "He is ten times a citizen, who can perform a citizen's part in ten different positions; and more than this, when he is ready and willing to teach others to be as useful as himself."

Warren would certainly not have objected to empty-handed Central American immigrants coming to Modern Times. For one thing, diversity of all kinds tested and reinforced the idea of individual sovereignty. For another, Warren's entire economic philosophy was specifically designed for the have-nots. "If our efforts do not secure homes for the homeless," he wrote, "we work to no purpose, and these homes cannot be secured in the cities now built." But they could be secured on this remote stretch of Long Island. Codman described the first two years at Modern Times as "days of large hopes and scanty realizations." The flame of idealism had flared up among a forest of pine stumps, and if it was, as Codman wrote, a time of "low living," it was also an era of "high thinking." According to Codman, the early settlers believed "that they were founding a true Commonwealth on a broader foundation than had been conceived or attempted during all Human History." And he added, "In their lexicon, there was no such word as fail." By 1853, sixty pioneers had taken up Warren's utopian experiment. Many were lured out to Long Island by the publication a year earlier of *The Science of Society*, in which Andrews promised that, at Modern Times, "the laboring classes might *step out from under* the present system, and place themselves in a condition of independence *above* that system." The early sovereigns built modest cottages by exchanging labor for labor, and they planted shade and fruit trees along the avenues. "If they were lacking in capital, they were flush in enthusiasm," wrote Codman (who hadn't yet arrived). "In short, they banked on the future, cast their bread on the water and hoped it might return many fold in Spiritual wealth, and to this end they were willing to sacrifice much in building an Equitable Village which should be an example of Harmony and Justice and which should be a bright and shining light to all the world—a beacon to show the way out from the many evils of competition and tyranny which had for all time dominated in human relations." A visitor confirmed Codman's enthusiasm when he observed that Warren's movement "does inspire its votaries with a confidence and zeal that cannot be surpassed."

In his usual perceptive way, John Humphrey Noyes once described Modern Times as "the electric negative of New Harmony." If you got a house built at Modern Times, it meant you spent a great deal of time helping others build their houses: labor for labor. This exchange of labor incidentally built up a great amount of social capital among the sovereigns. No benevolent overseer was bankrolling the experiment. The labor philosophy of Modern Times inoculated the community against sloth and graft. Because all parties agreed beforehand on the value of all work, class grievances never arose. Two women who needing washing and sewing, respectively, from each other could agree—this actually happened—that washing was the harder job and deserved a larger payment in labor notes. The community did not have to debate five different constitutions, as happened at New Harmony, because there never existed one constitution, or any other written and signed set of laws, at Modern Times.

What did get written at Modern Times, or at least reprinted, was Warren's manifesto *Equitable Commerce*. George Ripley, whose own utopian experiment, Brook Farm, had literally gone up in flames six years earlier, reviewed the book for Horace Greeley's *New-York Tribune*. Ripley allowed that the case for individual sovereignty was never pleaded "more admirably," but, as he pointed out, Warren's second principle that cost must be the limit of price stands in direct contradiction to the individual's right to do as he or she pleases. "Could there be a more flagrant violation of Sovereignty of the Individual?" Ripley asked. Pearl Andrews jumped to Warren's defense, arguing that "cost the limit of price" was not a *compulsory law* of equitable commerce, but rather a *principle* on which the citizens of an equity village voluntarily agreed to act. As such, reasoned Andrews, it did not violate an individual's sovereignty. Still, it's easy to see Ripley's point, especially in a time when talk of individual sovereignty comes not from any socialist circles, but almost always from the libertarian right. But what Ripley saw as an inconsistency in Warren's thinking might be instead a radical solution to the tension between personal rights and the greater good of the larger community. Andrews believed that the *end* of equitable commerce would be a socialist society, but the *means* to it would not be the traditional, coercive system of a Robert Owen or a Vladimir Lenin. The principle of "cost the limit of price," manifested through the exchange of labor notes, would draw people together in a reciprocating society that would in turn organically develop into something that closely resembled the ideals of socialism: worker ownership, nonexploitive labor, the absence of wealthy overlords.

By 1843, thirty-seven families were living at Modern Times, and Warren expected new ones every day. He complained, however, that some of the new arrivals "were full of 'crotchets.'" There was a blind nudist. Another man paraded his children naked through the streets of Modern Times because he believed the young should not wear clothes. One woman tried, and failed, to survive on a diet of unsalted beans. Warren rued the weekly arrival of some new homeopathy, as if "Lord Bacon has not entirely secured us against the delusion of mere fancies, instead of building our theories on experience." Codman confirmed that at Modern Times, "every kind of reform was advocated, from that of Abolition of chattel slavery, women's rights, vegetarianism, hydropathy (and all the -pathies), peace, anti-tobacco, total abstinence and the bloomer costume and every new and strange proposition was welcomed by a respectful hearing." Yet what could Warren say? These eccentrics were flying their freak flags as the fullest expression of individual sovereignty. They had, as he admitted, "the great sacred right of freedom to do silly things." In what seems an obvious violation of his own live-and-let-live principles, Warren even carped about a woman who walked the streets in men's clothing: "She cut such a hideous figure that women shut down their windows and men averted their heads as she passed." And in rather unenlightened prose, he went on: "It seemed not to have occurred to the woman in men's clothes, that the influence of woman is one of the greatest civilizing powers we have, and we need to know when we are in their presence." It was, in many ways, the question of women's rights, and Warren's inability to take the issue seriously, that began the slow decline of Modern Times.

The couple that rankled Warren the most were the free-love proselytizers Mary Gove and Thomas Low Nichols. While today in the collective consciousness, we tend to equate free love with open marriage, swingers, and key parties, the term itself originated in the nineteenth century as a feminist argument for the rights of women to marry and divorce whom they wished and to bear children when and with whom they chose, with no interruption or oversight by the church or the state. Robert Owen, of course, had made these arguments twenty-five years earlier, at New Harmony, but Mary Gove Nichols was the first woman to put them forward in the United States, and her autobiographical novel, *Mary Lyndon, or, Revelations of a Life*, made the first case in print against marriage from a woman's point of view. If her actual wedding vows to Thomas Low Nichols were anything like those of her fictional stand-in Mary Lyndon, they went something like this: "I enter into no compact to be faithful to you. I only promise to be faithful to the deepest love of my heart. If that love is yours, it will bear fruit for you and enrich your life—our life. If my love leads you from me, I must go." Alas, having given herself permission to stray, Mary remained as faithful to Thomas as the waves to the shore. Like Stephen Pearl Andrews and his wife, Mary Anne, the Nicholses' connubial happiness seemed only to increase in proportion to the energy with which they denounced the Procrustean marriage bed.

Charles Codman contended (rightly, I think) that the Nicholses were simply applying Warren's individual sovereignty to "the Marriage relation," though Warren himself seemed oddly obtuse to this point of view. Still, thanks to the Nicholses, Modern Times could not shake its reputation for licentiousness. Finally, the very name of the town became so tainted by insinuation that, in 1864, it was changed to the inoffensive Brentwood. Warren, no doubt, felt that his founding philosophies had been hijacked by an issue that he saw as a peripheral distraction. He maintained that individualism meant monogamy ("one man to one woman for a definite, specified length of time, renewable to consent of both parties") or, in his case, serial monogamy. While Caroline Warren had refused to join her husband at Modern Times, Warren wrote in a letter to Andrews that he and a certain Mrs. Jane Crane were reading Andrews's work to each other at night. As the Long Island historian Roger Wunderlich dryly noted, "People who read at night together tend to be more than casual friends." Thus it might be argued that Warren was, at least in practice, a greater advocate for free love than the faithful Nicholses, but he of course did not see it that way.

Aside from making Modern Times notorious, the Nicholses were, in Warren's view, attempting to speak *for* the village—the greatest heresy against individual sovereignty he could imagine. To put an end to it all, in 1853 he posted his own anti-free-love position on the village bulletin board and asked all who agreed with him to sign it. Apparently many did, and soon the Nicholses were packing their bags. But if Warren spent his entire adult life expounding two basic principles—sovereignty of the individual and cost the limit of price—the Nicholses seemed to flit from one world-mending scheme to the next. By the time they reached Yellow Springs, Ohio, they had abandoned the cause of free love and were instead attempting to form a Shaker-like community based on chastity. In 1857 they converted to Roman Catholicism, arguably the greatest protector of traditional marriage this side of the Koran.

Warren, for his part, was greatly relieved when Charles Codman's more straitlaced entourage arrived from Boston in 1857. One of them, a carpenter named William Upham Dame, built an octagonal house that still stands, now covered in white vinyl siding, at the corner of Brentwood and Third, where it is home to the Sisters of St. Joseph. Dame designated the second floor as an "Archimedian Hall," where meetings and dances took place. (Like the meetinghouse back at Pleasant Hill, it had no interior walls.) There was a glee club, a thespian club, a Shakespeare reading club, and even a short-lived football club, which ended when, as Codman wrote, "the philosophers" of Modern Times realized they "were better at talking than kicking each other's shins." Indeed, for twenty-five years, long after Warren departed Modern Times, a philosophers' club met weekly at Codman's house to discuss all manner of social reform. (Codman called his home the Hermitage of the Red Owl because one stormy night, he spotted said owl outside his window. He coaxed the nocturnal creature inside, whereupon it began to channel the spirit of an Indian chief once hacked to death and left beside a ravine on Codman's property. The owl asked Codman to retrieve the chief's bones and give them a proper burial. This Codman claimed to have done, and "since that hour, all has been well with me.")

To Warren's way of thinking, Modern Times could be judged a success for what it didn't have: There were "no quarrels about what is called 'religion.' No demand for jails. No grog shops. No houses of prostitution. No fighting about politics." And by 1860, Modern Times had brought together a rather diverse population that peaked at 250 sovereigns. There were farmers, dentists, physicians, merchants, mechanics, masons, harness makers, blacksmiths, and cobblers. The women of Modern Times adopted the skirt-and-pantaloons of the bloomer craze, and, Codman wrote, "the male reformers wore their hair long, a sort of badge—an outward sign of their affiliation with progress."

The fact that so much of the village's economic life was carried out with its own labor notes meant that it fared far better than other towns when the financial Panic of 1857 hit. Indeed, Warren argued that all three national panics—1814, 1837, and 1857— were caused by excessive importing of foreign goods and a lack of self-sufficiency at home. "A money that will not circulate beyond its own neighborhood is the true and legitimate remedy for these evils," Warren countered; "while, at the same time it would shape foreign commerce into an exchange of products, mutually beneficial to the nations concerned." One hundred years before writers like Jane Jacobs, E. F. Schumacher, and Wendell Berry began articulating the value of a local economy, we hear some of the first intimations of it in Warren. The labor notes at Modern Times insulated the village to a great degree from the larger financial markets back in New York City because they were symbols of real labor and real goods.

However, the community's five-year real estate contract for price stability also ended that year, and soon speculators moved in to claim unsold lots. In the end, Modern Times hadn't grown large enough to completely keep the world of finance out of its pine barren paradise. Codman lamented that the purer motives of the Modern Timers were no match for Wall Street: "We may have been Speculators in Morality, but not in Land or its products." The presence of the new capitalists slowly eroded the village's commitment to equitable commerce.

There were other problems. Modern Times never grew large enough to be truly self-reliant. "The fundamental mistake that we made," Codman wrote toward the end of his history, "was in thinking that even a small percent of those who are clamorous and insistent for Justice are honest and in earnest; they are not, and with sadness I write it, they want to prate and shout for it but are far from ready to practice." Because of its size, Modern Times had never built a successful manufacturing base. If only it had built a water tower, Codman mused, perhaps it could have encouraged "some kind of manufacturing and by it earned a living."

He also blamed Warren for not being the kind of electrifying leader that a radical movement needs. "He lacked the fit of languages and especially in addressing a public audience," Codman wrote. "Also he was a timid man and hated to wrangle, and after a discussion would retire to his home for 1–6 weeks at a time. He thus lacked the ability to present and maintain his views—I think that if he had had the gift or art of leadership the fortune of this Village and its founder would have been very different, that we should have won success, even if not the aims we strove for." No doubt Warren would have replied that a "leader" is anathema to an equity village. But one can't help agreeing with Codman on some level that if Stephen Pearl Andrews had spent a decade living at Modern Times instead of Warren, more aspirants might have come, and might have clung longer to the two men's original vision. Perhaps without a charismatic leader, a utopian movement needs a system to sustain it. After Mother Ann Lee died, Father Joseph Meacham forged her rather murky beliefs into both a community credo and a rigorous set of rules. The egalitarians at Twin Oaks reject the idea of a charismatic leader, but they have an intricate system that keeps things humming. Modern Times had neither the leader nor the system.

The other idea that drove a wedge between Warren and the community was his attitude toward the impending Civil War. The South had every right to secede from the Union, Warren argued, just as every slave had the right to secede from his master. The potential for secession was built into the Declaration of Independence. As far as Warren was concerned, every individual should ultimately be his or her own country, and a fully enlightened state would allow such liberty. But to force a man to fight and die for a country to which he didn't wish to belong and for a principle in which he didn't believe was the grossest violation of liberty Warren could imagine. None of this should have surprised the citizens of Modern Times, but after the Confederate attack on Fort Sumter in 1861, many of them felt a greater allegiance to Lincoln than to Warren. Zealous patriotism won out over practical anarchy. Feeling either chastened or betrayed by the villagers' decisions, Warren left Modern Times for good in October 1862 and moved to Boston, where he remained for the rest of his life. He died in 1874 and was buried at the Mount Auburn Cemetery, across from Harvard Square.

Many Long Islanders returned from the war and lived out their days in Brentwood. Modern Times did not come to a dramatic, colossal end like Brook Farm or New Harmony. It died the slow, smoldering death of a campfire. Gradually the people of Brentwood gave up on labor notes and Time Stores. Dollars were easier to use, and they could buy so much more.

In his essay's conclusion, written near the eve of World War I, Charles Codman worried that "happy times seem more distant than ever, that I shall have passed without a glimpse of the 'Promised Land,' that my eyes may not see the Millennium Dawn, and my query is, will anyone see it? Is it only a Chimera? I dunno—" The indefinite flatness of that "I dunno" seems rather heartbreaking, like a jilted lover abruptly slamming the door on a woman he thought he understood.

I slide Codman's manuscript back into its folder and take out an old photograph of the Modern Times schoolhouse, another of William Upham Dame's octagons, built in 1857 and kept in use for fifty years. In the photo, the octagon is a handsome work of board and batten, crowned with a small octagonal cupola. The caption says that the building still sits on the property of the current high school, waiting for restoration. I thank the librarian for her help and drive over to look for the city's first one-room school. As it turns out, the grounds of the high school are quite expansive, and I drive around for a while until, in a far corner of the campus, I find the old school's crumbling remains. Whenever that photograph was taken and its caption written, the building now appears far beyond repair. The siding is badly warped, and all the windows and doors are boarded up. The dormers have fallen through the roof, where moss long ago replaced the shingles. A large wooden sign, now covered in dark mold, says that restoration of the schoolhouse will "begin in 2005." Obviously that did not happen, and now it looks like it never will.

I suppose this is the end of the road as far as my search for Josiah Warren goes. Everywhere I look for some evidence of his life, of his life's work, I find nothing, or next to nothing. Was Brentwood too embarrassed by the free-love reputation of Modern Times that it preserved almost none of the original village? Did Warren's insistence that no constitutions be written add to the ephemeral nature of his legacy? Did his great distrust of language mean that little of it would be used to claim a place for him in this country's history? Perhaps the answer to all these questions is yes. Yet it still seems to me that of all the American utopianists, only Josiah Warren found a scheme to balance absolute liberty for the individual with absolute fairness—justice, if you will—for the community. Warren's two principles of equitable commerce both protected individual freedom and kept the individual from being exploited by larger economic forces. In a capitalist economy, the absence of the cost principle is what robs men of their liberty and makes them wage slaves. The second principle must therefore exist to protect the first. That was the genius of Warren's particular version of utopian anarchy.

The next morning, I myself feel almost catapulted over Queens and the Bronx by the flying buttress of a freeway that Robert Moses built above these boroughs. Soon enough, though, I'm tooling through the eastern Hudson Valley along the leafy Taconic Parkway, which gets its name from the mountains out my driver's-side window, which get their name from the Native American word for "in the trees." The novelist William Kennedy called this road a 110-mile postcard.

Right before I turn east into the Berkshire range, I see a huge, looming sign, circa 1950s, that reads CHIEF MARTINDALE DINER. The chief himself, in full cartoonish headdress, waves from atop the block letters. A giant red arrow sweeps around and under him, pointing to something I am always helpless to resist: a stainless-steel diner. However, no sooner have I settled into my booth and read these words on the menu, "Don't complain about the coffee; you may be weak someday too," than I reflexively pad my pants pocket and realize that the thing I have feared the whole trip has finally happened: my keys are locked in my car's ignition.

I surreptitiously take a butter knife from the table, go back outside, and use it to pop open the small window on the back of my cab. I reach my right arm through the window, but the knife is still a good foot from the lock on the driver's door. I go back inside the diner and borrow a coat hanger from the waitress. The wire is long enough unwound, but its hook won't get any purchase on the lock. There is a family with a little boy sitting in the corner of the diner. In my mind, I'm already coaxing him through the small window and into the driver's seat. But that seems like a last-ditch scenario. In the meantime, a pretty young waitress has emerged from the diner and says she'll try to shimmy through the window. I like this idea just fine, but alas, even her narrow shoulders are too wide to scrunch through. We both go back inside. By now the entire diner has taken an interest in my plight. Patrons are ready with suggestions, all except for the family in the corner, who does not offer up their small child as the obvious solution.

One older gentleman retrieves a garden fork from his truck. The handle seems just long enough to work. And when I reach through the back window with it, one of the tines digs into my lock and, with a flick of my wrist, lifts it one glorious inch: open. I retrieve my keys and reenter the diner to a smattering of applause. I smile and, for some reason, feel compelled to do something that resembles a stage wave. But now I'm unfortunately short on time. The waitress boxes up my burger, and I pull away from the Chief's eatery, feeling strangely proud of myself for rallying the diner to my rescue.

I point my truck east, toward Massachusetts. I pass stately clapboard houses with wood-shingled roofs. Bracken fern grows at the base of stone walls that mark the perimeters of immaculate lawns. There really is an undeniable *neatness* to rural New England, a quality that I suppose still surprises me because it never seemed to translate down past the Mason-Dixon Line. The rural South is many things, but neat it is not. Even the firewood around here looks meticulously stacked. It's as if everybody is preparing at all times for their calendar photo. I drive along the wide valley floor, past ponds where I notice a beaver lodge or two. Then this pastoral tableau gently deposits me in the town of Stockbridge. I drive past the whitewashed carpenter's Gothic-style church where *Alice's Restaurant* was filmed, past the white clapboard home where Norman Rockwell lived and painted, past the white brick institution where James Taylor kicked heroin and is said to have written "Fire and Rain." I follow the Housatonic River until it leads me through the town of Great Barrington, whose Main Street looks like a simulacrum built from paintings of the region's most famous and omnipresent artist.

I came here with the hunch that Josiah Warren's influence could be seen, even measured. At the branch bank, I exchange ninety-five U.S. dollars for one hundred notes of a local currency called BerkShares. These handsome dollars, slightly larger than the federal scrip, bear the images of local heroes such as Norman Rockwell, Herman Melville, and W.E.B. Du Bois. Despite a general misperception that it's illegal to print your own money in the United States, there are in fact thirty-six different local currencies throughout the country. Of those, BerkShares are probably the most fully evolved.

This alternative currency was the brainchild of two lifelong radicals, Robert Swann and Susan Witt. Swann was a conscientious objector during World War II and served two years at a federal prison in Ashland, Kentucky. In stir, he and other COs organized their own covert university of radical thought. Swann was released in 1944, and in the 1960s he discovered the writings of the British economist E. F. Schumacher. Swann was particularly taken with Schumacher's idea of a "Buddhist economics," which aimed to maximize people's well-being while minimalizing consumption, environmental destruction, and the violence that came from fighting over natural resources and land. ("People who live in highly self-sufficient local communities are less likely to get involved in large-scale violence than people whose existence depends on world-wide systems of trade," wrote Schumacher.) Swann urged the British publisher John Papworth to collect Schumacher's essays into a book. The result was the 1960s bestseller *Small Is Beautiful*. In 1980, Swann was instrumental in founding the E. F. Schumacher Society, which eventually found a home here in the Berkshires. Around that same time, as Swann wrote in an autobiographical sketch, he fell in love with Susan Witt, a high school teacher with a literature background. Witt had heard Swann speak about land reform on a local radio show and asked if she could join his cause. Swann was named president of the Schumacher Society, and soon Witt became its executive director.

Witt and Swann began to spend a lot of time thinking about how a local currency might strengthen their community just as Warren's labor notes had voluntarily bound together the citizens of Utopia, Ohio, and Modern Times, New York. But they took it slow. "We knew we would only have one chance to get this right," Witt told me by phone as I was driving to Great Barrington. In 1988 they coauthored the pamphlet *Local Currency: Catalysts for Sustainable Regional Economies*. But it wasn't until 2006, three years after Swann died, that BerkShares hit the banks. Today there are more than 2.5 million BerkShares in circulation throughout the region that gives the currency its name. About four hundred businesses accept the homemade currency, including the Riverhead Café, a popular coffee and lunch place driven by a locavore philosophy. It's there where I've planned to meet up with Will Conklin, a local arborist who serves on the BerkShares board.

Indeed, when we meet at the counter and place our orders, a bearded Conklin does look as if he's just climbed down from a tree, or spent the morning planting some. I buy my lunch and Conklin's coffee refill with a twenty BerkShare note, and the young woman at the cash register digs under her drawer for some ones, but she comes up short.

"Can I give you a real dollar instead?" she asks.

"As opposed to a surreal dollar," Conklin jokes.

When we take a seat at a table with a view of the Housatonic River (Mohican for "beyond the mountain place"), Conklin tells me, "If somebody has no idea what a BerkShare is or why to use it, this is the first important thing: it makes value stay local. By staying local, it creates more jobs and keeps wealth in the community." By its very nature, of course, a local currency has to stay within the region, since it has no value outside the community where it circulates. Research has shown that a local currency will keep wealth within a community three to four times longer than the federal dollar. That, in turn, creates what economists call the multiplier effect: more jobs, more income, more wealth for that particular place. This is also the reason for the 5 percent differential between the ninety-five U.S. dollars you take to Berkshire Bank and the one hundred BerkShare notes you receive in return. That 5 percent is meant to keep you circulating BerkShares instead of returning them to the bank for dollars. The BerkShare becomes both a symbol and a kind of glue for the community.

Not coincidentally, nearly all businesses that accept Berk-Shares are locally owned—by people who have an incentive to keep wealth in Great Barrington and Stockbridge and Pittsfield. Earlier, at a Rite-Aid, when I tried to pay for batteries and sunscreen with BerkShares, the woman at the counter said, "We don't take those." I tell Conklin this, and he says, "It's a debate among the board about whether we would even want the chain stores to take BerkShares, because they're not locally owned." And since they're not, the money spent there quickly leaves town and heads for the corporate headquarters.

Of course, one could argue that the BerkShare itself isn't really necessary, that a "buy local" campaign, using regular dollars, would achieve the same result. Or the dollar could be eliminated altogether. In another iteration of local currency, the Canadian computer expert Michael Linton created the Local Exchange Trading System (LETS) in 1982. Much like Josiah Warren's labor exchange, LETS simply sets up a clearinghouse where members can swap goods and services for credit. The computer program keeps track of how much credit someone has and how many debits he or she has withdrawn. No physical money changes hands, and the "backing" is simply one's promise to return into the system an equal supply of the goods or services withdrawn. The economist Thomas H. Greco has taken this approach further with what he calls a mutual credit clearing system. Greco points out that when a commercial bank lends money, it simply creates that debt as a computer entry. ("The process by which banks create money is so simple that the mind is repelled," John Kenneth Galbraith once remarked.) The bank isn't actually lending out money, and it "lends" much more money than it has. That is to say, it loans out the *same money* many times over. But *we* have to pay it back as real money—with interest. The problem here—and it's a problem that extends all the way up to the country's nearly insurmountable debt—is that since the bank demands interest in return for its principal, there's actually never enough money in circulation to pay back all debts. The bank generates $100, for instance, but demands $110 back. That extra $10 doesn't exist, so someone is *always* in debt, and thus the economy always needs to "grow." Greco likens this to a game of musical chairs, in which there is one chair short for those playing the game, and his solution is to create exchanges that, in essence, make banks irrelevant and so make paying interest unnecessary. Credit, Greco argues in *The End of Money and the*

Future of Civilization, is a perfectly good backing for money, but banks have perverted such trust between lender and recipient by turning credit-backed money into debt money that demands high interest. As with LETS, direct credit clearing eliminates the need for money altogether. Once participants agree on the value of one another's goods and services, trading can begin, and debits and credits can be calculated electronically. The term *clearing* refers to the process by which claims by participants are offset against one another. Banks clear, or cancel out, millions of checks each day rather than sending, say, two one-hundred-dollar checks from one bank to the other. Greco's approach simply takes interest out of the picture. This would make goods and services much more affordable, and it would take away from banks the interest they did *nothing* to earn beyond loaning nonexistent money into circulation. And since we are now obviously soaring in the realm of utopian thinking, consider what would happen if the U.S. government issued its own currency, alongside local currencies, instead of paying massive interest to the cabal of private bankers otherwise known as the Federal Reserve, which is actually neither federal nor a reserve. For every hundred dollars we borrowed at, say, 5 percent interest, the government would pay five dollars back into the economy as funding for all manner of worthy civic projects: education, infrastructure, non–fossil fuel sources of energy. That money would return to circulation; it wouldn't end up in the coffers of the very rich or in the Wall Street casino of day trading. And, argues the former banker Ellen Hodgson Brown, it wouldn't create inflation, because the government spending would deliberately balance out supply and demand.

Still, Will Conklin maintains that an actual paper currency does things that a computer transaction cannot. It functions as a reminder of its own value. "A local currency connects people to their own goods and services and to each other in a way the federal currency can't," Conklin says. The BerkShare reinforces the idea—Josiah Warren's idea, really—that a community with its own currency is a more self-reliant community because it has a more self-reliant economy. "That builds resilience into the system," says

Conklin. Recall Warren's claim that excessive importing caused the financial panics of the nineteenth century, and that a local currency was "the true and legitimate remedy for these evils." Conklin agrees and thinks that BerkShares are leading to an import-replacement mentality in the region. "Why are two-by-fours coming from two thousand miles away?" he asks, when there's plenty of tall timber right here in the Northeast. With a local wood industry, says Conklin, "you're not only cutting supply lines and reducing your carbon footprint, you're also paying the sawyer of the wood a decent wage."

There have been problems. Some business owners chafe at the 5 percent differential between the dollar and the BerkShare; it's a 5 percent loss for them, after all. And businesses such as the co-op, where many who support the idea of a local currency do their shopping, found that they were taking in more BerkShares than they could recirculate, given that many of their suppliers accepted only dollars. Local farmers have run up against similar issues.

Conklin's phone rings. He has to get back to his trees. "Ask Susan Witt about that stuff," he says as we both rise to leave. "She can tell you more than I can."

I had in fact made an appointment to talk with Witt later this afternoon. So I head back along Great Barrington's Main Street, and then I'm quickly out of town and wandering past small farms in the Berkshire foothills. Mount Washington looms in the distance, but my GPS keeps sending me up dead-end roads or private drives. Finally, at the base of a hillside on Jug End Road, I see a modest wooden sign engraved with my destination. At the top of a gravel drive, I park beside the barnlike library that also operates as the headquarters of the Schumacher Society, recently renamed the New Economy Coalition.

Wearing a trim pink dress and pink pumps, Susan Witt belies certain received images of the counterculture matriarch in Birkenstock sandals and an alpaca sweater. She leads me into the open-air library where sun pours into the room. Shelves of more than fifteen thousand books on topics ranging from alternative agriculture to land reform to nonviolent resistance stand beneath a vaulted ceiling of white pine. Since it began, the Schumacher Society has sponsored a lecture series that has brought to this building the most revolutionary thinkers in the country. And drawing on Thomas Paine's tradition of pamphleteering, all those lectures have been bound by a local printer and now line one wall of the library. I imagine the kind of radical education one might receive merely by sitting in the room, day after day, reading through those lectures by men and women such as Jane Jacobs, Wes Jackson, Deborah Meier, Kirkpatrick Sale, and Peter Barnes.

I try to pick up with Witt where I left off with Will Conklin on the matter of merchants who've resisted accepting BerkShares, but Witt seems decidedly impatient with those who can't see the grander vision of a just economy detached from the ugly Siamese twin of our current financial system. While the BerkShare has received a lot of media attention in its seven years of existence, the reporters really came too early, Witt says in a slow husky voice. While a local currency is everything Conklin claims it to be, it has not finished evolving; nor is it the only vehicle to the truly sovereign economy that Witt imagines. Much more could be done to strengthen the local economy and inoculate it against the whims of the larger financial markets. Take Will Conklin, for example. It turns out his idea about better supporting local sawyers was not just a theoretical point. Right now the New Economy Coalition is taking the next step to begin a loan program with BerkShares. Recently, the Doen Foundation of the Netherlands ponied up five hundred thousand dollars to collateralize the new venture. Its director, Nina Tellegen, told Al Jazeera America, "Partly as a result of the financial crisis, people no longer believe in banks, and banks are no longer willing to support many of the small [to] medium-size enterprises. So by introducing this loan system within the BerkShares currency, that's a very important next step." These loans will go to local businesses that provide goods that local people need—import replacement goods, ideally.

Conklin, for instance, would use the loan to outfit his portable sawmill and begin producing locally milled wood products. The BerkShare loan would be interest-free, says Witt, because "there's no cost to the money coming down from the Fed."* And since the loan is issued in BerkShares, Conklin would be buying his own supplies locally as well as offering a local product—the multiplier at work again. But what about things he couldn't find locally, such as parts for his sawmill, or gasoline? In that situation, Conklin would trade willing customers BerkShares for dollars, and then he would use the federal currency to import what had no local replacement.

The Dutch loan might even help nudge the BerkShares collective toward another of its long-term goals: independence from the dollar. "As long as BerkShares are tied to the federal dollar, we haven't created a new system," Witt admits. "The only legitimate way to untie it is to have greater value standing behind the issuing than other currencies. So you tie it to the value created in the community. That means if all of your loans are to farmers, you have a sound currency. You have a little bit of money chasing a lot of goods. You can begin to determine a value separate from the federal dollar." You can back a local currency with anything that the region has in stable, consistent supply. Wendell Berry has suggested that in Kentucky we could back a local currency with chickens; everybody likes chicken, there's a lot of them back home, and almost all are shipped out of state by Big Poultry. When I tell Witt that Josiah Warren's labor notes were backed by corn, she smiles at this and says, "Those midwesterners still knew it in their gut: they hadn't forgotten parity. They hadn't forgotten basic economic concepts. For the rest of us it's so abstract."

---

*That is to say, Federal Reserve notes cost consumers interest because they are collateralized by the national debt. Part of the taxes we pay on the national debt underwrites the operating expenses of the Federal Reserve Bank. And since 66 percent of Fed currency circulates overseas, according to the economist Benjamin Gisin, Americans end up paying a lot of taxes on money they never see or use. A BerkShare loan program would be a small corrective to that element of globalization, and of course it would lower the cost of a loan.

Perhaps, I suggest, we as a country are finally making a turn back in that direction; perhaps the Great Recession has opened our eyes a little to the zero-sum game of the financial industry and the blackmail tactics of "too big to fail." Witt smiles again, as if this time I've said something so obvious that it barely deserves a response. Finally she responds: "Before the financial collapse, we were seen as a boutique organization, kind of sweet and irrelevant. Since the collapse, the glint is off the global economy and its promise of raising all boats. Now there is much more serious investigation of what we do. We remain serious, committed long-term thinkers on this."

From an equitable commerce point of view, Witt and Conklin are slowly turning currency back into what it should be: a *symbol* of real wealth that cannot be manipulated or despoiled by the speculators that Thomas Jefferson once dismissed as "the stock-jobbing herd." A BerkShare represents real goods, not a bogus "financial product." As with Warren's labor notes, one of the more important impulses behind the BerkShare is fending off a predatory financial system. Such a truly independent currency would exist entirely outside the realm of bubbles, junk bonds, and derivatives, and thus it would be immune to the regular failures of that system. Such a decentralized currency is immune to the coercive thinking of "too big to fail," and even if it did fail, it wouldn't take the entire country down with it.

It also represents an economy based on trust, honest accounting, and reciprocity. After all, for someone to make money on a credit-default swap, someone else must lose money. A BerkShare economy is not based on winners and losers, but rather on reciprocal exchanges in which both parties benefit from the transaction. In a famous computer experiment called the Prisoner's Dilemma, the American political scientist Robert Axelrod found the programs that ran the longest involved "players" who cooperated, tit for tat, instead of taking advantage of one another. They simply pushed players such as the CEO of Duke Energy out of the game by isolating aggressive behavior and rewarding cooperation. The reason Modern Times was free of "law-courts, jails and crime" is because it refused to engage in a mutual exchange of labor with anyone who would take advantage of others and therefore deserve, in the conventional sense, to be punished with jails, by judges. A contemporary community might accomplish similar results by subverting and decentralizing the power and wealth of Duke Energy, while at the same time increasing local wealth through a local currency.

I tell Witt all this by way of trying to connect Josiah Warren's ideas to the local currency movement.

"What about land?" she asks.

"Land?" I say.

"You can't have a utopian movement without land reform." Witt flashes a smiling yet withering look that seems to suggest she might be wasting her time with me after all. But I realize she's right. It was ultimately the *lack* of land reform that strangled and squelched all of Warren's experimental villages. There simply wasn't room enough to expand after rents went up and speculators moved in. The villages couldn't become large enough and self-sufficient enough to continue. It was Warren himself who said that the world's greatest crime was "the monopoly of the soil." How could I have come this far in my trip and still neglected something so obvious?

"In prison," Witt begins, "Bob Swann spent a great deal of time in solitary because he and the other COs refused to participate in the prison's segregation. So they sat with their black friends and got written up and thrown in solitary for ten days. Bob could handle that; some couldn't. He'd just come out and get thrown back in, come out and get thrown back in. He had a lot of time to think about the root causes of war. And he came out thinking there were two root causes of war. One was the issuing of currency by nation-states that allowed for the financing of war outside of taxation. And the other was the commodification of land where a few people benefit from the need of all to own land." So when Swann's five-year sentence was cut in half at the end of the war, he entered civilian life with plans of addressing both problems.

BerkShares became the solution, or at least a partial solution, to escaping from a monetary system that financed a war machine. As for the commodification of land, Swann started something he called the Community Land Trust. The idea is simple enough, though radical in its simplicity: the land is a God-given (Swann said "Earth-given") entity that cannot rightly be treated as a commodity. It must therefore be held in trust by those who use it and live on it. Any improvements that people make on the land, such as house building, belong to those who made those improvements. Those things can be sold, but the land cannot.

"Land and natural resources are limited in supply," says Witt, explaining Swann's initial thinking about the land trust idea. "Economic wealth occurs when human labor organized by human ingenuity transforms the natural world into new products. The natural world itself is not the new wealth. So it doesn't rightly belong to be traded in the economic sphere. The fact that it does creates lots of inequities. So, often at the core of any utopian movement, intentional community of any kind is a new approach to holding land." The Shakers and the Twin Oaks communitarians held and hold land in common. Winstanley's Diggers took to the English commons because, as the song says, "No man has the right to sell the earth for private gain." Dissension spread at New Harmony in part because Robert Owen refused to deed the town over to its inhabitants. The sovereigns at Modern Times bought land together, and then split it up among themselves. And of course, when Josiah Warren refused any profit when he returned the eight blocks of real estate in Cincinnati to the man he had leased it from, he was operating on the same principles that led Swann to the land trust idea. Swann even stipulated that the lease on such land should run for ninety-nine years, the exact amount of time spelled out in Warren's Cincinnati lease. During that time, a leaseholder owns buildings and agricultural improvements on the land, but on resale, wrote Swann, "leaseholders are restricted to selling their buildings and improvements at current replacement cost, excluding the land's market value from the transfer." It's Warren's "cost the limit of price" idea all over again. The resale restrictions mean the land will not again be capitalized and therefore will remain affordable to future generations.

Swann believed that a local economy stagnates when its capital is tied up in land instead of in the farms and businesses *on* the land. In that sense, one can see how a local currency and a land trust are two sides of the same BerkShare; both prevent speculation on things that should not act as commodities: land and money. "When land and natural resources are treated as commodities and traded on the market, as in the current system, an imbalance occurs in the economy," Witt explains. "A few people can then profit from the need of all for access. No new wealth is generated, only a speculative value, with all the consequences of a speculative economy, including social inequity and ecological degradation."

Witt rises to retrieve a small wooden box from a shelf in the library. The box contains a piece from a small spinning wheel. The little contraption was a gift to Swann from Govind Deshpande. Witt explains that Deshpande walked with Gandhi's spiritual successor Vinoba Bhave through the Gramdan Villages of India. In each place he visited, Bhave told the villagers, "My brothers and sisters, those of you with more land than you can use, won't you share that land with your brothers and sisters who are in need?" Many did. The practice became known as *Bhoodan*, or "land gift." The titles from that gifted land were transferred to the villages themselves, and then leased out to farmers too poor to buy their own land.

"It was the practice of Gandhians to engage in productive labor while holding meetings," Witt tells me. "When arriving at a village, Vinoba and his followers would sit on the ground, open the cases of the spinning wheels they carried with them, assemble the parts, and spin. Gandhi taught that the spinning of cotton was both a symbol of, and a practical step toward, freeing India from the economic oppression of Europe. The cotton was later woven into khadi cloth, a homespun substitute for the silk and linens from Belgium and England." In 1967, Robert Swann helped start this country's first land trust in a poor African American community in Albany, Georgia. He organized a group that purchased a five-thousand-acre farm, which was then leased out to local black farmers who couldn't otherwise afford arable land. Vinoba Bhave gave his spinning wheel to Swann, says Witt, as a recognition that he was carrying on Gandhi's work in this country. "Bob taught us that it is not land and natural resources that create wealth," Witt says, "but rather the transformation of those resources into products that others need."

The ten-acre hillside where the Schumacher Center for a New Economics sits is itself a community land trust. I can see Witt's own modest house up the hill, beside a handsome vegetable garden lined with raspberry vines. A couple of other homes sit over the swell. And if those families decide to sell their homes, that is all they sell; the land remains a commons.

Though there are now hundreds of community land trusts around the country, Witt is under no illusions that there will be an imminent transformation concerning the way Americans think about land as real estate. In that sense, it is yet another "utopian" dream. But as Victor Hugo said, and as Jimmy Carter's former adviser James Gustave Speth repeated in a speech he delivered in this very room, "There's nothing like a dream to create the future. Utopia today, flesh and blood tomorrow."

Hunger Not to Have but to Be

WALDEN POND: CONCORD, MASSACHUSETTS
Mile: 001901

The first thing you see driving into Concord from the west is the Massachusetts Correctional Institution. Built in 1878 with the mission of teaching incarcerated males under thirty a viable trade that would ease their return to society, the prison today is a medium-security facility ringed with high fences, razor wire, and guard towers positioned at every corner of the yard. Suffice it to say it doesn't look much like the homey Concord jail where Henry David Thoreau famously spent one night, an experience from which arose this country's most important essay, "Resistance to Civil Government." It's just a few miles farther to Walden Pond, where a distressing sign at the park entrance reads PARKING CAPACITY—FULL. Is this some joke? I have made my nearly two-thousand-mile pilgrimage to the world's most revered utopia of solitude—and it's too crowded even to get in?

I make a left turn toward town. A quarter mile down the road is a small parking area, but the sign there says that it's only for Massachusetts residents; cars with any other tags will be towed. I drive on. A half mile farther, I come to the local high school. A group of men and women in Lycra are unlocking racing bikes from atop their cars. A sign here says that parking for Walden Pond is prohibited. It's beginning to seem like I'll have to drive all the way to the Old Manse, where Thoreau once planted a large garden for his new neighbor, Nathaniel Hawthorne, and hoof it from there, just as Thoreau would have done. Yet there are plenty of empty spaces here at the high school, so I pull into one, shoulder my combination backpack/folding chair, and start walking.

Walking. Thoreau claimed to do at least four hours of it each day. At the beginning of his essay called "Walking," he even invents his own etymology for the word *saunter*. It came from the root *Sainte Terre*, Thoreau conjectured, meaning a "Holy Lander," a religious wanderer, a mendicant. Having no home, he is at home everywhere: "For this is the secret of successful sauntering. He who sits still in a house all the time may be the greatest vagrant of all; but the saunterer, in the good sense, is no more vagrant than the meandering river." Thoreau was known to walk with an umbrella, and wear a top hat into which he had built a compartment that held the plants, fish, and turtles he collected along the way. (He joked that his brain kept the specimens moist.) He donated some of these, including smelts and shiners from Walden Pond, to the world-famous ichthyologist Louis Agassiz, who had arrived from Europe to set up a Harvard lab.

In the gnostic Gospel of Thomas, we find this saying by Jesus: "Be passersby." Though that gospel was not discovered in Thoreau's time, if it had been, Thoreau would have known exactly what that other, Mediterranean wanderer meant: Don't accumulate what will only weigh you down—physically, spiritually, financially, psychologically. Travel light through this world. In "Walking," Thoreau paraphrases one of Jesus' sternest sayings when he writes, "If you are ready to leave father and mother, and brother and sister, and wife and child and friends, and never see them again—if you have paid your debts, and made your will, and settled all your affairs, and are a free man, then you are ready for a walk." In that essay, Thoreau declares walking to be his main line of work, and he further claims that no wealth can buy "the requisite leisure, freedom, and independence, which are the capital of this profession." Of course, what Thoreau saw as requisite leisure many of his townspeople saw as indolence; what he called freedom they called vagrancy. They were, in short, deeply suspicious of the jobless Harvard graduate. That's the fun of "Walking": Thoreau is at once acknowledging the criticisms of his neighbors while upbraiding them for not having chosen a profession as elevated as his own. ("It requires a direct dispensation from Heaven to become a walker.") As for those who held jobs in town, tending shops or working as mechanics, "I think that they deserve some credit for not having all committed suicide long ago." Thoreau could give as good as he got.

Putting forth an idea he inherited from both his transcendentalist mentor Ralph Waldo Emerson and the ancient Stoic philosophers, Thoreau writes, "I believe there is a subtle magnetism in Nature, which, if we unconsciously yield to it, will direct us aright." We can trust our own nature as a moral compass because it is part of a grander Nature. Said the Stoics: the laws of nature are also the laws of man, and we should seek a union between the two. Thus for Thoreau, the outward walk through the natural world was simultaneously an inward walk through the soul's landscape, its spiritual terrain. *Sainte Terre*. If the world's orientation was westward, Thoreau said he was walking east. That is to say, he wasn't seeking his fortune; he was migrating inward, toward the soul's earliest impulses. It's a theme he returns to again and again in *Walden* and in his journals—this idea that the soul has its own terrain, one that mirrored Thoreau's native landscape. "Nay, be a Columbus to whole new continents and worlds within you, opening new channels, not of trade, but of thought," he writes in the conclusion of *Walden*. To wander the woods of Concord was simultaneously to explore the soul's unseen but very real topography.

The point of such a walk was to remind readers of Thoreau's famous dictum, the one you see printed on national park brochures all across the country: "In Wildness is the preservation of the world." "Walking" was, in fact, originally called "The Wild," and the point of all Thoreau's walking and writing was to inform us over and over that our bourgeois American lives had become too tame, too comfortable, too compromised, too degenerate. "A town is saved, not more by the righteous men in it than by the woods and swamps that surround it," he maintained. "Out of such a wilderness comes the Reformer eating locusts and wild honey." Out of such a wilderness would come Henry David Thoreau.

When Thoreau trekked a half mile out of town to live at Walden Pond for two years and two months, he was walking away not only from a rapidly industrializing society for which he felt increasing contempt, but also from a life that had lately dealt him a number of profound losses. In the summer of 1839, Thoreau and his brother, John, undertook a two-week rowing expedition up the Concord and Merrimack Rivers. That same summer, they both fell in love with the same seventeen-year-old girl, Ellen Sewall. Her aunt Prudence Ward boarded with the Thoreau family. John had escorted Ellen on walks around Walden Pond, and Henry, not to be outdone, took her rowing there in a wooden boat he had built at age sixteen. By all accounts, John and Henry Thoreau were best friends. It was John who first led Henry, two years younger, roaming through the Concord woods and who later made for him a catalog of all its native birds. But the brothers were also tuned in very different keys. John was easygoing, charming, at home in a crowd. Henry was aloof, tight-lipped, awkward among strangers. His humor wasn't gentle like John's, but cutting and ironic. Henry was bookish and exacting; John wore his learning lightly. It was Henry who had a Harvard education, but John who was said to have a future.

By the time the brothers returned from their river trip, Ellen Sewall had returned home to the coastal Massachusetts town of Scituate, and what's more, her parents were away at Niagara Falls vacationing. John immediately set out to pay her a visit, while Henry lamented in his journal that a parcel of heaven had been annexed from his heart. Montaigne, in his essay "On Friendship," argues that brothers could never truly be great friends because they "must of necessity often jostle and hinder one another." Thoreau, as the younger brother, did indeed feel jostled out of the way by John's pursuit of Ellen. When John and Ellen were out walking on the beach at Scituate, the older Thoreau suddenly proposed marriage. Startled, Ellen said yes, but by the time they returned home, she was having second thoughts. And when her conservative, Unitarian father arrived, he cemented those thoughts by informing his daughter that there was no way she would be marrying into a family that was friendly with the transcendentalist heretic Emerson. John gallantly accepted the bad news, while Henry saw it as an opening, slim though it might have been. Deploying nautical metaphors, he proposed to Ellen in a letter that no longer exists. What does exist is a letter from Ellen's father telling her to reject Henry in terms that were *short, explicit,* and *cold.*"

Ellen never visited the Thoreaus again, and for that, John seemed to blame Henry's obtuse attempt to win Ellen for himself. A distance developed between the brothers, one that troubled Henry greatly. Then, in January 1841, he had a dream about "a Friend" who suddenly forgave him, and Henry woke up feeling "unspeakably soothed and rejoiced." On New Year's Day 1842, John nicked his finger shaving. A week later, his limbs began to ache, and then he developed lockjaw. Three days later, he died of tetanus, in his brother's arms. A week after that, Henry developed the same symptoms as John. "You may judge that we are alarmed," Emerson wrote to his brother, William. But Thoreau's symptoms were psychosomatic, a stoic brother's form of grieving. However, as soon as Henry's symptoms disappeared, Emerson's five-year-old son, Waldo, died of scarlet fever. Thoreau, who had lived with the Emersons for two years as a general handyman and caregiver, had loved the child and devoted to him endless hours of avuncular attention, carving him toy boats and building him birdhouses.

A month after Waldo's death, Thoreau sent to Emerson's sister-in-law Lucy Brown a letter that is a beautiful meditation on loss. "What right have I to grieve," he wrote, "who have not ceased to wonder? We feel at first as if some opportunities of kindness and sympathy were lost, but learn afterward that any *pure grief* is ample recompense for all. That is, if we are faithful; for a great grief is but sympathy with the soul that disposes events, and is as house while her husband was away lecturing in Europe. I don't mean to suggest something salacious about that request, only that Thoreau immediately heeded it and called a halt to one of literature's most famous solitary sojourns.

It is not an exaggeration, I think, to say that when Thoreau left society for solitude, he left for good the romantic company of women, the chance that he would ever marry. His failed attempts to win the affection of Ellen Sewall, along with what must have seemed to him the unattainable love of Lucy Brown and Lydia Emerson, convinced him (correctly, it turned out) that if he were to be happy, he must make nature his bride. All the secular utopianists whose paths I've crossed saw marriage as a crime against women; the religious utopianists saw it as a crime against God. But what of Thoreau? Had Ellen Sewall accepted his proposal, as her daughter years later said she wanted to, the world would certainly have been without *Walden*. Would Thoreau have been happier? Probably. Would we, the readers of *Walden*? Of course not. Of all the utopianists, Thoreau alone seemed to *want* a wife, but the unlikeliness of that drove him to enact, and then transform into literature, the world's great utopia of solitude.

When I reach the four-lane Cambridge and Concord Turnpike, I
ss over to the Walden Pond State Reservation proper, along
a dozen other pedestrians. Most of them take the main road
d the pond, the road that also leads to the gift shop, the re-
cted cabin, and the main beach. I wander off a sandy side
no real sense of where it leads. Fortunately, it leads to
l site of the famous cabin. Emerson, the founder of
talism (a philosophy that said we must transcend the
ody and soul because the divine exists, however la-
f us), had bought some land around Walden Pond
t from the woodcutter's ax and because he had
ams of building a solitary place to write. Nine
ted by an iron chain, frame the site of Tho-
ered in 1945. Aside from a few flat stones

natural as the resin of Arabian trees. Only Nature has a right to grieve perpetually, for she only is innocent." For his solace, his recompense, Thoreau would turn to the natural world; he would turn to Walden Pond. There he would wonder, instead of grieving for the loss of John, Ellen, and Waldo.

It may even be that Thoreau was in some ways lamenting the loss of his correspondent Lucy Brown. She was twenty years older than he, and had come to live in Concord after her bankrupt husband abruptly fled for Europe. One day the young Thoreau, home from college, tossed a bunch of violets through her window, accompanied by a poem that began, "I am a parcel of vain strivings tied / By a chance bond together . . ." Members of the Emerson family later recalled that the staid Thoreau liked to entertain Lucy Brown with . . . solo dancing. Yet Lucy was still married, and twice his age, and in the end, she moved back to Plymouth. Nor was she the only older Emerson female whom Thoreau admired in a way that was laced with romantic, if unrealistic, affection. In the two years that Thoreau lived with the Emersons, he devel-oped what looks from a distance like real, unrequited feelin Lydia Emerson, something perhaps akin to the love Nietzsche felt for the wife of his hero and mentor Ric (The day Nietzsche went insane, he dashed identifying himself as the husband of Cosi copy of Emerson's essays in his coat p Thoreau had moved to Staten Islar ing tutoring job, Lydia Emerson now lost, that must have exp Thoreau sent back som voice seems not a v as from the pap elevate my life behold, as when knew that Lydia w. evening star, but this he finally left Walden P him to. Specifically, she a.

that might have been part of the foundation, none of the original structure survives.

When Thoreau returned to Concord from Staten Island, he went to work in the family's pencil-making business. In fact, Henry, the supposedly impractical son, made fundamental improvements in the American pencil so that what the family sold looked pretty much like the No. 2 pencil modern schoolchildren pack to class. Those improvements allowed the Thoreaus finally to buy a lot in town. There Henry worked as an apprentice to his father, John Sr., and the two men built the family's first house in 1844. After that, it was an easy affair for Henry to translate those skills into a ten-by-fifteen-foot cabin.

Thoreau sited his cabin between the new railroad embankment and the pond. Indeed, I'm surprised to see how closely the railroad runs behind the cabin site. It has almost become a trope of environmentalism to bemoan how much Walden Pond has changed since Thoreau's time, but the place was changing rapidly before its famous hermit ever arrived. When Thoreau returned from Staten Island, the Fitchburg Railroad had already reached Concord. A thousand Irishmen were making fifty cents for a sixteen-hour day of work, and Emerson had written earlier to Thoreau that it all looked like a kind of voluntary slavery. Irish shanties were strung out all along the encroaching railroad. Between the time Thoreau lived at Walden and the time he published *Walden*, the chestnut trees he depended on for sustenance had been converted to railroad ties, or "sleepers," as they were called; Thoreau writes ruefully that the ties slumbered beneath an "iron horse." While Walt Whitman celebrated the Transcontinental Railroad, not only as a symbol of industrial progress but as a spiritual passage back to the world's oldest religions of India, Thoreau mocked such notions of progress and claimed that his own travels to his own India could be done inwardly, in Concord. In a world where writers were traveling great distances, and writing about those adventures, Thoreau argued that he would never live long enough—and he didn't—to exhaust the fields, ponds, and forests of Concord. Emerson had written in "Self-Reliance" that traveling was a fool's errand, yet he traveled constantly. Thoreau, however, took the sentiment very seriously. The belief that one might "expand one's horizons" by ranging farther and faster was, to him, just one more ruse of that great myth Progress. The iron horse, powered by a coal-fired combustion engine, was in actuality a Trojan horse that would need hundreds of thousands of soldiers to procure and protect the natural resources of the new industrial economy. "My muse may be excused if she is silent henceforth," Thoreau writes in *Walden* of all the constant sounds of the train and the ax. "How can you expect the birds to sing when their groves are cut down?"

Thoreau was twenty-seven when, near the end of March 1845, he himself borrowed a friend's ax and starting chopping down some "tall arrowy white pines" in the woods around Walden Pond. Thoreau hewed the main supports of his cabin into six-by-six-inch timbers, and he laid a puncheon floor by squaring the logs only on the visible side. When finished with the timbers, Thoreau asked Bronson Alcott, Emerson, and a few others from the transcendentalist circle to help him raise the frame, not because he needed the help, he wrote, but rather as a "good occasion for neighborliness." He then bought an Irish railroad worker's shanty, dismantled it, and sheathed his own cabin with the boards. Wooden shingles went on the roof. He crushed clamshells from the pond to make his own lime, with which he plastered the interior walls. When winter came, Thoreau finally got around to setting a hearth and chimney, with stones from the pond. Taking his cue from a local woodchuck, he dug his cellar into the side of a south-facing slope on the north side of the pond. He was much pleased with his effort, comparing the cabin to a temple where a goddess might trail her garment. Walter Harding, Thoreau's most reliable biographer, gives us the (mostly borrowed) contents of the famous cabin: a caned bed, a table, a desk, three chairs ("one for solitude, two for friendship, three for society"), a small mirror, a kettle, a skillet, a frying pan, a dipper, a washbowl, two knives and forks, three plates, one cup, one spoon, a jug of oil, a jug of molasses, and a japanned lamp. In the end, Thoreau's careful tabulation shows that the entire venture cost him $28.12½. James Collins, the Irish railroad worker who sold Thoreau the cabin, apparently insisted on the last half-cent.

A wooden sign that stands beside the cabin site repeats the now-hallowed words from *Walden*: I WENT TO THE WOODS BECAUSE I WISHED TO LIVE DELIBERATELY, TO FRONT ONLY THE ESSENTIAL FACTS OF LIFE, AND SEE IF I COULD NOT LEARN WHAT IT HAD TO TEACH, AND NOT, WHEN I CAME TO DIE, DISCOVER THAT I HAD NOT LIVED. It is true that almost all Thoreau's thinking resides somewhere in that sentence. The word *deliberately* suggests the ontological and even "mystical" (Thoreau's word) elements of that philosophy; the phrase "essential facts of life" hints at Thoreau's political economy; the setting of the sentence in the woods reveals that, for Thoreau, the most important laws would be the laws of nature.

Thoreau had first to develop his own microeconomics, as it were, so he could then build a philosophy of life upon it, and within its limits. The great question of *Walden* is the same for all the utopianists: "How should I live?" Thoreau first reduced that question to the absolute foundations of life—literally, of staying alive—by deciding that a human being cannot survive without body heat. So how does one supply the body with that warmth? Four ways, he decided: food, fuel, shelter, and clothing. These in turn became the main subject of *Walden*'s first and longest chapter, "Economy."

The central tenet of transcendentalism is self-reliance. For Emerson, this was principally a philosophical position: one must be true to divine "Intuitions" of one's "aboriginal Self." Those were far more important than the secondary "tuitions" of the Bible, which were not the inspired word of God (certainly not the inerrant word of God), but simply the work of mere mortals. What's more, repentance, Thoreau writes in his journal, is not "a free and fair highway to God." The real divine teachings always arise from the soul's capacious chambers. Thoreau bought into this wholeheartedly, but he took it further into the practical realm of providing for oneself through one's own labors. Emerson had warned in his essay "Self-Reliance" that the world would whip the nonconformist with its displeasure, and certainly Thoreau felt the sting of his townspeople's ridicule. Indeed, he wrote *Walden* as an explanation for his experiment in self-reliance, and he turned the justification of his own life into a critique of his neighbors'. And it could be a very truculent critique. Thoreau's captious nature ultimately became a great bother to Emerson, and their friendship suffered for it. *Walden* also suffers for it in places, as when Thoreau claims he can do without the post office because he never received a letter worth reading. (We know good and well that he treasured, at the very least, letters from Lydia Emerson.) But it is Thoreau's uncompromising nature, the purity of his venture, that makes *Walden* the great manifesto of solitude.

One of Thoreau's most self-righteous critiques of his neighbors came in comparing his dwelling with theirs. Thoreau sided, as he did throughout his life, with the Native Americans, in this case the local Penobscot, who chose a teepee over a manse. If the Indian owned his dwelling and the bank owned the white man's house, who exactly was "savage" and who "civilized"? Thoreau wanted to know. The New Englander doesn't own the house; the house owns him. He is his own kind of slave. From this follows Thoreau's fundamental economic principle: "the cost of a thing is the amount of what I will call life which is required to be exchanged for it." He and the Penobscot had too much living to do; they couldn't fritter away those hours sitting in a shop or behind a desk all day. Such was not a life. What's more, the Gospels warned against laying up treasures on earth; Thoreau was always beating his neighbors about the head with their own Testament.

By the time he was a senior at Harvard, Emerson's most rigorous student had invented for himself what we might call a Sabbath economy. "The order of things should be somewhat reversed," Thoreau told the graduating class of 1837 at its commencement; "the seventh should be man's day of toil, wherein to earn his living by the sweat of his brow; and the other six his Sabbath of the affections and the soul—in which to range this widespread garden, and drink in the soft influences and sublime revelations of nature." Thoreau was twenty years old at the time, yet was expounding a philosophy that would guide him through the rest of his life. His greatest skill, he said, was to want very little. "I found, that by working about six weeks in a year, I could meet all the expenses of living," he writes in the "Economy" chapter of *Walden*. "The whole of my winters, as well as most of my summers, I had free and clear for study." One day of surveying or simply working as a laborer could secure all the material wealth he needed to spend the other six days exploring what his friend Walt Whitman called nature's "realm of budding bibles." This Sabbath economy so pleased Thoreau that he would write to his editor, Horace Greeley, and repeat in *Walden*, "I am convinced, both by faith and experience, that to maintain one's self on this earth is not a hardship but a pastime, if we will live simply and wisely."

Such a leisurely economy was of course the very antithesis of what Adam Smith had in mind when he wrote *The Wealth of Nations*. If all economies were based on the division of labor, Smith argued, the efficiency of such a system would reward everyone with some degree of wealth. Thoreau argued that this would only turn men and women (and children) into machines. Thus *Walden* became one of the most unexpected and strangely influential replies to Smith. It was at once an argument and a demonstration that a man *could* live completely outside any division of labor, and that such a life would be more just and more poetic. Indeed, the utopia of solitude *must* by definition be a self-reliant enterprise. While living at Walden Pond, Thoreau became a country of one. Critics carp that, now and then, he went to his mother's house to do laundry or get a cucumber sandwich, but the basic fact remains that Thoreau provided for all his human needs during those two years. Luxuries, he argued, like many philosophers before him, were a hindrance to the elevation of the race. To be a true philosopher *required* voluntary poverty. "There are nowadays professors of philosophy, but not philosophers," Thoreau charged. "Yet it is admirable to profess because it was once admirable to live. To be a philosopher is not merely to have subtle thoughts, nor even to found a school, but so to love wisdom as to live according to its dictates, a life of simplicity, independence, magnanimity, and trust. It is to solve some of the problems of life, not only theoretically, but practically." Here we find the humus in which the American school of pragmatism took root: in the idea *that* an idea is only as good as its actual consequences. By reducing his needs and eschewing "the so-called comforts of life," Thoreau could practice both independence and simplicity in a way that allied him with the Eastern philosophers and religious men he most admired. As far as a practical form of magnanimity at Walden, we know that Thoreau gave succor to slaves making their way along the Underground Railroad.

Thoreau scholars have long puzzled over this cryptic sentence from *Walden*: "I long ago lost a hound, a bay horse, and a turtledove, and am still on their trail." The answer, in fact, can be found in the other book Thoreau was writing at Walden, *A Week on the Concord and Merrimack Rivers*. There he quotes the Chinese philosopher Mencius, who wrote, "If one loses a fowl or a dog, he knows well how to seek them again; if one loses the sentiments of his heart, he does not know how to seek them again. The duties of practical philosophy consist only in seeking after the sentiments of the heart which we have lost; that is all." Thoreau's turtledove and hound could be found again, Mencius is saying. But the bay horse (the sentiments of the heart, the laws of one's own nature) we can recover only through a practical philosophy, the kind Thoreau was inventing at Walden.

Back in Great Barrington, Will Conklin had mentioned that the words *economy* and *ecology* both derived from the same Greek word, which meant pertaining to a household. In a very strict sense, Thoreau was reducing the idea of an economy to the idea of running a household in a way and in a place where nature was the measure of what was aesthetically, spiritually, and fiscally right. Arguing against the bourgeois "home journals" that had begun proliferating at the advent of mass media in this country, Thoreau maintained that a home should be only an emanation, a manifestation, of the person or people who would dwell therein. It should reflect a certain truthfulness and nobleness. Thoreau's philosophy of elemental simplicity called for an equally modest cabin. "Who knows," he wrote, "but if men constructed their dwelling with their own hands, and provided food for themselves and families simply and honestly enough, the poetic faculty would be universally developed, as birds universally sing when they are so engaged?" Instead, most of us act like parasitic cowbirds, laying our eggs in a nest other birds have built. In such instances, said Thoreau, the carpenter is only a coffin maker, and we move from one tomb to the next. For his part, Thoreau was satisfied that, with his cabin, he had caged himself among the wild birds rather than trying to cage them inside the bourgeois tomb. It was as if he had placed himself inside a Joseph Cornell box and freed all the birds.

As for his other sources of heat, Thoreau defended his rather shabby style of dress—gray pants and brown shirts "the color of a pasture with patches of withered sweet-fern and lechea"—by opining, rightly, "Every generation laughs at the old fashions but follows religiously the new." He went on to warn his readers to "beware of all enterprises that require new clothes, and not rather a new wearer of clothes." (I've actually spent a great deal of my life making career decisions based on that advice, and indeed it has saved me money on clothes, though it may have prevented me from attaining work that would have afforded me a nicer wardrobe—but, as Thoreau would have said, therein lies the cyclical folly of consumer logic.) As for his fuel, Thoreau burned driftwood from the pond and tree stumps from the garden he had dug for his final source of heat: food. According to his account, that garden contained seven miles of bean rows, interspersed with some potatoes and corn. "I have come to love my rows—they attach me to the earth," he writes in his journal. While at Walden, Thoreau ate a plain fare of beans and potatoes, fish from the pond, and his one great culinary invention: raisin bread—it supposedly shocked Concord housewives. It was a diet, Thoreau maintained, worthy of any ancient philosopher. In good weather, he cooked outside over heated stones, clambake-style. The first summer at Walden, he waged constant war against a woodchuck; the second summer, he simply killed and ate the damn thing. Thoreau figured he needed about eight dollars a year to meet his meager expenses, and that's just about how much he made selling the vegetables he himself didn't eat. Concord farmers were struggling mightily because the Erie Canal was bringing cheap corn in from western New York State, but Thoreau crowed that since he owned no farm or farmhouse, he "could follow the bent of my genius, which is a very crooked one, every moment." Emerson had borrowed the word *genius* from the Neoplatonist philosophers to mean an individual's deepest intuitions. A similar genius led Walt Whitman to write, contemporaneously, those famous early lines from "Song of Myself": "I loafe and invite my soul, / I lean and loafe at my ease observing a spear of summer grass." Thoreau, who needed so little to survive, could also afford to loaf at Walden Pond, "for a man is rich in proportion to the number of things which he can afford to let alone." Yet what looked to the townspeople like loafing was in fact a sacred vigil Thoreau conducted each morning before what he called the "poem of creation." Many mornings he sat on his stoop listening to the birdsong all around him, "rapt in revery, amidst the pines and hickories." In the chapter "Where I Lived, and What I Lived For," Thoreau is forthright in declaiming the purpose of his book: he aims to "brag as lustily as chanticleer in the morning, standing on his roost, if only to wake my neighbors up." What Thoreau has to brag about is this: he has discovered a philosophy of the individual that is thoroughly just—it depends on no slaves, on no tea imported from China—and thoroughly satisfying to the soul. He meant for that philosophy to rouse his neighbors from the torpor of their famously comfortable "lives of quiet desperation."

To be *awake*—it is a frequent theme throughout *Walden*. Thoreau meant it two ways: we must be awakened from our too-casual complicity in an unjust economy, and we must wake to the luminous present. At Harvard, Thoreau would have read Heraclitus, who wrote, "One must talk about everything according to its nature, how it comes to be and how it grows. Men have talked about the world without paying attention to the world or to their own minds, as if they were asleep or absent-minded." One can hardly imagine a more Thoreauvian sentiment. Thoreau would find in the natural world the clues to his own nature, the dispensations of his own soul. He would not follow the laws of institutions invented by absent-minded men who did not know their own minds. Follow your own nature, your own genius, he wrote; it will never let you down, it will never "fail to show you a fresh prospect every hour." Yet too often we merely succumb to the business and busyness of the world. In doing so, we refuse to see—here comes again that bulwark of utopian thinking—the kingdom of God laid out before us. Thoreau refused to place that sacred realm in either the future or the past. "God himself culminates in the present moment," he writes, "and will never be more divine in the lapse of all the ages." As for some golden age, "No dust has settled on that robe; no time has elapsed since that divinity was revealed." Thoreau rejected the British fascination with historical heroes; every age could be heroic, he argues, if men learned to follow "the gospel according to the present." Time was not a forward march called History or Progress; it was a present that must be eternally renewed by our *attention*, our awakeness. The problem is that most men and women do not wake to their genius, are not called to see the natural sacraments of light on a pond or spring peepers cheeping along its banks. They are awakened, said Thoreau, by factory bells. "The millions are awake enough for physical labor," Thoreau writes; "but only one in a million is awake enough for effective intellectual exertion, only one in a hundred million to a poetic or divine life." But that is what Thoreau aspired to; that was the epitome of his practical philosophy: to transform one's life into a work of art, into something *worthy* of contemplation. That was the truly heroic feat. "To affect the quality of the day, that is the highest of the arts. Every man is tasked to make his life, even in its details, worthy of the contemplation of his most elevated and critical hour." To contemplate the masterpiece called *Walden* and to contemplate Thoreau's experience beside this pond would amount to the same thing. The artist becomes inseparable from the work of art. The poet's experience becomes the poem.

In truth, no one today seems much interested in this particular spot where I alone am standing: the cabin site itself, this empty space, this non-monument to the utopia of solitude. Everyone at Walden Pond today is sunbathing or swimming, splashing around or telling children to quit splashing around. I hear a large group in the cove that stretches into the northernmost section of the pond, so I decide to start walking in the opposite direction. Walden Pond is a glacial lake; there are hundreds spread throughout New England. The scouring motion of the retreating glaciers drilled deep into this bedrock—some New Englanders during Thoreau's time thought Walden bottomless—and then left the ice behind to melt gradually into this pond. It's a sixty-one-acre body of still water that stretches three-quarters of a mile in length and a half mile wide. I'm a bit surprised at how small the pond actually is. As I wander around its eastern shore, I realize that I could easily circumnavigate the whole thing in about an hour. Swimming from shore to shore in either direction would be no great feat.

A narrow path does stretch around the pond's perimeter, though a wire fence usually separates the trail from the shore. In only a few places is there a break in the fence where a set of stone steps leads down to the water. At each of these openings, a cluster of sunbathers has gathered, talking in either German or something Scandinavian. I don't hear any English being spoken along the entire southern side of the pond. It's true that those countries have far superior environmental records than we do, though that's hardly saying much. Did *Walden* play some role in the German and Scandinavian enthusiasm for alternative fuel sources? Have these tourists really come this far on pilgrimage? I don't speak any European languages, so I don't ask. Instead, I finally locate my own pebbly little beach—solitude at last!—and unfold my chair at the edge of the water.

On warm evenings, Thoreau liked to drift out over the pond and play his flute, charming the perch that swam around his boat, or so he imagined. Sometimes he fished by moonlight. His thoughts would wander to "vast and cosmogonal themes" until a jerk at his line brought him back to the tactile world. "Thus I caught two fishes, as it were, with one hook." Today out on the water, two teenage boys and a girl, ostensibly lifeguards, cut the small engine on an inflatable lifeboat and start laughing about how drunk one of the boys got at a party last night. Hardly cosmogonal thoughts, but then, these kids obviously came to Walden Pond to find summer jobs, not a philosophy of life. Today the pond is green at a distance and absolutely pellucid, as Thoreau said it was, up close. Clouds move low above the tree line on the opposite side of the pond. A forest, said Thoreau, is never as beautiful as when seen from the middle of a pond. From that vantage, one sees not only the forest but also its reflection in the water. But it puzzled Thoreau that Walden Pond could be blue at one time and green at another. "Lying between the earth and the heavens," he writes, "it partakes of the color of both." Thoreau says more than once in *Walden* that a pond is the earth's eye, "looking into which the beholder measures the depth of his own nature." I wade out into the water about twenty feet, not to take a measure of my own nature, but to call my wife on a very un-Thoreauvian device and tell her I'm standing in Walden Pond. She doesn't answer, so I return to my chair, take out my copy of *Walden*, and turn to the chapter on New England's ponds.

John Muir said there was nothing in nature more beautiful than a mountain stream; Thoreau averred that a pond was nature's greatest glory. It was a crystal on the surface of the earth. "Nations come and go without defiling it," he writes. Then Thoreau issues the kind of sentence that makes him the greatest prose stylist this country has ever had:

> It is a mirror which no stone can crack, whose quicksilver will never wear off, whose gilding Nature continually repairs; no storms, no dust, can dim its surface ever fresh; a mirror in which all impurity presented to it sinks, swept and dusted by the sun's hazy brush—this the light dust-cloth—which retains no breath that is breathed on it, but sends its own to float as clouds high above its surface, and be reflected in its bosom still.

At the end of Thoreau's chapter on ponds, he becomes so stirred by the serene repose of Walden—"How much more beautiful than our lives, how much more transparent than our characters"—that he accuses all humanity of not deserving "her." Only he, Henry David Thoreau, was worthy to call this pond his betrothed. "Talk of heaven!" he tells his townspeople rhetorically, "ye disgrace earth." There was heaven enough a half mile from Concord.

Long before he took up residence at Walden, a young Thoreau wrote in his journal, "Drifting in a sultry day on the sluggish waters of the pond, I almost cease to live and begin to be." My own experience confirms this sentiment that there is indeed no better place than inside a small wooden boat, especially one you've built, to make the subtle glide from being to Being, from existence into that intense experience of pure, unmediated presence in the world, an experience that has no language because it needs none.

On the best nights, Thoreau's whole body became one sense "and imbibes delight through every pore." He became Emerson's famous "transparent eye-ball." In *Nature*, transcendentalism's first manifesto, Emerson effuses, "I am nothing; I see all; the currents of the Universal Being circulate through me; I am part or particle of God." At Walden, Thoreau lived in that same unfallen world. He was Adam alone, but never lonely, he insists: "I have never found the companion that was so companionable as solitude." To be alone in the woods meant the greatest companionship of all. Thoreau declared himself blessed by God to have been given such a life. In Nathaniel Hawthorne's short story "Young Goodman Brown," the natural world becomes darker and more malicious the farther into it the title character walks, until he finally comes upon a black mass where his wife, Faith, is standing over a font of blood and intoning prayers to the Dark One. *Walden* is, of course, the antidote to Hawthorne's malignant vision. The witches were all hanged (some by Hawthorne's own relatives), so why be afraid of the dark? asked a bemused Thoreau. The farther he ventured into the natural world, the closer Thoreau came to "the perennial source of our life," the closer he came to the Universal Being.

Organized around the cycle of the seasons, *Walden* begins in summer and ends in spring, that time of year when, wrote Thoreau, "all men's sins are forgiven." One day, toward the end of his stay beside the pond, Thoreau watched with fascination the thawing sand and clay along the edge of the railroad embankment. The sands (gray, yellow, and red) flowed down like lava after the last frost, and to Thoreau it appeared as if "the Artist" were still at work, sculpting the world with fresh designs. "I feel as if I were nearer to the vitals of the globe," he wrote, "for this sandy overflow is something such a foliaceous mass as the vitals of the animal body. You find thus in the very sands an anticipation of the vegetable leaf." The arteries that gravity was carving into the bank seemed to mimic the veins in the leaf. The leaf mapped the streams and tributaries of a watershed. The bird's wing was another version of the leaf, as were our own hands and feet. The microcosm was reflected everywhere in the macrocosm. "What is man but a mass of thawing clay?" Thoreau asks. A man's ear was but a fanciful lichen on the side of his head, his cheeks flowed down his face like a mud slide, and the nose emerged as "a manifest congealed drop or stalactite." Is Thoreau talking about his own famously aquiline nose here, his own long, sad face? His friend, the poet William Ellery Channing, described Thoreau's whole bearing as an "active earnestness," and at the embankment, Thoreau seemed to be looking into a kind of mirror and finding himself once again reflected best in the natural world.

The earth, Thoreau concluded, is not dead matter—"There is nothing inorganic"—but rather a living thing, and it is constantly changing. Though he had not yet read Darwin's *On the Origin of Species*, he was already beginning to sense, on his own intuitive level, that Louis Agassiz's theory of special creation was wrong. And when Thoreau did discover Darwin, he found a man much more to his liking than Agassiz. The Artist is always at work, and the world is in a constant state of transformation: that idea aligned with Thoreau's observations in the woods and fields around Concord. The transcendentalists had early on rejected any literal interpretation of the Bible, but Thoreau took that idea furthest by making the natural world the only scripture a person would ever need. "What sweet and tender, the most innocent and divinely encouraging society there is in every natural object," he writes in his journal only days after arriving at Walden Pond, "and so in universal nature even for the poor misanthrope and most melancholy man. There can be no really *black* melancholy to him who lives in the midst of nature, and has still his sense." The preacher, said Thoreau, could dismiss his congregation. The woods of Concord were as sacred as were the great oak groves of the Romans. It was time we started acting as such.

The year Thoreau moved to Walden Pond, Robert Owen came to Concord and issued one of his characteristic, rousing pleas to abandon commerce for community, individualism for socialism. Indeed, between 1843 and 1845, thirty-three utopian communities blazed into being, most of them fired by the country's newfound passion for the writings of Charles Fourier. This was the second, and last, wave of utopianism in the United States. Owen's version was dead, though he knew it not, and Fourierism, or associationism as it was called in America, would thrive for a decade. The Unitarian minister George Ripley, a friend of both Thoreau and

Emerson, quit his church in 1841 to try to establish the kingdom of God on earth in West Roxbury. He eventually recruited thirty others to join his cause. Thoreau, for his part, believed that individuals needed to reform themselves before they got around to reforming society. Regarding Brook Farm and all the other associationists, Thoreau wrote in his journal, "As for these communities, I think I had rather keep bachelor's hall in hell than go to board in heaven." He was deeply sympathetic to George Ripley's countercultural idealism, but while Ripley called together a utopia of solidarity, Thoreau mounted a solitary counteraction at Walden Pond. The Brook Farmers officially took on the trappings of Fourierism in 1844, but only so they could secure funding from Albert Brisbane's larger American Union of Associationists. Their hearts were never in it, and when the Brook Farm phalanstery burned down in 1846, they called it quits. The original farmhouse, which Ripley's collective called the "hive," still stands on a hill in a Roxbury neighborhood—barn swallows are its only current inhabitants—but Brook Farm was always more an idea in the American imagination than an actual, viable utopian community. It is best known through Nathaniel Hawthorne's satirical treatment of it, *The Blithedale Romance*, and for all the transcendentalists who refused to join: Thoreau, Emerson, Bronson Alcott, and Margaret Fuller among them.

The extent to which Thoreau thought he could establish himself wholly as his own state was tested one afternoon in July 1846, when he had been living at Walden Pond for just over a year. On the twenty-third or twenty-fourth, he walked into Concord to pick up a shoe from the cobbler's shop and was stopped on the street by the local constable, Sam Staples, who pointed out that Thoreau hadn't paid the compulsory poll tax for several years running. Though he distrusted the transcendentalists, Staples liked Thoreau and even offered to pay the tax for him, if he was "hard up." Thoreau, who was hard up in the conventional sense, replied that he was refusing to pay the tax on principle: he would not support a country that condoned human slavery and had just attacked its neighboring country, Mexico.

"Henry, if you don't pay, I shall have to lock you up pretty soon," Staples replied.

"As well now as any time, Sam," Thoreau is said to have replied. This is how he came to spend his famous night in the Concord jail. Staples had already arrested Bronson Alcott on the same charge, for the same reasons, three years earlier. Yet Alcott didn't turn the experience into an essay about the ways in which human beings were obliged to respond to the actions of an unjust government. Thoreau did.

The essay "Resistance to Civil Government," now universally known as "Civil Disobedience," published in 1849, begins with the Jeffersonian motto "That government is best which governs least." Thoreau pushed this sentiment further to say, "That government is best which governs not at all," and that is what we would have if we were truly prepared for it. Because of this opening salvo, American anarchists and libertarians often claim Thoreau as one of their own. Yet Thoreau goes on to insist that he isn't a "no-government man," but rather a better-government man. "Let every man make known what kind of government would command his respect," he wrote, "and that will be one step toward obtaining it." Such was the purpose of his essay: to make government better by making it face up to its faults.

Thoreau, the lover of personal liberty, did not object to government's role in ensuring that citizens left one another alone to follow their however crooked genius. And when he left jail to lead a huckleberry-picking party the next morning, he cheerfully agreed to pay a highway tax because he said he wanted to be as good a neighbor as he was a bad subject of the state. That is to say, he *used* the highway and was therefore ready to support its maintenance. To settle matters of expedience was government's role, Thoreau contended: Where would the best road serve the most people, and so on. In such instances, majority rule was fine. The problem arose when the government perpetuated an injustice and then compelled a citizen to finance, or be party to, that injustice. Then honest men and women must disassociate themselves from that government. It wasn't their responsibility to *solve* the injustice, he emphasized. Life is short, after all, and there are grosbeak nests to inspect, water lilies to examine, books to write. "I came into this world, not chiefly to make it a better place to live in," he explains, "but to live in it, be it good or bad." Yet a man must at least "wash his hands" of such a corrupt state. He must walk away from it. This is exactly what Thoreau was doing at Walden Pond: living outside the state. Though the country was only seventy-three years old the year "Civil Disobedience" was published, Thoreau already saw what it would become: a great maw that sent its soldiers all across the globe fighting for foreign resources, fighting to defend a culture of accumulation that Thoreau had grown to despise. If one can do without tea and coffee and meat, he wrote, one should not be compelled to support a government that perpetuates all manner of injustice to secure such luxuries. Thoreau's abstemious pescatarianism (the woodchuck notwithstanding) was a deliberate decision to set himself apart from a state that didn't deserve his allegiance.

Eight years later, when the slave Anthony Burns was arrested in Massachusetts under the Fugitive Slave Act and returned to his Virginia slave owner, Thoreau would change his mind: he would see that simply walking away *wasn't* enough. Yet back in 1846, at age twenty-nine, Thoreau had mounted a successful experiment in individual self-sovereignty, and he had gained the moral high ground from which, once again, to point out the hypocrisies of his townspeople, who allegedly wanted to eliminate slavery but continued paying taxes that perpetuated a slave-owning nation. "If a thousand men were not to pay their tax-bills this year, that would not be a violent and bloody measure, as it would be to pay them, and enable the State to commit violence and shed innocent blood," Thoreau writes. "This is, in fact, the definition of a peaceable revolution." This is why Thoreau insisted that true reform must begin first with the individual. Abolitionists who would not refuse to pay the poll tax were reformers by no definition he accepted. It was the same thing that so frustrated Martin Luther King, Jr., about the "white moderates" who in speech supported the civil rights movement but would take no action or break no laws. Merely to have a conscience means little if one isn't compelled to begin the hard work of change. "Action from principle," urged Thoreau. Words must become flesh or they are meaningless. Words must become acts.

"Resistance to Civil Government" was published in 1849 in Elizabeth Peabody's small journal, *Aesthetic Papers*. As it happened, Josiah Warren was living in Boston that year, after leaving Ohio and before moving on to Long Island to start Modern Times. I bring this up only because I wonder if he saw the essay, and only because I believe he would have agreed with every word in it. Warren would have seen the power of his own philosophy put into the words of a man whose prose style was as powerful as his ideas. He surely would have recognized a coconspirator in Thoreau, with his conclusion that, to be strictly just, a government must have the sanction and consent of the governed, and can have no right over person and property, except what the individual concedes: "I please myself with imagining a state at last which can afford to be just to all men, and to treat the individual with respect as a neighbor; which even would not think it inconsistent with its own repose, if a few were to live aloof from it, not meddling with it, nor embraced by it, who fulfilled all the duties of neighbors and fellow-men."

One day, when Thoreau went out to his woodpile, he found a great internecine war being waged between black and red ants. They tumbled over the wood chips and gnawed off one another's heads and feelers. One large red ant approached from the far side of the woodpile like some Achilles come to avenge his Patroclus, or so Thoreau imagined. He further imagined that respective military bands were stationed "on some imminent chip" to play each faction's "national airs." He marveled that the ants' battle seemed to show little difference from human hostilities. He even conjectured that their warfare was nobler than what had begun in Boston and Concord some seventy-odd years earlier; it certainly wasn't waged over "a three-penny tax on their tea." He carried one wood chip into his cabin and placed it under a tumbler so he could better watch a black ant sever the heads of two red ants even as they tore him limb from limb. When Thoreau lifted the glass dome, the victorious black ant limped away on his one remaining leg. "The battle which I witnessed," wrote the ants' official historian, "took place in the Presidency of Polk, five years before the passage of Webster's Fugitive-Slave Bill."

That bill would do much to change Thoreau's solitary thinking, his isolationist politics. While living at Walden, he boasted that he was doing his bit to abolish slavery by living apart from, morally above, the state. All the other utopianists I have come across in my travels felt exactly the same sense of superiority to the abolitionist movement. But when the state of Massachusetts returned Anthony Burns to the South in chains, Thoreau wrote in his journal, "I had never respected this government, but I had foolishly thought that I might manage to live here, attending to my private affairs, and forget it." How, he wondered, could he contemplate the beauty of nature when humanity was so base. On July 4, 1854, Thoreau delivered his most sulfurous speech, at a rally organized by the abolitionist William Lloyd Garrison in Framingham, Massachusetts. Extending his argument in "Civil Disobedience," Thoreau asked why the people of Massachusetts would care to uphold a constitution that found it legal to force into slavery three million men and women. Under such a system, judges and justices were nothing more than inspectors of an executioner's tools. But whoever could discern truth for him- or herself, whoever knew that slavery was an abomination, did not have to wait for or follow the laws handed down by Daniel Webster and the Supreme Court. They needed rather to obey "that eternal and only just CONSTITUTION, which He, and not any Jefferson or Adams, has written into your being." They needed actively to reject a state that would send an innocent man back into slavery. "I dwelt, before, perhaps, in the illusion that my life passed somewhere only *between* heaven and hell," Thoreau told his audience at Framingham, "but now I cannot persuade myself that I do not dwell *wholly within* hell."

Thoreau would finally see the publication of *Walden* that same year, but the Anthony Burns incident had pulled him away from his earlier utopian thinking. Thoreau, who had in *Walden* declared that all men were slaves, clearly had begun to see the difference between those who were slaves to their possessions and those who were literally beaten into subjugation. Years later, the leader of Concord's Underground Railroad remembered that Thoreau, who died on the eve of the Civil War, had done more to help fugitive slaves than anyone else in the town.

Thoreau left his cabin at Walden Pond on September 6, 1847. He had, he said, other lives to live. *Walden's* conclusion is a distillation of all the themes that came before. In it, Thoreau returns to his exhortation that men and women wake up from the "restless, nervous, bustling, trivial nineteenth century" and aspire to nobler virtues, nobler lives. That meant listening to the soul's own drummer, and marching to that tune, though it led away from the customs of the day. Variety is the law of nature; dullness and uniformity the law of man. Forget the common sense of the masses: that "is the sense of men asleep." Like Friedrich Nietzsche, a solitary philosopher for whom Thoreau would have recognized deep sympathies, the hermit of Walden Pond called his readers to awaken to their, to our, higher selves. At Walden, Thoreau had put meat and bones on Emerson's airy notions of self-reliance. He had shown that it wasn't just a philosophical position, but a political and an economic stance. He had been jailed for believing in individual conscience over constitutional law, and he had shown that abstract virtue meant nothing if it led to no action. That is the meaning of the apocryphal story in which the imprisoned Thoreau answers Emerson's question "What are you doing in there, Henry?" with "What are you doing out there, Rafe?" The laws of one's own being, said Thoreau, will never exist in opposition to a just government, if such a government ever exists.

In his "Conclusion," Thoreau also issues an attack on writers who "go round the world to count the cats in Zanzibar." Was this a veiled, or not-so-veiled, reference to Emerson, whose departure for Europe had occasioned Thoreau's own departure from Walden? Within days of his mentor's embarkation, Thoreau took up residence again with Lydia and the Emerson children. Still, Thoreau maintained, his two-year experiment at Walden Pond had been an unmitigated success. He learned

> that if one advances confidently in the direction of his dreams, and endeavors to live the life which he has imagined, he will meet with a success unexpected in common hours. He will put some things behind, will pass an invisible boundary; new, universal, and more liberal laws will begin to establish themselves around and within him; or the old laws be expanded, and interpreted in his favor in a more liberal sense, and he will live with the license of a higher order of beings. In proportion as he simplifies his life, the laws of the universe will appear less complex, and solitude will not be solitude, nor poverty poverty, nor weakness weakness. If you have built castles in the air, your work need not be lost; that is where they should be. Now put the foundations under them.

There it is, the utopian mission: to realize one's greatest moral aspirations, to build a scaffolding beneath one's waking dreams. Thoreau grounded transcendentalism's lofty idealism beside this pond where I now sit and watch the small yellow shiners swim around my feet. He enacted a prelapsarian dream, brought it to waking life, if only for two years, and with no Eve beside him.

Speaking of awakenings, I wonder: What if the spirit of Edna Pontellier had somehow seized Lydia Emerson and she abandoned her husband and children to join Thoreau in this nineteenth-century Eden? Or what if, more realistically, Ellen Sewall had answered her own drummer, defied her father's will, and returned to Concord to marry Thoreau? Would he have stayed on at Walden, enlarged the cabin, and continued to live a self-sufficient, though perhaps more gastronomically adventurous,

life? I raise the possibility only because that's exactly what happened to the remarkable artist Harlan Hubbard, back in my home
state of Kentucky.

Like Thoreau, Hubbard was painfully shy around women, and
he remained a bachelor until age forty-three, when he fell in love
with Anna Wonder Eikenhout, a librarian who lived just across
the Ohio River, in Cincinnati. Hubbard would pay her visits in
his johnboat and check out books by Henry David Thoreau. One
day Hubbard wrote Anna a letter proposing marriage. He said
that he would be on the Number 8 train coming into Cincinnati
on a certain day. If Anna stepped onto the train, he would consider that a yes. If she didn't, he would go back to his solitary life
painting landscapes and farming on the Kentucky banks of the
Ohio. When the appointed day came, Anna appeared on the train.
Harlan had his answer. For the next six years they floated down
the Ohio and Mississippi Rivers on a shanty boat they built, like
Thoreau's cabin and Joseph Cornell's boxes, from salvaged materials. Indeed, the cabin was as deliberately designed as, and in
many ways resembled, a Cornell box. There was just enough space
for a woodstove and cooking stove, choice books, canned goods,
a small closet, painting supplies, a cello, and a violin. Yet, whereas
Thoreau and Cornell eschewed travel for the most part, the in-
trepid Hubbards set out in search of the dangerous, unpredictable
world along the big rivers. At first Harlan worried that Anna
would find this life wanting, but he "was confident that she would
evolve a pattern of living which, while still giving scope to my
wild longings, would satisfy her innate delicacy, her femininity and
self-respect." It's a line one can easily imagine Thoreau writing
had Ellen Sewall come to live with him at Walden.

"The river, being of finite length, should always be taken in
small amounts to make it last longer," Hubbard wrote in his account of the voyage, *Shanty Boat*. (Like Thoreau, Hubbard published two books in his lifetime, one about rivers and one about
homesteading in the utopia of solitude.) Anna agreed, and by the
end of their trip, she also seemed in agreement with Harlan (and
Thoreau) that "surely refinement of living does not consist in

gadgets and machinery, but in such elements as leisure, contentment, lack of confusion, small niceties." When the Hubbards finally reached the Gulf of Mexico, they sold the shanty boat, bought an old Dodge, and headed back to Kentucky. There they found a remote piece of land called Payne Hollow, where Harlan built a small, beautiful house out of rough-hewn timber. Together for thirty-four years until Anna's death in 1986, the Hubbards lived almost completely off the land and the sun.* They cultivated a garden and raised goats for food and milk, baited a trotline every evening for catfish, and cut firewood for the stone hearth that Hubbard had set by hand. They were rebelling against the twentieth century in the same way Thoreau was reacting to the nineteenth. "Against what I thought wrong and false, I have been conducting a one-man revolution," wrote Hubbard. Except it was a one-man and one-*woman* revolution. His life, Hubbard said, would have made no sense without Anna. She brought "a degree of refinement and even elegance" to his Thoreauvian dream, something he "would not have thought possible without the sacrifice of simplicity and honesty." You see Anna's presence most obviously in old photos of her Steinway grand piano standing next to Harlan's homemade furniture. Each evening, they played duets, with Harlan on violin. He loved, he said, to send a little Brahms out into the woods. Indeed, detached from the power grid, they lived a very acoustic life. It was rich in sounds, as was Thoreau's life at Walden, and it was rich in silences. "Our truest communion and understanding," Hubbard wrote in *Payne Hollow*, "is attained with only a few words between periods of communicative silence." I love that phrase: "communicative silence." If, as Nietzsche said, a successful marriage is a long conversation, it seems to me that it must also be a long series of communicative silences.

When I told a friend about the Hubbards recently, she said, "Well, isn't marriage itself a utopian venture?" I realized she was right. Who believes in the potential for happiness more than newly-

* I would have visited Payne Hollow on my trip, but an inexplicable argument over one of Hubbard's paintings caused the current caretaker to refuse me access.

weds? (As for people like me, it was Dr. Johnson who said a second marriage is the victory of hope over experience.) One would be hard-pressed to find a better description of the utopia of marriage than this passage from Hubbard's journal: "To arise in the frosty morning at the point of daybreak, climb the hill and cut wood, while the sky lightens above the soaring trees; to eat this wholesome sweet food; to use my body, hands and mind at the endless work I have to do; to read by firelight, to sleep warm and snug; all this shared and enjoyed by my loving partner—what manner of a man originated this idea of a happier life beyond death?" Hubbard's kingdom of God was at Payne Hollow, Kentucky. Hubbard compulsively painted its hillsides and woods so as to see them better and help others see them as he did. He kept and dressed the land in accordance with the first chapters of Genesis. As far as Harlan Hubbard was concerned, he and Anna were the first man and woman, cultivating the garden of an unfallen world. It's a life one would have wished on Thoreau, and the success of that life can be measured by the fact that the Hubbards stayed at it for thirty-eight more years than Thoreau.

Still, Thoreau wrote that when he considered his life as a whole, he felt blessed by the gods. Emerson once said that nature is a good mistress but a poor wife. After moving to Walden Pond, Thoreau spent the rest of his life trying to prove that sentiment wrong. *Walden* ends with the true story of a "beautiful bug" that one day emerged from the wood of a table that had stood in a farmer's kitchen for sixty years. The insect hatched from an egg that had been deposited in a living tree all those years earlier, and had, perhaps, been finally incubated by the heat of an urn set on the table. "Who does not feel his faith in a resurrection and immortality strengthened by hearing of this?" asked Thoreau. It is the final awakening of *Walden*. Might we not also finally crawl out of "the dead dry life of society," rustle our wings, and take flight? Might we not also be resurrected into a luminous present where we stop existing and begin to be? It isn't too late, wrote Thoreau: "The sun is but a morning star."

Some Heartbreak, Much Happiness

ONEIDA, NEW YORK

Mile: 002184

The next morning, I leave behind Thoreau's crowded utopia of solitude, and soon I'm cruising through the swamps and swales along Route 2, otherwise known as the Mohawk Trail. As the name suggests, it was originally an Indian path that led to prime fishing spots along the Connecticut and Deerfield Rivers. The English Puritans later used the trail to spread disease among the Massachusetts and Wampanoag tribes, reducing their populations by half. Then they worked to pit one tribe against the other and gained, as it were, a right-of-way along the Mohawk Trail. It's the old sad story, so I won't dredge it up again.

For now, I'm happy again to be following a road that follows a flowing river, Millers River, up through northwestern Massachusetts. I'm remembering another line by the poet Richard Hugo: "When I see a river, I want to say, 'Exactly.'" When I see the sign that promises GLACIAL POTHOLES, I hang a left toward a place called Shelburne Falls, which turns out to be another small New England town that seems recently to have built a successful economy around local cuisine, local artisans, and a dependable river. The water spills over Salmon Falls, where the Mohawk and

Penobscot tribes forged a 1714 treaty to fish in peace. Below the falls, large sections of gray limestone, streaked with the orange evidence of iron oxide, have indeed been hollowed out to look like potholes. Some are the size of kettledrums; others are large enough to swim in, a practice that was recently banned. How these cavities came about apparently remained a mystery for hundreds of years. In *A Week on the Concord and Merrimack Rivers*, Henry David Thoreau explains that tribes at war with the Mohawks hid their provisions in these potholes, believing their god had cut the cavities for that purpose. That, Thoreau said, was at least a better hypothesis than the one put forth by the Royal Society, which concluded that the potholes "seem plainly to be artificial." Thoreau himself casually remarked that "their origin is apparent to the most careless observer." Whirlpools of water caused stones to spin in a gyrating motion for centuries, like an inverse potter's wheel, slowly cutting down into the limestone, "doing Sisyphus-like penance for stony sins," according to Thoreau—and he was right, at least about the geology of it.

I'm determined to keep rivers out my window for as long as I can. I head up along the North River into Vermont, past small sawmills, and soon I'm winding through the Green Mountain National Forest. Across the state line into New York, I pick up the Mohawk River in Troy and head west. Farms spread out across the Upper Hudson River Valley on my right. I'm driving roughly parallel to the Erie Canal, or what's left of it, so I pull off at Lock 20 in Whitesboro to watch a few sailboats, with their booms lowered, released through the sluice gates on their way east to Lake Erie. A completely black, slightly sinister-looking canal boat is docked just above the downstream lock chamber. It's called the *Memory Motel*, named, I presume, after my favorite Rolling Stones song, about Hannah, "a peachy kind of girl" from Boston, who leaves the singer halfway through the song, causing Mick to wail, "I hit the bottle and hit the sack and cried." I've always loved that line for some reason. Anyway, the original Erie Canal was an integral part of the early 1800s Transportation Revolution. Along with new railroads and steamboat routes, it allowed utopian proselytizers to move around the country and address audiences of the popular Lyceum speaker series. Even the home-bound Thoreau couldn't resist making a little money on the Lyceum circuit. The Transportation Revolution also made possible both the commerce that the utopianists fled and their own success at transporting their goods to market. With the possible exception of the Shakers, no community was more successful at this than the perfectionists of Oneida, New York, just down the road from here.

The perfectionists offer a curious bookend to my original des-tination, the Shaker village of Pleasant Hill. Like the Shakers, the perfectionists were founded as a religious community, though they were the only theocratic utopia of American origins. Their founder, John Humphrey Noyes, imagined his New England community as analogous in many ways to Brook Farm. If transcendentalism spawned Brook Farm, then the Congregational and Presbyterian Churches "ripened into Perfectionism." Noyes also liked to point out that his original community began the year after the fire at Brook Farm, as if it were the phoenix rising from that abandoned dream.

Unlike the residents of Brook Farm, though, and very much like the Shakers, the perfectionists flourished for many years. They grew wealthy by their own labor and ingenuity, and they shared the fruits of their labor equally among themselves, like the origi-nal Christians as recounted in the Book of Acts. Like the Shakers, the perfectionists were agrarians as well as ceaseless inventors of labor-saving devices. They made and grew most of what they needed. They were millennialists who believed they could hasten the resurrection by creating that heavenly state of being here on earth. Really the only important thing the Shakers and the perfec-tionists disagreed about was sex. On that score, John Humphrey Noyes reached exactly the opposite conclusions as Mother Ann Lee—though for the same reason. Both groups wanted to avoid sexual division and nuclear families. According to Noyes, the only two ways to do that were: to ban sex altogether, or to make it open to all. The Shakers chose the first course, the perfectionists the latter.

While Noyes claimed to have invented the term *free love*, he also came to rue doing so when the words were later applied, with much scandal, to the perfectionists of Oneida. Nevertheless, one still sees evidence of the founder's ample free-love progeny when driving through town, such as the sign for the Noyes Real Estate Agency, situated on a corner where I turn toward the original community's Mansion House. This sprawling brick structure is the closest any American utopian community came to realizing Charles Fourier's dream of a palatial phalanstery or Robert Owen's vision of a self-contained equity village. Begun in the early 1860s, and built by the Oneidans with bricks they fired themselves, the three-story Victorian Gothic structure is built on a quadrangle and dominated by two square turrets that resolve into a mansard roof. It sits on a rise overlooking what was once an orchard and is now a small neighborhood of handsome Greek Revival and Queen Anne–style homes, a few still occupied by descendants of the original community.

The Mansion House itself is dark inside and completely quiet. The office door is locked. A wide staircase rises at the back of the entry hall, and to my left stretches a long hallway where a small sign stands, reading NO VISITORS PAST THIS POINT PLEASE. Beyond the sign, I see a woman with a walker slowly moving down the barely lit hall. People live here, I realize. Old people. Are they, too, the descendants of the original perfectionists?

I have made a reservation to spend tonight in the John Humphrey Noyes Suite, a two-story accommodation situated in the north turret. But unable to locate a key to that once-revered chamber, I decide to have a look around the mansion. The main stairway leads to the Great Hall, which was the central gathering place of the Oneida Community. It is still painted in the original warm tan, and its cornices and moldings are trimmed in light blue. Sun pours in through three-story-tall windows behind a large stage where a grand piano stands. A tiered balcony wraps around three sides of the room, above twelve long Shaker-style wooden benches that fill most of the Great Hall. Along the back wall hang three more-flattering-than-life oil portraits of John Humphrey Noyes, his long-suffering wife, Harriet Noyes, and his spiritual and sexual muse, Mary Cragin. It was this curious love triangle that gave perfectionism its infamous form.

Noyes was born "of respectable parentage" (a phrase the disapproving historian Charles Nordhoff couldn't resist) in Brattleboro, Vermont, in 1811. He graduated from Dartmouth College and studied law for a time. Yet after a year of clerking, Noyes went, at his mother's urging, to a revival led by Charles Finney, the same evangelist who as a child found the Cane Ridge Revival so repulsive. In 1831, Finney was leading the country's Second Great Awakening and the fervor swept up Noyes, who said he wrestled with Satan for four days during the revival before giving his soul over to God. The main thrust of the Second Awakening was to steer Americans away from the Calvinist doctrines of predestination and man's innate depravity, and Noyes immediately enrolled in Yale Divinity School, where his professors encouraged a similar theology. The founder of Methodism, John Wesley, had been preaching a doctrine of "holiness" that said that men and women could attain a state of perfect love with God. Those who took up this belief were called perfectionists, and soon Noyes followed their view to what he saw as its logical conclusion: Christians could not only escape their Calvinist fate, but release themselves from sin altogether. That, he decided, was in fact the whole crux of Christianity: to be "saved" was to become sinless, to be perfect in the eyes of God. To give oneself wholly to God meant to be governed by grace and liberated from the laws of man. Noyes spoke in the language of "born again" Christians; only, he argued that the second birth was a release into spiritual perfection. That inner perfection, that "purity of heart," would then work to transform the actions of the outer self. In 1310, Marguerite Porete, author of *Mirror of the Simple Soul*, was burned at the stake for professing this same belief. Seven centuries later, it didn't win John Humphrey Noyes many friends, either. When a classmate visited Noyes's room to ask if he really thought he was sinless, Noyes answered in the affirmative, and word spread quickly around New Haven. The date was February 20, 1834, an anniversary that the Oneida Community would later celebrate as their equivalent of Christmas.

Yale revoked Noyes's license to preach in the region and asked him to leave the Divinity School. Nearly penniless, he wandered the streets of New York City preaching his new religion to whoever would listen. He was either a deranged homeless person or a direct spiritual descendant of a Mediterranean street preacher, depending on your perspective. Noyes, like Mother Ann Lee and George Rapp, chose to believe the latter and became convinced that God had chosen him directly and exclusively to lead the world back to the Promised Land.

Then, in 1837, he wrote a letter "in the nakedness of privacy" to David Harrison, one of his converts, revealing his new belief that marriage was an impediment to spiritual ascendancy. "When the will of God is done on earth as it is in Heaven," Noyes wrote, "there will be no marriage. Exclusiveness, jealousy, quarrelling have no place in the marriage supper of the Lamb." Harrison showed the letter to a friend, who showed it to a friend, and so on, until it finally wound up in print, in a paper run by a publisher who reviled Noyes.

The wandering visionary immediately lost most of his few followers. He was about to be kicked out of his boardinghouse for failing to pay back rent when a woman named Harriet Holton sent him eighty dollars to settle his bills and keep his magazine, *The Perfectionist*, going. Holton, who was later remembered in the Oneida newspaper as "not brilliant, but plodding," was the granddaughter of a wealthy Vermont lawyer, an orphan who stood to inherit her grandfather's fortune. Noyes immediately did what any destitute man who had just rejected the bonds of matrimony would do: he proposed marriage—but in the strangest, most circumscribed of ways. He wrote Holton a letter (more a legal document, really) in which he suggested "a partnership which I will not call marriage till I have defined it." He went on: "We can enter into no engagement with each other which shall limit the range of our affections as they are limited in matrimonial engagements by the fashion of the world." Noyes added, just to be absolutely clear about what he was proposing, that his "yoke-fellow will love all who love God," and love "as freely as if she stood in no particular connection to me." Holton accepted Noyes's terms immediately, and the two were married, under her grandfather's skeptical eye, in June 1838.

They set up house in Putney, Vermont, where Noyes continued to publish *The Perfectionist* and slowly gathered a small congregation around him. By 1843 there were thirty-five members of what Noyes called the Society of Inquiry of Putney. They lived together on a farm and followed the precept of the Primitive Church about holding things in common. But that, Noyes decided in 1846, was not enough. It was time to act on the sentiments he had expressed in his letter to David Harrison nearly ten years earlier. And he gave this new dispensation a name: complex marriage. In the beginning, Noyes thought such an arrangement could exist only after the resurrection of the physical body; but at Putney, he came to believe that by instituting complex marriage immediately, he and his followers could hasten the Second Coming.

This belief grew out of Noyes's theory, based on rather flimsy biblical justification, that the *first* Second Coming of Christ had already happened. As a divinity school student, Noyes could not get past the passage in John where Jesus says, "If I will that he [John] tarry till I come, what is that to thee?" To Noyes, this implied that John would live to see Christ's return. Noyes claimed to have "read the New Testament through ten times with my eye on the question as to the time of Christ's Second Coming." At last he reached the conclusion that the judgment of mankind had been split "into two acts occupying two distinct periods of time." The first act occurred in 70 BCE, when the Romans, under Titus, sacked the Second Temple of Jerusalem. That, according to Noyes, was God's judgment on the Jews. All the righteous members of the Primitive Church ascended into heaven, which, he said, is why Christianity changed so radically after that generation, devolving into the legalistic, ritualistic Church of Rome. However, Christ's judgment of the gentiles, the *second* Second Coming, hadn't happened yet, but was extremely imminent. Furthermore, Noyes had come to believe, he was the sole millennial messenger, and the sole instigator, of that return. Eighteen hundred years after the "primary resurrection and judgment in the spirit world," that spiritual kingdom above was finally descending to meet an earthly kingdom of God that was simultaneously rising, under the guidance of Noyes, to embrace its heavenly reflection. Their millennial confluence would bring about the second and final resurrection. Again like the Shakers, Noyes and his followers would actually *call down* the kingdom through their example of sinless perfection.

The only difference, of course, was that the Shakers eliminated sin by eliminating sex; the perfectionists eliminated sin by eliminating shame—the shame of adultery. The Creation story that Noyes invented for the perfectionists began with what the literary critic Harold Bloom would call a "strong misreading" of the first three chapters of Genesis. As Noyes saw it, the Fall involved "two great manifestations of original sin": Adam and Eve's alienation from God and their erotic separation from each other, brought on by the shame of nakedness. No other living creatures felt such human shame—Walt Whitman famously wrote in *Leaves of Grass* that he sometimes wished he could "turn and live with the animals" because "they do not lie awake in the dark and weep for their sins"—and such innocence made their burdens infinitely lighter than humankind's. "To be ashamed of sexual conjunction," said Noyes, "is to be ashamed of the image of the glory of God—the physical symbol of life indwelling in life, which is the mystery of the gospel." Noyes's plan to reverse the Fall involved, first, a reconciliation with God and, second, a "true union of the sexes." That true union meant a return not to prelapsarian monogamy but, rather, to the unshackled sexual purity of the angels: a preprelapsarianism, as it were.

More than one historian has attributed Noyes's idiosyncratic reading of scripture to the pretty obvious fact that he had developed uncontrollable sexual feelings for one of his parishioners' wives, Mary Cragin. In the only photo that survives, Mary Cragin appears gaunt, with dark, oily hair plastered to the side of her head. She was, wrote Spencer Klaw in his excellent history of Oneida, "far from beautiful." To Noyes, though, she embodied the "wisdom of love." One evening, when the two went out for a walk, Noyes was overwhelmed by a desire so free from guilt and shame that he concluded that it must have been divinely inspired. "I took some personal liberties," he later confessed in an article called "My First Act in Sexual Freedom." On June 1, 1847, he proposed the practice of complex marriage to the Society of Inquiry and, as he later wrote, "it was unanimously adopted as the declaration of the believers assembled that *The Kingdom of God Has Come.*"

All members of the Putney community signed a "Statement of Principles" that read, in part, "All individual proprietorship of either persons or things is surrendered and absolute community of interests takes the place of the laws and fashions which preside over property and family relations in the world." It said that only God was the community's "supreme regulator," but that Noyes was "the father and overseer whom the Holy Ghost has set over the family thus constituted." As a constitution for the kingdom of God, the "Statement" is admirable in its clarity and conciseness, but the Putney utopia proved short-lived. On October 26, 1847, some local parishioners who did not think Noyes was God's chosen intermediary had him arrested on the charge of adultery. He was quickly granted bail and released, with a court date set, but he responded to the danger as he would throughout his life: he fled. A month later, while he hunkered down with a small group of perfectionists in Madison County, New York, Mary Cragin and her husband learned that warrants for their arrest had also been issued. Their lawyer, fearing a mob attack, advised any of Noyes's followers who were not residents of Putney to get out of town.

Jonathan Burt, a perfectionist who had bought a small farm from the Oneida Indians in upstate New York, offered to resettle the Putney deportees on his land. Some of the cabins on Burt's farm had been built by the Oneida tribe, a fact that pleased Noyes. He quickly accepted Burt's offer and gave him five hundred dollars as a down payment. With that, thirty-one adults, along with fourteen children, joined Burt's small group to form the Oneida Association.

"You must be Mr. Reece," I hear a female voice say while I'm staring at the rather girlish portrait of Mary Cragin. Startled, I turn toward the stairs. "You're staying in the Noyes Suite tonight, yes?"

"I couldn't find anyone around when I got here," I say.

She explains that I'm the only guest tonight, and it must have slipped the afternoon staffer's mind. The woman leads me down some narrow corridors—the whole dark interior feels disorienting and labyrinthine, partly, I suspect, because the mansion was built in stages, in a rather hodgepodge fashion—and then hands over my key. The door of my suite overlooks the community's main sitting room, a rather ornate space that Noyes apparently designed to look like the grand decks of Hudson River steamboats. The suite itself fills the second and third floors of the front turret. Indeed, when I stare out from that tower's highest window, this mansion on a hill does feel something like a great ship cresting over a green swell. I stand here in the forecastle of this lumbering vessel, with the galleys, dance floor, and hundreds of narrow cabins to my back.

The walls and molding of the suite's lower sitting room are painted white, and the room is furnished with Shaker side tables and Queen Anne chairs. I take a seat and pull from my book bag a thin volume called *Bible Communism*. Before arriving here, Noyes still harbored the illusion that he could convert the Congregational churches of New England to what he called the "communism of love." Yet, once ensconced at Oneida, he came to understand the hard truth that eventually settled over all the utopianists of the nineteenth century: for their vision to succeed, it had to develop in isolation from the prejudices of the masses. So, instead, Noyes shifted to an argument put forward by embattled religious groups from the Mormons to the Rastafarians: the practices of the Oneidan perfectionists, though offensive to mainstream congregations, were sanctioned by their God and therefore protected by the Constitution's First Amendment right to freedom of religion. The perfectionists, Noyes maintained, only wished to protect their beliefs, not proselytize outside their community. Of course they would publish, three times a week, their *Oneida Circular*, but only better to explain and justify their ways to the world.

Soon after arriving at Oneida, Noyes sat down to write his most thorough justification for perfectionism and complex marriage. The world needed to know exactly what the perfectionists believed, and once Noyes had established the scriptural justification for their beliefs, the world, he hoped, would leave them alone. Noyes set up *Bible Communism* as a series of "Propositions," perhaps meant to emulate the structure of Spinoza's *Tractatus Theologico-Politicus*. His initial proposition got right to the question of marriage. If the Shakers, and most Christians along with them, had interpreted Matthew 22:30—"At the resurrection people will neither marry nor be given in marriage; they will be like the angels in heaven"—to mean there's no sex in heaven, Noyes read the verse as justification for his rejection of conventional marriage and monogamy. After the resurrection, Noyes maintained, "the intimate union of life and interest," which on earth has been confined to one man and one woman, "extends through the whole body of believers." If the sacrifice of Jesus on the Cross means that Christians are "dead to the world," then the worldly law of marriage no longer applies to them. Furthermore, argued Noyes, Christ's commandment to love one another meant that such loving should be done not in pairs but en masse. Finally, we must, following 1 Peter 1:22, love one another "burningly." For Noyes, there was only one way to interpret that charge—hot, polygamous sex. Such abandon was in keeping with what Noyes called the "anti-legality" of the Gospels. He compared monogamy to kosher restrictions: outdated. "The secret of the human heart," Noyes wrote, was that "the more it loves the more it can love. This is the law of nature, thrust out of sight, and condemned by common consent, and yet secretly known to all. There is no occasion to find fault with it. Variety is the nature of things, as beautiful and useful in love as in eating and drinking."

Charles Fourier certainly would have endorsed that sentiment. Fourier and Robert Owen would have further agreed with Noyes that traditional marriage "provokes the secret of adultery, actual or of the heart," and that it "gives to sexual appetite only a scanty and monotonous allowance." Such monogamy leads to jealousy, and jealousy leads to division—the devil of a utopian community. All the nineteenth-century utopianists were in accord that women could be liberated from the perils of patriarchy by being liberated from monogamous marriage. "We are not 'Free Lovers,'" Noyes insisted, "in any sense that makes love less binding or responsible than it is in marriage." Sexual "license and anarchy" was not what perfectionism was about. Rather, it was the fundamental reconciliation with God in the heart of the Oneida Christians that sanctioned the heavenly state where monogamy ceased to exist. Everyone at Oneida was *married* within the kingdom of God—they were simply all married to one another. Noyes, therefore, replaced that form of matrimony with what he called a new form of divinely inspired, social marriage, whereby all God's children, even close relatives, could have sex with whomever they chose. Far from the abomination that mainstream religion claimed polygamy to be, complex marriage was actually a spiritual duty for Christians who had perfected themselves and so lived sinlessly. By releasing sexual love from the acquisitive, human institution of marriage, the perfectionists were hastening the final resurrection.

There were four things, Noyes wrote in *Bible Communism*, that prevented human beings from finding God's kingdom. The first was a breach with our Creator, the second was disruption between the sexes, the third was the curse of oppressive labor, and the fourth was disease and death. Wrote Noyes, "The sin-system, the marriage-system, the work-system, and the death-system, are all one, and must be abolished together." To reconcile with God would mean to reconcile men and women to their natural state of divine polygamy. (Noyes here ignored the obvious problem that Adam and Eve *had* to be monogamous unless they were to take up bestiality.) To reconcile the sexes would mean to free both from oppressive labor: the labor of birth for women and the labor of too much difficult work for men. With fewer kids to take care of, men and women would share labor, and thus make it at once diminished and more attractive. In this way, work would become so effortless that the workers would never tire, never get ground down, and so never taste death. It all made sense to Noyes; when all this sin and shame and work was abolished, "we arrive regularly at the tree of life."

I decide to walk the grounds and look for some of the actual trees the Oneidans planted during the heady 1860s, when they seemed determined to replicate the floral richness and variety of the original Garden. From the north lawn, I gaze back at the Mansion House. The black and gray slate tiles on the mansard roof make a handsome pattern, as does the alternating red and yellow brickwork over each of the mansion's many windows. All the doors are painted forest green, and all the porches white. New wings were added as the community gradually expanded to 250 members. "We do not look for architectural purity and precision which would belong to a statehouse or a church," one member wrote in the *Circular*. "Our eye is rather pleased, and our interest piqued by noticing the evidences of time, and the successive stages of progress that have passed over the work."

An undated photograph taken sometime during the perfectionists' thirty-two-year existence shows a cluster of children, ages three to five, posing with their schoolmaster, William "Papa" Kelly, in front of an arbor made from rough-hewn cedar and covered with a thatch roof. The structure still stands here on the north lawn, and I stop inside it to get out of the sticky July heat. One of Noyes's greatest challenges at Oneida was separating children from their mothers. (Even greater, it turned out, was separating mothers from their children.) Yet, again like the Shakers, Noyes felt such distance crucial if the community were to avoid the balkanization caused by members retreating into biological families. Children were reared in their own wing of the mansion, though they often spent the night in the rooms of adults who were not their actual parents. Vital to the spirit of Bible communism was Noyes's insistence that children did not "belong" to their mothers but, rather, to the entire community. All adults were to act as their mothers and fathers. Noyes exhorted his followers thusly: "So if the old saying is true that 'blood is stronger than water,' we must add to it that 'love is stronger than blood.'" Of course, given Oneida's system of complex marriage, many children did not know who their fathers were, and the men who could identify their progeny seemed to form far weaker attachments to their biological children than did the mothers. Women who developed what Noyes called "philoprogenitiveness" (an excessive love of one's own offspring) were sometimes forced to avoid their children for weeks at a time. No doubt the initial separation of mother and child after weaning was rough on both parties, but the anguish seemed temporary. Jessie Catherine Kinsley, who grew up in the community, wrote years later of Oneida's children, "Indeed we were a happy lot—far happier than are children made tyrants by petting, or nagged by anxious and over-worked mothers."

Mary Cragin became Oneida's first schoolmistress, and taught the children her own brand of nursery rhyme socialism:

I-*spirit*
With me never shall stay,
We-*spirit*
Makes us happy and gay.

One of Noyes's many children, Pierrepont Noyes, was born in 1870. In a beautiful memoir written sixty-seven years later, he maintained, "The Community adopted communism only that the members might live the unselfish lives ordained by Jesus Christ." By the time he was born, Oneida "must have exorcised the spirit of acquisitiveness very completely," because the younger Noyes never remembered growing up with any sense that some toy, some object, might *belong* to him. "For instance," he remembered, "we were keen for our favorite sleds, but it never occurred, to me at least, that I could possess a sled to the exclusion of other boys."

As in Maclure's school back at New Harmony, the Oneida children worked for an hour or two each day, and then they studied reading, writing, math, and geography for a few more hours. At five o'clock they were subjected to an hour-long Bible lesson, which they all dreaded. Pierrepont Noyes took from these lessons that "God seemed rather terrible, but a friend of the Community." However, Papa Kelly's ultimate lesson to the children was "Do good for evil." The children's formal schooling ended when their sexual education began, at puberty, though they were encouraged to continue their studies into adulthood, as all the Oneidans were.

Not long after the arrival of the perfectionists, a rumor began spreading throughout Oneida County that John Humphrey Noyes was initiating girls into sexual adulthood as soon as they began to menstruate—and the rumor was true. In *Bible Communism*, Noyes complains that females hit puberty at age fourteen but usually don't marry until twenty-four. "For ten years, therefore, and that in the very flush of life, the sexual appetite is starved." Noyes set out to reclaim that lost decade, and he did. Up until his late sixties, when fourteen-year-old girls were no longer obliging of him, Noyes initiated most of Oneida's virgins into womanhood. After that rite of passage into the spiritual world of polyamorous socialism, a rite that usually took place in the suite where I'm staying, the young women could have sex with, or not have sex with, whomever they chose. To the Oneida County district attorney

Samuel Garvin's way of thinking, this violated about every moral standard he could imagine. In 1851, Garvin brought charges of "adultery and fornication" against the community. Noyes relented and issued a statement to the effect that complex marriage would cease. However, many in the surrounding community actually stepped up to the perfectionists' defense, calling them good neighbors who minded their own business—and also made some pretty good fruit preserves. When Garvin, apparently satisfied with Noyes's retreat, decided not to press charges, the ecstatic Oneidas threw a party on the west lawn for their defenders. I wander over in that direction, where a well-tended perennial garden still survives, the work, I suspect, of the descendants who still live here. (The original Oneidans kept five acres of fruits and vegetables under cultivation, and one member, in a prelapsarian spirit, urged others "not to talk about the *farm* any more, but the *garden*.") The perfectionists' agreement to abstain from complex marriage didn't last long, but the tradition of picnics on the lawn continued. Almost every summer Sunday, hundreds of New Yorkers walked, rode, or took the train up to the Mansion House. Clearly they were curious to see the community caught up in what the *New York Observer* called "a state of vile concubinage," but what they got instead was lemonade and innocuous bowls of strawberries and cream. Eager to disprove their scandalous reputation, the perfectionists never engaged in public displays of affection; and eager to gain support in the likelihood of future legal battles, they grew enough strawberries to feed an army. On July 4, 1866, more than six thousand guests came to picnic, listen to the children's choir, and tour the mansion. Many were disappointed not to find the "orgy room" they had expected.

In the morning, I check the literature left in my suite and learn that, since this is the off-season, I will have to conduct my own self-guided tour. During his visit in the early 1870s, the historian Charles Nordhoff asked for a definition of perfectionism and was told, we're not sure by whom, "Salvation from sin, as we understand it, is not a system of duty-doing under a code of dry laws, Scriptural or natural; but is a special phase of *religious experience*, having for its basis spiritual intercourse with God." This emphasis on religion as an experience puts the perfectionists squarely in the realm of the religious pragmatism advocated by William James, wherein a belief is justified only if it becomes what he called a habit of action. One would be hard-pressed to find a group of American Christians who so thoroughly put their beliefs into action—say what you want about those beliefs—as the Oneida perfectionists.

The Mansion House still seems decidedly empty except for a woman I find sitting at a computer in the small gift shop/book-store. She looks up and smiles as I enter, and then asks how I liked the Noyes Suite.

"It's very nice," I say. "I guess some of the perfectionists were more equal than others."

"Hey, that's from *Animal House*, isn't it?"

"*Animal Farm*, I think."

"Right. Sorry. Definitely not a John Belushi line."

Speaking of animals, I mention that I noticed on my way down a locked room that contained a lot of old traps.

"We keep it locked because it kind of freaks out children," she says, grabbing a set of keys.

As we walk down the hall, I ask about the current residents at the Mansion House. Many, she says, are simply single mothers who work at Oneida Ltd., the famous silverware company into which the Oneida Community eventually transformed. Only about 20 percent of the residents, like the older woman I saw yesterday, are direct descendants of the original perfectionists.

"But my husband is one of them," she says. "We live here part of the year." I ask if I might speak with him. "He's at our apartment in New York right now, but I think he's coming back later today. I'll tell him you asked."

When she unlocks the door to the trap room, I see that it resembles a torture chamber, with fifty or so steel maws hanging from the walls. In one corner, the community's most important trap is mounted on top of an oak stump. Inch-long spikes protrude from its jaws, clasped shut by two steel arms. Even in this closed formation, though, the contraption is intimidating. This is the now-famous Newhouse trap, invented by Sewell Newhouse, a blacksmith and trapper who joined the community in 1848. At that time, the perfectionists were struggling, selling their preserves and canned vegetables, and they lived in a much more modest, wooden dormitory. The Newhouse trap, with its more reliable spring system, changed all that. By the late 1850s, the Oneidas were selling more than one hundred thousand traps a year. Newhouse diversified to make smaller traps for otters, beavers, and mink, like the ones that hang on the walls here. When the perfectionists added their famous line of silverware to the trap business, the community grew quite wealthy.

In her study, *Oneida: Utopian Community to Modern Corporation*, Maren Lockwood Carden expresses shock that no one saw a contradiction in building a Christian utopia with the profits of such a cruel invention as the Newhouse trap. However, there seems to be no record of such qualms, and it was women as well as men who helped manufacture so many of these snares. Indeed, the historian Lawrence Foster wrote, "Few societies in human history have done more to break down arbitrary distinctions between the sexes than did Oneida." Oneida freed women from almost every traditional role that had been assigned them in the realms of work, dress, motherhood, and sex. Oneida certainly freed women from the cage of the Victorian bodice. Instead, the perfectionist women wore bloomer-style short skirts over functional pantalets, an outfit first instituted by Mary Cragin and Harriet Noyes, presumably as a utilitarian function for women who were often changing jobs during the day. Men who visited Oneida were universally disparaging of this getup, with some going so far as to wonder how a community based on free love could allow women to look so dowdy in public. However the women appeared to outsiders, they had at least achieved Robert Owen's earlier hope of transcending the vanity and superficiality of fashion. Noyes, for his part, constantly warned against the "dress spirit" that would only lead a woman to haughtiness, to think herself better than other women or, worse, too good for certain men. More important, part of Owen's argument had been that marriage makes women economic slaves to their husbands. Noyes solved that problem by both getting rid of husbands and getting rid of property. Yet whereas Owen's argument had been grounded in the secular unfairness of nineteenth-century law, Noyes's appealed to the higher law of the Primitive Church, the Garden of Eden, and his own interpretation of heaven.

Women at Oneida were free to choose work that had, everywhere else in nineteenth-century America, been closed off to them. Several young women worked as carpenters and were prized for the delicate way they worked a lathe. The perfectionists had essentially the same governing structure as does Twin Oaks today, with a small central committee and numerous subcommittees that each oversaw one branch of community activity: agriculture, education, printing, and so on. Women headed up many of those committees and subcommittees. The one key difference is that, at Oneida, everyone ultimately answered to John Humphrey Noyes.

Like Charles Fourier's imaginary Harmonians, the actual perfectionists divided their days into various kinds of work, and Noyes made sure that no one was pressed to do the least rewarding work, which usually involved the kitchen, for longer than a month. (Noyes did not make Robert Owen's mistake of taking in any soul who professed allegiance to his vision of utopia. He scrupulously screened applicants and accepted only those who had skills, or capital, or both.) When a large job needed doing in a short amount of time (picking strawberries, peas, or apples, for instance), the perfectionists organized a "storming company" to attack the work as a unified front. In the case of harvesting, someone would read a novel by Dickens to entertain the pickers, or caroling would commence during these "bees." Noyes maintained that since his community lived in a resurrected state, its people possessed "the vigor of resurrection." Still, like Fourier, he tried to make labor as attractive as possible by creating work environments that were varied, unhurried, and social. As the *Circular* announced in 1853, "We believe that the great secret of securing enthusiasm in labor and producing a free, healthy, social equilibrium, is contained in the proposition, 'loving companionship and labor, and especially the mingling of the sexes, makes labor attractive.'" All work was equally valued, and community members never handled money. However, while Fourier justified dirtier work as tasks that little boys would want to do anyway, the perfectionists took a more practical and less idyllic approach: they hired out the more menial work to locals. This allowed the community members to approach their own work leisurely and noncompulsively, and it also made the surrounding towns beholden to Oneida in some ways, an advantage Noyes hoped to exploit if new charges of concubinage arose.

However, if the local philistines had seen where the perfectionists actually performed the sex act, it might have tempered their lurid fantasies. Upstairs from the trap room, one private quarters has been preserved as it was in the 1800s. The room is a cramped eight feet wide by fifteen long, the same size as a solitary confinement cell in a federal prison. A very narrow twin bed lines one wall. There is a chest of drawers, a nightstand with a sink beneath it, two chairs, and a small Wanzer lamp. Everything about the Mansion House (the large sitting room, the Great Hall, the library downstairs, and this narrow bedroom) proclaims the utopia of solidarity over the utopia of solitude. The Mansion House was meant to resemble a circulatory system where everyone moved through the public spaces, and privacy was only for sleep and sex. Yet the sex one could have in such a small space, on such a small bed, would have been a much different affair from the nightly bacchanalia that Fourier envisioned in what he called the Court of Love. One learns from the archives of the Kinsey Institute for Research in Sex, Gender and Reproduction that the "perfectionist position" was this: the lovers lay on their sides, and the man entered from behind so he could also offer manual stimulation. There is no record of homosexuality at Oneida, and given Noyes's theology of polyamory, it seems slightly odd that no record exists of sexual combinations that went beyond one man and one woman. Not that this attenuated room is exactly conducive to threesomes or anything beyond what a college freshman might get away with in his dorm. After the perfectionists' sexual assignations— "interviews" they were called—they must have found the single bed uncomfortable to share: in fact, it was meant to discourage too much postcoital time together. That would only have led to "partiality" and monogamy among lovers. Once the interview was over, the sated couple was expected to get back out into the social circulatory system of the Mansion House and its grounds.

To push the feminist line of argument a little further, it might also be argued that what looks at first glance like a flimsy theological scheme to justify John Humphrey Noyes's louche behavior was in fact a form of liberation for the women of Oneida. Apart from the fact that they could choose and refuse sexual partners (assuming Noyes's approval), women also could take comfort in knowing this: they would not get pregnant. The reason was simple: Noyes forbade the men of Oneida from ejaculating. In fact, one of his more convincing theological arguments in *Bible Communism* is that back in the Garden of Earthly Delights, sex was originally meant for pleasure, not procreation.

Noyes divided sex into two categories: the amative and the propagative. The latter was intended solely to produce offspring, and was greatly inferior to the former, which was pleasing to God because it brought erotic pleasure to his creations. Because the First Man was not meant to be alone, as Genesis states, the amative act of sex came first. Indeed, the propagative effects of sex occurred only east of Eden, where the pain of childbirth was meant to punish Eve for choosing the wisdom of the serpent over divine admonitions. Noyes proposed to return his perfectionists to the erotic bliss of the original Garden by returning men and women to the amative state. Still today we hear the argument from religious conservatives that the fundamental justification for marriage—and for banning gays from marriage—is procreation, and that sex for the sake of pleasure is a sign of suspect morals. In fact, this summer the governor of my own state will appeal a federal judge's ruling for the constitutionality of gay marriage, and he will base that appeal solely on the procreation argument. Nothing, said Noyes, could be farther from scriptural truth. "Such persons do not only dishonor God's creation," he claimed, "but despise that part of human nature which is noblest of all except that which communicates with God. They profane the very sanctuary of the affections—the first and best channel of the life and love of God." Noyes reinterpreted the Genesis Creation story to say that sex was not the work of the devil; rather, the devil's work was to trick us into thinking that such glorious pleasures were base.

As with the Shaker founder, Mother Ann Lee, the physical and psychological pain of losing children at the point of pregnancy seemed to inform Noyes's sexual theodicy. Whereas Mother Ann Lee renounced sex entirely after none of her four infants survived childbirth, Noyes, after his wife, Harriet, gave birth to five stillborn children, arrived at a completely different conclusion. It wasn't the amative act of intercourse that caused women so much pain, he argued; it was the propagative act of childbirth. And Noyes had a solution. The perfectionists abolished the curse of pregnancy through a birth-control method that Noyes called "male continence." This was not the same thing as coitus interruptus, which Noyes found vulgar and unscriptural: "God cannot have designed that men should sow seed by the wayside, where they do not expect it to grow." Noyes also rejected early condoms, which he dismissed as "French sacks." (Besides, in 1890, one of Noyes's mortal enemies, Anthony Comstock of the New York Society for the Suppression of Vice, saw to the arrest of a local businessman found in the possession of seven hundred condoms.) Rather, in Noyes's *coitus reservatus*, the male partner did not ejaculate at all. Noyes insisted that this method bestowed much more pleasure on the female—she could have sex for as long as she wanted, after all, without repercussions—and it would ultimately yield more pleasure for the male as soon as he learned the appropriate self-control. The trick, said Noyes, was never to paddle too close to the rapids of sexual release, but to confine one's desire upstream, in "the region of easy rowing." This created a kind of positive feedback loop that encouraged men to control themselves: those who couldn't usually found fewer sexual partners than those who could, and men who repeatedly violated the sanction were singled out for public criticism. At Oneida, women avoided both unwanted children and also the shame of raising them if the father absconded or otherwise shirked his responsibilities. At Oneida, if a woman chose to become pregnant, the father had no filial responsibilities. The child belonged to the community.

Noyes also instituted a system that he called "ascending fellowship," whereby older, more spiritually ascendant members initiated the younger ones into the mysterious waters of concupiscence. This ensured that older members were not neglected in matters of complex marriage, while novitiates were trained by their more perfect elders in matters both sexual and spiritual. Noyes often advised younger members on whom they should couple with on their quest for a more perfect state of spiritual communism. The system wasn't perfect, but a physician who interviewed former members of Oneida in the 1890s estimated that most women in the community had sex every two to four days, even though one more "ascendant" ex-member complained that younger women had sex seven times a week, sometimes more. One of those younger women, Jessie Kinsley, remembered Oneida as a place of endless variety in work and play; its one constant was "the changing and the steadfast lovers—some heartache, much happiness." The heartache came when exclusive lovers were forced apart by Noyes, or when an unrequited lover was rejected through a third party. (One man, Charles Guiteau, was rejected so often that he stormed off and eventually assassinated President Garfield, though what role his sexual frustration played in that act remains unclear.) The happiness implies a sexual love that circulated unhindered and unconditionally throughout the community.

I make my way back to the Great Hall, where the perfectionists performed their one act of censure. The perfectionists at Oneida had no constitution and no bylaws, but instead maintained that the New Testament, refracted through the peculiar hermeneutic lens of their leader, was the only governing document they needed. When visitors asked the same question over and over— "What do you do with the lazy ones?"—the answer was simple: mutual criticism. Something that began as a game Noyes played with other divinity students at Yale became the single form for, as the community's "First Annual Report" of 1849 stated, "regulating character and stimulating improvement." Throughout each year, everyone at Oneida had to submit to a session in which four spiritual elders sat on the stage here in the Great Hall and enumerated "everything objectionable in his character and conduct." Some commendations were made as well, but uncomfortable revelations formed the thrust of each mutual criticism. Such hard truths, Noyes claimed, were the sole "agents of perfection to all classes," and really, it's hard to argue with his results. For three decades, Oneida became the most productive and harmonious utopia of the nineteenth century, rivaled only by those of the Shakers and Rappites. As one anonymous member wrote in the *Circular*, "We have to criticize members for working too much, oftener than for being lazy."

The Shakers of course had to confess all their own sins to an elder, but that is a different thing from being told, by a presumably objective committee, *how others perceive your faults*. As such, and as bracing and unnerving as a session of criticism must have been, one can see its value. On some level, I would like to screw up the courage to hear how my family and friends perceive my shortcomings. I would, no doubt, learn a great deal about myself from such a "many-sided mirror," as the Oneidans called mutual criticism. With very few exceptions (such as interventions performed as last-ditch efforts to help addicts), we as a culture do not have any mechanism like the perfectionists' mutual criticism. Yet I think one might do us some good, as bracing and unnerving as the process would be. Our therapists, who might be the best trained to offer something of the sort, seem trained instead to *avoid* at all times telling us what they truly think. Parents cannot be trusted, because their criticism too often seems as skewed and as suspect as the warped perceptions we have of ourselves. What we all say we want, at least in our more aspirational moments, is greater self-actualization. Mutual criticism might reveal to us, at the very least, that most elusive of information: how others see us, what they truly think of us. To act on that knowledge might give us, at the very least, an alternate version of our selves that we could then compare with the highly subjective one we carry around inside us. Perhaps the two wouldn't look all that different, and we could congratulate ourselves on how well-adjusted we were, how skillful we navigated the daily ontological. Or perhaps we would learn that we deceived ourselves mightily, and serious recalibrations were in order. Isn't that something we would want to know? Perhaps we would finally face up to, and try to change, the hypocrisies and insincerities we have secretly, or not so secretly, suspected in ourselves. The perfectionists promised, "By this channel the resistless spirit of truth courses through the whole body." Within the community, that truth seemed to defuse problems associated with inflated egos and a lack of awareness of one's effect on others. As Spencer Klaw concluded, "At Oneida it was very hard to lead an unexamined life."

There was, however, one Oneidan who didn't submit to criticism: John Humphrey Noyes. When someone dared to ask why, Noyes responded that, as God's ambassador to North America, there was obviously nothing in him to criticize. Yet on more than one level Noyes was a deeply flawed progenitor of God's kingdom. He was, by most accounts, a terrible fiddle player—one son called him "far from a musical genius." To criticize that deficiency would have been petty, of course, yet in some weird act of transference, Noyes criticized an accomplished community violinist, Frank Wayland-Smith, for taking too much pride in his own playing. A petulant Noyes even confiscated the poor man's instrument for a time, along with all his sheet music. Certainly that display of naked envy was not beyond reproof. On July 19, 1855, the *Circular* included the criticism of one unnamed member whose faults included "large self-esteem and extraordinary practical judgment in some respects, which together with an ardent temperament, and large language, make him naturally forward, dogmatic, and oppressive in his intercourse with others." What, at a distance, seems amusing about this passage, given the cumulative portrait we now have of John Humphrey Noyes, is that every word of the criticism could have applied to him had he been willing to hear it. Yet one thing we can say about the seductive visionaries who led the utopian movement in America—the men most of all—is that they did not lead the most self-examined lives.

For a while, Noyes believed that mutual criticism could cure sickness and disease, reasoning that such illness was God's punishment for being less than perfect in the ascending kingdom of God. When diphtheria spread among the Oneidans, all manner of scorn was heaped upon the sick, and later the *Circular* proudly proclaimed that of the fifty-nine cases, all had recovered. Yet soon Noyes himself was suffering from chronic throat disease, along with deafness, and since he couldn't, or wouldn't, submit to mutual criticism himself, he allowed that some scientific remedies could be of use. Later, in an effort to serve the community further, he sent his son Theodore to Yale to study medicine.

However, the Great Hall was far more than a place for the individual to be humbled before the larger cause of community. In most instances, this was a space for much levity. The three muses waft around the chandeliers on the ceiling above me as if they have taken the place of the standard grim Christian iconography of the three crosses on Golgotha. In fact, there are not now, nor were there ever, any visible vestiges of Christianity on display here in the closest thing the Mansion House has to a sanctuary. The Oneidans did not pray out loud—Jesus had, after all, warned against such ostentation—nor did they have anything like the impressive hymn collection of the Shakers. They did not take communion, presumably for the same reason Ralph Waldo Emerson quit his Unitarian pulpit: it seemed redundant. The perfectionists already embodied the sinless state of which Christ's blood was but a mere symbol. Because the Oneidans lived in such a state of spiritual perfection (mutual criticism notwithstanding), they needed no reminders of how that salvation was achieved. The closest thing to a sermon the community heard was the informal "Home Talks" that Noyes delivered most nights after dinner here in the Great Hall. These were followed by discussions of community business. Men read the many newspapers that the community subscribed to, while women knitted. Pierrepont Noyes remembered that perfectionism "was a happy religion, never a gloomy one, nor did Bible communism appear to demand ascetic living." The community formed an orchestra, led by Frank Wayland-Smith (presumably after Noyes returned his violin). The orchestra played overtures from Mozart and Handel, waltzes by Strauss, and military marches. The perfectionists were also great lovers of musical theater, and they often reprised, for themselves and the larger community, Gilbert and Sullivan's *H.M.S. Pinafore*. Once, the children put on a pantomime called *When I Was a Bachelor*, in which a boy tried to stomp out a pack of stuffed rats who had invaded his bachelor pad. The bachelor concluded that he needed "to go to London and get myself a wife." However: "The streets were so broad and the lanes were so narrow, / I had to take my wife home in a wheelbarrow." As a child, Pierrepont Noyes took from this tale the lesson that wives in the world outside Oneida were largely needed to protect a husband's bread and cheese. It seemed so absurd—the wife, the wheelbarrow, the gendered division of labor—why wouldn't anyone rather live as a Bible communist?

The perfectionists loved dancing as much as the Shakers, though they of course shunned the segregated ring dances of their Communist brethren. Instead, a band led the community dancers through quadrilles, Virginia reels, and country dances. Still, John Humphrey Noyes must have felt a deep sympathy for the leader of the Massachusetts Shakers, Frederick Evans, who convinced President Lincoln not to draft Shaker men into the Civil War. (Because the Mansion House stood on the border dividing Madison and Oneida Counties, each county seat thought the other had drafted the perfectionist young men; as a result, none of them was forced to serve.) Before converting to Shakerism, Evans wrote tracts advocating land reform, women's rights, and, perhaps most radical of all, mail delivery on the Sabbath. He converted to socialism in 1830 and soon joined the New Lebanon Shakers because theirs was the only community he could find that truly embodied the tenets of socialism. Noyes often invited the New Lebanon Shakers to Oneida for dancing in the Great Hall. Pierrepont Noyes remembered as a child watching his father and Elder Evans talking together after the dancing, and he was struck by the fact that, for once, John Humphrey Noyes treated another man as his equal.

If Noyes was a demagogue, he could be a very pliant one. Though he never changed any of his fundamental convictions about Bible communism or the Second Coming, he greatly modified the latter after immersing himself in the work of the British evolutionists Charles Darwin and Charles Lyell. Noyes was the uncharacteristic American religious visionary who didn't feel threatened by the emerging science. The library downstairs, which contains more than four thousand volumes, few of them religious in nature, is evidence of that. A long wooden reading table, with two sides slightly tilted like a draftsman's bench, runs down the middle of the room. Here the perfectionists were encouraged to study everything from astronomy to metallurgy.

The geologist Lyell convinced Noyes that the world was much older than six thousand years, and that discovery seemed to soften Noyes's fervent millennialism. Perhaps the kingdom of God would not come as quickly as he had told his followers. Ever since his own conversion to Bible communism, Noyes had convinced himself that he would not die, not before the heavenly kingdom merged with his own social experiment in perfectibility. Yet, as he grew older and more infirm, and as other Oneidans died, he backed off his earlier prophecies. Then he read Darwin's *On the Origin of Species* and decided not that it represented a godless universe but that humans could actually be *bred to achieve spiritual perfection*. It had happened once with the Jews, he reasoned.

Why couldn't Noyes be the St. Paul of evolution, breeding a superior gentile?

Thus Noyes, who had always discouraged pregnancy and advocated male continence at Oneida, now trod boldly into the new world of eugenics. He called his new experiment "stirpiculture," derived from the Latin *stirps*, meaning "stem," or "root." In 1869 he selected fifty-three young women to act as vessels for the so-called stirpicults, and they all signed a statement that "we do not belong to ourselves in any respect, but that we *do* belong first to God, and second to Mr. Noyes as God's true representative." The women were to be paired with men of deep spiritual development so that their offspring would inherit those traits. Sixteen years earlier, Henry David Thoreau, a man who had little in common with Noyes, wrote a letter in which he seemed to affirm both Noyes's amative arguments and his belief in selective breeding. "The only excuse for reproduction is improvement," Thoreau wrote. "Nature abhors repetition. Beasts merely propagate their kind; but the offspring of noble men and women will be superior to themselves, as their aspirations are. By their fruits ye shall know them." To speed this evolution along, Noyes himself sired ten of the fifty-eight children born at Oneida between 1859 and 1879. Pierrepont Noyes was one of the spiritual purebreds. And while most of the stirpicults grew up to be, in the later words of a Johns Hopkins Medical School study, "robust and well built," not many turned out to be modern Zarathustras; they didn't even turn out to be particularly religious. Few attended church as adults, and only one claimed to be a perfectionist.

Did the failure of stirpiculture signify the end of Noyes's grand experiment in Bible communism? Throughout the late 1860s, Noyes was transforming all the journalist A. J. Macdonald's notes into what became the first important document of nineteenth-century utopianism, one I have referred to throughout this trip, *History of American Socialisms*. But where Macdonald perceived one failed community after another, Noyes observed, correctly at the time, that only the utopian communities that were not grounded in religion unraveled; those like his own were almost always a success. They succeeded because they answered to a higher calling than Owen's brotherhood of man, and they were almost always held together by a dynamic leader with some unorthodox interpretation of the New Testament.

When Noyes's health began to fail in the early 1870s, he tried to hand power over to his son Theodore. The only problem was, Theodore had gone away to Yale Medical School and returned to Oneida an agnostic with newfound doubts about his father's divine revelations. Nevertheless, Noyes put Theodore in charge of the community's daily operations while he withdrew to a smaller perfectionist community, in Wallingford, Connecticut. Theodore's tenure proved to be something of a disaster, however, and when his father returned to take back the reins, dissent spread throughout the community. Some newer members, mostly men, no longer believed that Noyes was God's chosen emissary meant to call down the Second Coming. If he were, they reasoned, it would already have happened. They also chafed at the way Noyes ran Oneida like a family monarchy. They wanted a more democratic form of decision making. More important than any of that, though, they wanted to have sex with more virgins. Why did Noyes get to decide who slept with whom? And why should Noyes reserve for himself the right to initiate girls into sexual adulthood? The end of perfectionism, the end of the Oneida Community, lay in the inability to resolve those two questions.

The downfall of John Humphrey Noyes was the same as that of many men before and after: teenage girls. It seems really as simple as that. A faction of Oneidans led by a man named James Towner threatened to bring charges of statutory rape against Noyes. That seems like something of a hollow threat, because what Towner and his followers wanted was the opportunity to perform statutory rape themselves. More threatening to Noyes, however, was a group of fifty-odd clergymen who were meeting at the same time in Syracuse to plan some kind of legal action against the perfectionists. "Testimony is being taken," reported the *Syracuse Standard*, "which stamps the Oneida community as far worse in their practices than the polygamists of Utah."

Around midnight on June 23, 1879, two of Noyes's closest advisers, Otis Kellogg and Myron Kinsley, knocked quietly on his door and implored, "You should go away immediately! Tonight! Tomorrow will be too late. Tomorrow the community, your children, all of us, may be dragged into a publicity that could blight many lives." A few minutes later, Noyes crept down the stairs of the Mansion House in his stocking feet, carrying his boots. Kellogg hitched two horses to a buggy a short distance away. The two men rode thirty miles to the U.S. border, where Noyes caught a ferry across the Saint Lawrence River into Canada. Noyes later said he felt hounded the whole way by "the shadow of a life and perhaps a death in the State Prison." Historians have since pointed out that such threats existed largely in Noyes's mind. The leader of the offended clergy even admitted that he didn't have legal ground for prosecuting the perfectionist leader. Yet to Noyes, the threat was very real, and despite pleading from community members, despite the fact that James Towner soon departed with his own followers for California's free-love frontier, Noyes never returned to Oneida. His millennial dreams were over, his libido was waning, and he no longer had the unquestioning devotion of all perfectionists. So Noyes did what he had always done when faced with failure: he declared it a success. "We made a raid into an unknown country, charted it, and returned without the loss of a man, woman or child," he wrote to the remaining community from Canada. To that, his son Pierrepont replied with uncharacteristic exasperation, "Could anything be more dramatic—a man now in his seventieth year, standing amid the ruins of his lifework, shouting, 'Victory!'?"

With Noyes gone, the three things that held the perfectionists together—complex marriage, communal property, and mutual criticism—quickly came to an end. Acrimonious nightly meetings made mutual criticism redundant. As for complex marriage, the women, particularly the young women of Oneida, were ready to be done with it. They wanted husbands, or rather, *one* husband, and they wanted children that they'd raise themselves. Frank Wayland-Smith wrote to Noyes, "This feeling has taken such a hold that some of us find ourselves practically monogamists, or nearly, perforce." Without Noyes there to reassure reluctant women that polyamory was God's will, men such as Wayland-Smith had no alternative but to seek out the affections of the women with whom they first arrived at Oneida: their actual wives. To nearly everyone's surprise, however, Noyes wrote from Canada to offer his blessing on monogamous marriage. Complex marriage had not been a mistake, he said, but the world was not ready for it, even when restricted to the spiritual laboratory that was Oneida. Therefore, in order not to cause further "offense" to the Comstock crowd, Noyes declared his version of sexual socialism over.

Those who still wished to live as free lovers followed James Towner's westward migration. By the end of 1880, thirty-seven weddings had taken place at the Mansion House. Many of the new couples chose to live there, where walls were knocked down to expand the spartan sleeping quarters and turn them into family apartments. Unfortunately for some, thirty years of complex marriage had made more traditional arrangements awkward or impossible. As one woman wrote, "Our relations are no longer 'complex,' but they are dreadfully complicated." Men and women who had always secretly loved one another were sometimes prevented from marrying because the men felt duty-bound to the mothers of their biological children. Many women had more than one suitor; others had none. There were women, such as Pierrepont Noyes's mother, who couldn't marry the fathers of their children. Noyes's wife, Harriet, was still alive, and anyway, John Humphrey Noyes had sired many children other than Pierrepont. Such single mothers wouldn't fare well in the judgmental world outside Oneida. During the year of the community's disintegration, a child named Earl, whose parents had recently joined Oneida, conferred upon Pierrepont a new sobriquet, "illegitimate." The worldly Earl informed Pierrepont that "while our parents' offense was a thing of the past, we, the improperly born products of the community system, would be continuing reminders of its unforgivable defiance of Victorian morality and as such would suffer the reproach of illegitimacy through all our lives." What's more, the young Pierrepont suddenly realized that Papa Kelly's instructions to resist selfishness and turn the other cheek might not serve him well in the world outside Oneida. If existence is struggle, then Pierrepont, even at age nine, knew he had experienced little of it. He knew he would eventually have to pass from "the green pastures of a protected childhood into that forest of problems wherein all active lives are spent," and he made that passage more successfully perhaps than anyone at Oneida. Many did not. So as to avoid both the world's harsh glances and its acquisitive ways, a number of mothers and their children stayed in or near the safe confines of the Mansion House for many years, sometimes for many generations.

As soon as complex marriage ended, many in the community seemed to look back at those years like the shame-filled Adam and Eve grasping for fig leaves. In 1914, Jessie Kinsley wrote to her adult daughter, "I cannot tell you much about that part of my life in the Community because it is too strange to be understood." Then, perhaps sensing that her silence might be mistaken for guilt or an admission of wrongdoing, she went on to implore her daughter, "Dear Edith, if imagination carries you back into the unusual past that I cannot describe, you must think that religious devotion was a part of it all. In its religion you will find the key to this Community life." Pierrepont remembered that his own mother seemed greatly relieved to hear about John Humphrey Noyes's letter calling an end to complex marriage. Yet she told her son in earnest, "We will never give up communism."

However, communal property would indeed be the last pillar of perfectionism to fall. Once the Oneidans had splintered into traditional families, those families began to want things for themselves and themselves alone. Many years later, the adult Pierrepont Noyes would remember that time and reach the conclusion that Robert Owen and many other utopianists spent their lives both resisting and confirming: "Every serious student of social problems has discovered that possessiveness in sex and family relations makes economic communism unattainable. To put it the other way about, the family, monogamy, is the main support of economic individualism. For the sake of family, millions endure the chaos and misery of our competitive regime." Amid the factional sparring in the Mansion House, much work had gone neglected. The community was quickly drifting toward bankruptcy, and many no longer felt compelled to toil for the good of the whole, as that collective fabric had been torn asunder. Frank Wayland-Smith, who was running the nightly meetings in Noyes's absence, proposed converting the Oneida businesses into a joint-stock model to allow all parties at least to claim their financial interests and then go their own ways. At first, this sounded like heresy to most of the perfectionists; it violated, after all, their founding precept in the second Book of Acts. Again, to the surprise of all, Noyes condoned the change as the most sensible option, given the circumstances. It was then decided that all community property and businesses would be pooled into a new corporation whose shares would be held exclusively by the former perfectionists. (In the end, the only Oneidan who refused to sign on to the plan was Sewell Newhouse, who argued, quite reasonably, it seems to me, that since he'd invented the trap that saved the community, he was entitled to a larger share of the profits; the Newhouse shares were then held in trust until years later, when the old trap maker finally relented and accepted the standard share.) They estimated that their joint property was worth six hundred thousand dollars, which was then divided into twenty-five-dollar shares and distributed among the community based on members' original contributions and their length of time at Oneida. Widows and widowers were provided for, and children were paid one hundred dollars a year until age sixteen, when they would be given a two-hundred-dollar "bonus." In the end, the stock was divided among 226 members and soon-to-be former members. Those who wished to stay at the Mansion House could pay for their room and board at cost. They could retain all the furniture in their rooms up to a thirty-dollar value, and buy more if they chose.

Pierrepont Noyes admitted that such a prospect thrilled his

nine-year-old self. "Thereafter I looked at our bureaus and beds and chairs through new eyes," he wrote; "they would be ours—Mother's and mine." Moreover, the boy would be allowed to live *with* his mother, among their new possessions. A huge auction was held in the Great Hall to mark the end of communal ownership at Oneida. Families bid on all the things that had once been held in common. While it felt scandalous and just plain strange for some Oneidans finally to be handling actual dollars, they soon warmed to the spirit of the auction, and fierce bidding commenced. There was, Pierrepont observed, "a certain novel elation in thus wielding, for the first time, the age-old power of money to buy possessions of things desired." His mother made sure that she had enough money to buy Pierrepont what he once claimed not to covet: the sled.

I return to the Noyes Suite to pack my things. I've been traveling for two weeks now and have one last leg before me: the route John Humphrey Noyes followed when he escaped to Canada. I think (not for the first time, I will admit) of all the pubescent girls Noyes deflowered inside these turreted rooms. One young woman confided in a letter to a friend, "I went to his room and told him I could do one thing, and that was to submit myself to him and look for his spirit to enter into me and fill me." Such a spiritualized initiation into sex absolved the act of shame and brought the transformed girl into the universal family of Bible communism. Or so Noyes told her. Certainly he believed it, and through the cult of his personality he made his followers believe it, too. Or was it all a complicated ruse engineered so Noyes could surround himself with a harem of one hundred willing, if fashion-stunted, females? Perhaps it was that in part, but I can't bring myself to lump Noyes in with a bunker-building dimwit like David Koresh. While both men claimed a direct line to God and both met their demise over charges of statutory rape, Koresh surrounded himself with low-skilled misfits much like him. Noyes's followers were highly skilled and highly intelligent. They didn't arm themselves with illegal weapons; they disarmed their skeptics with straw-berries and cream. They enacted their peculiar version of utopia for three decades, a vision that didn't end in mass murder, but in assimilation. In the end, perhaps, flight was part of Noyes's genius: unlike the dug-in Koresh, his departure freed his followers from further persecution.

As I'm mulling all this over, the phone rings. The voice on the other end belongs to Giles Wayland-Smith, current secretary of the Oneida Community Mansion House board of trustees and direct descendant of John Humphrey Noyes's sister, Harriet Skinner. I'm thrilled when he suggests we talk down in the old dining hall built onto the back of the Mansion House.

Today the dining hall is, like the rest of the building, uncom-fortably hot. At ninety-three thousand square feet, the Mansion House is far too large to air-condition, except for individual rooms; the current board can't afford it. The fact that I'm this weekend's sole visitor suggests that the Mansion House doesn't pull in the tourist traffic of New Harmony or Pleasant Hill. When we shake hands, though, Wayland-Smith, a recently retired soci-ology professor at Allegheny College in Maryland, still seems happy to give me an audience. The spacious hall is almost com-pletely empty except for a sofa, where we take a seat. Wayland-Smith explains that the current residents have pocket kitchens in their rooms, so communal dining was abandoned, again as too expensive, a few years ago. We're sitting in front of a large fire-place where the older residents sometimes gather in the fall and winter for drinks and conversation. Above the hearth hangs a large portrait of the handsome, adult Pierrepont Noyes. After Oneida first became a joint-stock company, business floundered under inept management by older men whom John Humphrey Noyes had appointed. What's more, the trap business was on the decline as the country grew increasingly urban. Pierrepont, after two years of college, returned to Oneida and convinced the com-pany's board that its future was in flatware. By 1926, almost every home in America owned some utensil manufactured by Oneida Ltd. By then, Pierrepont's half-brother Theodore had returned to

Oneida with a degree in architecture, and he built a house for Pierrepont's family, and for eight others, down below the Mansion House where the orchards and gardens once grew.

"P. B. Noyes became the almost regal presence in the community," Wayland-Smith tells me as we gaze up at the painting. He became for the company what his father was to the original community. He appointed Theodore as the city planner of Sherrill, the company town down the road that grew up around the success of Oneida Ltd. Under Theodore's leadership, the company subsidized churches and schools, a golf course and a baseball field. (I watched a few innings of a game there last night.) When a union organizer arrived in 1916, he concluded that the Oneida workers were so well treated that a union would be redundant. Trying to carry on some of his father's socialist teachings, Pierrepont Noyes solicited the governor to make Sherrill an autonomous commune, overseen by his own benevolent hand. Governor Charles Whitman said he'd be goddamned if he was going to allow a commune in New York, but he did designate Sherrill a city—then and now the smallest in the state. Sherrill's schools were excellent, Wayland-Smith says, because Noyes recruited 50 percent of their teachers from the Seven Sisters women's colleges of New England, and he compensated the male workers who were drafted into the First and Second World Wars for losses in pay while they fought.

I ask Wayland-Smith, who grew up "about four hundred yards" from the Mansion House, what his grandparents and great-grandparents told him about life before Oneida Ltd. "They didn't pass on a lot," he confesses; nor did many of the other original perfectionists. "Which is interesting. It wasn't because they were embarrassed by it. In many ways they were very proud of it. But the old phase was behind them, and the new phase was there and was successful, and so they sort of rewrote the narrative. The irony is that the new narrative was a business narrative. They really abandoned ship on the most controversial aspects of the original community."

Yet, Wayland-Smith says, the shift wasn't as dramatic as it

might seem. Pierrepont Noyes was in many ways his father's son, and he tried to translate the spirit of perfectionism into what Wayland-Smith calls "terrestrial possibilities." "In one spiritual sense, the perfectionists were otherworldly," he says, "but then they were absolutely worldly in every other way. They were separate from the community but anchored in it. They were pushing forward the Industrial Revolution, and they were making money hand over fist and had enough money to build this," he says, gesturing all around him. There is no question that the founder knew how to bend his thinking to the times if it meant creating a more amenable environment for his Bible communists. "Perfection was not just something in the abstract," Wayland-Smith maintains. "So it's not a coincidence that early on they had central heating. The good society was also a comfortable, almost bourgeois society." He points to the "very bourgeois-looking" Mansion House as an example of how the perfectionists could at once look completely ordinary from the outside and practice the most radical social and sexual politics in the country within its walls. "You'd never know by looking at this building that there was complex marriage and mutual criticism and all these strange things going on," he says. "It's not Transylvania, surrounded by clouds and mystery. It's right out in the open and it looks like every other well-to-do house in Rochester or Syracuse at the time. And I thinks that's deliberate on their part. They were sensitive to the fact that they lived in a larger community and would only be successful if they could work with that community."

As for what went on within the Mansion House, Wayland-Smith suggests that Noyes's early shyness with women might be responsible, in part, for Bible communism. If Noyes could get what he wanted from women through theology, he didn't have to woo them or, worse, risk rejection. Whatever the libidinal forces behind Noyes's theocracy, his great-grandnephew still maintains, "I'm really a fan of his. To me, what's important is: he got a lot of it right that speaks to us today. Going back to Abraham Maslow, I think the perfectionists had their own early version of self-actualization, of becoming what you're capable of. I think that's an important insight. And education is critical to that. But also a stable and satisfying material life. There was a foundation of well-being here.

"It speaks to us today because another aspect of self-actualization is that each of us has our own capacity, and the community has its own capacity, but everybody is a part of that and is contributing to that. Everybody, then, should share in that well-being. One of the things we're facing today of course is the extraordinary gap between wealth and the people who are just struggling to make ends meet. The thing the perfectionists were insisting upon as a community, and later as a company, is that we're all in this together. We all succeed on the basis of the efforts we are making. During the Great Depression, the top executives at Oneida Ltd. took a thirty-percent cut, and those on the floor only a five percent; exact opposite of the golden parachute you have today. And that's a message that we need."

As for complex marriage, well, Wayland-Smith admits, "No one has adopted it recently, but now we have all kinds of ways of raising families. There's not just nuclear families. What they showed was that it's not so much gay parents or straight parents; what's really important is what kind of love and support is being created in the family. So their very unorthodox family just reinforced something that's a message for us today: that you can put yourself together in a lot of different ways, and it doesn't matter who those component parts are, but rather, what's going on there. So I think they got that right."

As for the community's demise, Wayland-Smith takes a larger, more sociological view than my own reductionist theory of sexual jealousy. "At the time of the community's formation, both at Putney and here, there was still a kind of open-endedness to America," he contends. "The frontier was opening up. There was a kind of social flux. People were moving beyond the Appalachians. And there was still a kind of innocence about the country in many ways. The Civil War killed that. I think the very idea of creating the perfect society no longer had any resonance. You can't lose a million dead and wounded and think that society can be revolutionized in that way. It just didn't take hold. It gets replaced by individual reform movements."

Still, of all the people I've spoken with during my travels, Giles Wayland-Smith is the first who still unapologetically embraces the word *utopia*. He points back to the distinction between the Greek *outopia*, "no place," and *eutopia*, "good place." "Utopia is a no-where, but it's also a good-where," he says. "And I think every utopia poses for society a vision of a better society. That's useful in its own right. I think just having a utopian vision is important because it can make people stop and think about the way they're living or what society looks like and whether there might be ways of making it better. I've always believed that good society is never fully possible, but it's a kind of horizon. It's always a disappearing horizon, but you can see its contours if not its details. You can see images of a better society. It's there, it's real, and it has its own gravitational force. That's where I think a utopian vision really helps." That's why Wayland-Smith still lives part-time in the Mansion House; that's why he serves on its board; that's why he's sitting here talking to me. "Any kind of utopic vision is especially important in terms of identifying the problems with the current society as well as understanding how that can be transcended. I think this community—like the Shakers, like the Owenites, like Twin Oaks—provides that stimulus to self-reflection. That's why it's so important to keep this place going. Hopefully people will think about what part of that earlier vision is translatable into what is needed today."

I think about this as I drive along the southern shoreline of Lake Ontario. And I think about Giles Wayland-Smith's apt horizon metaphor while, out in the distance, the lake's gray swells disappear against dark clouds that erase the actual horizon. In his midnight flight from Oneida, John Humphrey Noyes took the most direct route possible to Canada, due north, then across the Saint Lawrence River. But with no hellhounds on my trail, I'm driving a more leisurely, westerly route that will deposit me at the great falls where Noyes eventually settled and lived until his death on April 13, 1886, nearly seven years after he abandoned Oneida. I wanted, for one last day, to drive alongside a body of water, and thanks to the atrocious conditions of this potholed state road, I'm driving it almost alone.

When my teeth have about rattled out of my head, I veer south through a countryside of Amish farms. These aren't the corn monocultures of Indiana and Ohio, but rather, family farms, each with a wooden fruit stand built near the road to sell pints of cherries and apples. When I get closer to the small towns, it seems that every third house is operating some cottage industry: alpacas, split wood, grain stoves, hayrides. Then, all of a sudden, I find myself teetering in a vertiginous state on a winding road high above the Niagara River. The behemoth Robert Moses Niagara Power Plant, built on land taken from the Tuscarora tribe, blocks out the entire horizon. I pass over the dam and am soon sitting in traffic on a steel arch bridge that spans the plunging river gorge.

When I finally reach the checkpoint, a rather severe-looking border guard, her long hair pulled back into a ponytail, demands to know my license plate number. I am always helpless before authority figures in uniforms, before people who could potentially incarcerate me—who have in the past incarcerated me, multiple times—and I begin to stammer. I don't know my license plate number.

"It's on your registration," she says. "Don't get out of the vehicle."

I fumble in the glove box for my registration. It's in here somewhere with the bottle openers, broken sunglasses, and unpaid parking tickets.

"That's it, right there," she says. "Read it to me."

"Three-six-zero-DTD. Kentucky."

"What's your business at Niagara Falls?"

"I'm writing a book."

"What's it about?"

Here, for the sake of simplicity, I go for the quick lie: "Niagara Falls."

"How long are you staying?"

"A few days."

"Where's your wife?"

"I'm sorry?"

"Your wife. Where is she?"

Having been married only a short time, I'm suddenly bamboozled by the fact that this stranger has somehow heard about my marriage to Melissa. Or else she's psychic. Do all border guards possess the ability to suss out one's marital status? Have they honed the soul-searching ability to read one's true, perhaps nefarious, intentions for visiting Niagara Falls? Then the obvious finally occurs to me: I'm wearing a wedding ring. Highly visible. Right up there on the hand clutching the steering wheel.

"She's back home," I say.

"Why didn't you bring her?" Am I really being accused, already, of being a bad husband? Am I being hit on? Or, more likely, is the poor, bored woman simply trying to amuse herself at my expense. "She could have had a little vacation while you worked on your book," the guard explains helpfully.

"You make a good point."

"I think she deserves it," the woman adds, then points to a cardboard box that holds all my CDs for the trip and that once contained a small kitchen appliance that was, in fact, a gift from my wife. "I see your little Pampered Chef box there. I can tell you're taken care of."

I decide that my best option for ever getting across the border is simply to stare mutely at this woman. Seeming to sense this, she finally smiles and motions me through.

What If?

I had expected to stare across Niagara Falls at a gaudy pile of tourist restaurants, wax museums, and casinos on the American side, but in fact, that's what I find here in Canada, where kitsch clings to the Falls like barnacles. Still, I take up a position among a throng of posing tourists and gaze out at the raging cataract. As someone who has at times earned a marginal living as a "nature writer," I know I should be more impressed than I am. Hundreds of millions of gallons of water plunge every minute over a 176-foot precipice—one-fifth of the world's freshwater. That's impressive. Yet the fact that so many other people have been equally impressed before me and alongside me makes my own experience feel somehow less impressive. It's like in Don DeLillo's novel *White Noise*, when the narrator, Jack Gladney, and his university colleague Murray drive outside their anonymous college town to gaze upon what is reputed to be "the most photographed barn in America." Standing among a throng of shutterbugs, Murray finally says to Jack, "No one sees the barn." All anyone can see after so many photographs is the image of the barn, not the thing itself. That's how I feel standing before Niagara Falls. I see it and I don't see it. It won't come into focus.

Anyway, I didn't come here to look at the Falls; I came to look for Stone Cottage, the home where John Humphrey Noyes spent the last years of his life. Seven months after Noyes fled for Canada, the community back at Oneida voted unanimously to buy their former leader a Gothic-style cottage at Niagara, one with a view of both the American and the Canadian Falls. He was also given a horse and carriage, along with a $150-a-month expense account. Many of his loyalists eventually moved to Niagara to be near him, and Oneida Ltd. set up a silverware factory here so they would have work. Harriet Noyes, who outlived her husband by a decade, moved with him to Stone Cottage. "She had been more a disciple than a lover when she married my father in 1838," wrote Pierrepont Noyes, "and she remained his unfaltering disciple to the end." As did Noyes's sister Harriet Skinner and several of his biological children, who all moved to Niagara. Pierrepont spent a long visit there in 1886, though he seemed slightly wounded to be the last of Noyes's children invited. (He was suspected of possessing an entrepreneurial spirit, which he did, and which allowed all his elders to live very comfortable lives up until the end.) Pierrepont remembered that Noyes still delivered "Home Talks" in the evenings at the cottage, though they were much more informal than those back at Oneida, and the founder was by then stone deaf. He would stroll the three-sided veranda by day, gazing out at the Falls and, his son suspected, "thinking great thoughts." At Niagara, Pierrepont tried to decide whether his father was a religious fanatic or a man ahead of his time. "I think I concluded, if I actually reached any conclusion, that it was a little of both."

Unfortunately, Stone Cottage is long gone by now, replaced by Planet Hollywood, the Niagara SkyWheel, and suicide hotline phones scattered all along the Falls. The closest thing I find to Stone Cottage is a hotel called the Old Stone Inn. Its core is an old flour mill built in 1904, which functions now as a restaurant that, according to photos on the wall, has been patronized by several Canadian prime ministers. Rows of rooms were added on in the 1970s with no apparent concern for complementing the mill's original architecture. My own room overlooks a rather bleak scene of liquor stores and alleys filled with trash, so I quickly abandon it for the bar nestled inside the original stone mill. As at Oneida, I seem to be the only person here. One waitress also seems to be the only server. I wait for her at the empty bar for some time, looking back over all the notes I've scribbled during the last two weeks. Soon, without quite realizing it, I've taken over the bar with various piles of paper.

"What have we here?" says the waitress when she finally appears.

I briefly tell her the story of John Humphrey Noyes's escape to Niagara Falls.

"You drove all the way here to look for a building you knew didn't exist?"

I admit that's one way to look at it.

"And this is the closest thing you could find, this place?"

I say that's right.

"You poor man. I think that deserves a drink on the house."

I intrepidly order a double martini, figuring I might not see my server again for a while. She sets the drink in front of me and says to just come on into the dining room when I'm finished if I want to try the chef's much-heralded prime rib.

I take a big sip, crunch down on a pearl onion, and toast myself for having reached the end of this utopian sojourn. I feel at once triumphal and homesick. In the beginning, I had planned to linger here in Canada for several days, rest up, and see the sights. But now all I really want to do is jump on I-90 and make the long, fast plunge down through Cleveland, Columbus, Cincinnati, and then home to Melissa and Nonesuch. Unlike Henry David Thoreau, I managed in the middle of my life to find what I was always after: a solitary country life and a woman to share it with. I'm lucky, and for one of the rare times in my life, I can see that clearly.

I realize of course why Robert Owen, Mother Ann Lee, and the rest saw marriage as such an impediment to their utopian vision. The biological family meant the death of communal life, the end of sharing. The Shakers shared work and property, the perfectionists shared one another. Plus, marriage laws were diabolically unfair to nineteenth-century women. The institution had to go. Now most of those laws have been expunged from the books, and as with the end of Oneida, people still seem too pulled by biology to accept for long any real redefinitions of the nuclear family. For better or worse, evolution decided long ago that the best way for the species *Homo sapiens* to get its genes into the next generation is through one or two very attentive parents who have eighteen years to devote to the task. Still, as Giles Wayland-Smith told me back at Oneida, we have developed many expansive definitions of family that go beyond mere biology, even if the size of the immediate family hasn't changed that much. Much of this has to do with the fight for ongoing equal rights, obviously, and that *was* a very consistent utopian theme. In the 1800s, there were simply no other groups or organizations that extended equal rights to women, or to African Americans, as did the utopian communities.

What were their other successes, the other things we can still learn from these radical experiments in idealism? I flip again through my notes as the gin turns my mood expansive and once more full of affection for these unlikely dreamers. "How should people live?" That was their question, over and over. They enacted communities almost completely without violence, and therefore without jails. They rejected a financial system that treated money as anything other than a substitute for genuine wealth, and therefore they had no banks. That is to say, there was no physical or financial exploitation within what Josiah Warren accurately called these equity villages. Their inhabitants believed in the nobility of work because they believed that actual labor should be the only measure of value. They welcomed the poor and the homeless into their circles, assuming such men and women were willing to work alongside them. They were principally agrarian communities that acted with great care and stewardship toward the land they tended. They manufactured almost all of what they needed, and that self-sufficiency protected them, for the most part, from both the volatility of constant financial panics and the often cruel conditions of the nineteenth-century mill or factory. They kept their communities small enough to ensure accountability among the members. The religious communities realized to an astonishing degree the tenet of the earliest church: that all things should be held in common to ensure a true brotherhood of believers. In that, I would argue, they showed mainstream American Christians a far more elemental and more genuine version of the country's dominant religion—one based on cooperative sharing in this world, not the individual's salvation after death. Many of them contended that the laws of the heart and the laws of nature were synonymous with the laws of God. One could understand the natural world as a spiritual world and, in doing so, find a more authentic experience there, one that transcended the world of commerce and self-interest. The ideas and ideals of these daring people replaced a culture that seemed increasingly shallow, corporate, and corrupt. And yet—and yet—we are still so often quick to say that these communities failed. Indeed, as a culture, we need them to fail because that failure affirms the inevitability of the dominant economy, with its attendant violence, inequality, and injustice.

Yet the Shakers lasted one hundred years at Pleasant Hill; the perfectionists turned a completely successful experiment in socialism into a wildly successful joint-stock company; Modern Times gave up equitable commerce only after proving that it worked. To say that these communities no longer exist—and as Twin Oaks proves, many of them still do exist—is not the same thing as saying that they failed. The angel of history may yet salvage their blueprints from the detritus of the past. Because, after all, we still *need* these ideas so badly. In fact, we need them now more than ever before. During my utopian summer, the western ice sheet of Antarctica began breaking off into the ocean, which will cause sea levels to rise far more than scientists had predicted. Back in my hemisphere, the American Congress passed fifteen bills into law—total. Five percent of Americans continue to control 85 percent of this country's wealth, and since 1980, the wealthiest Americans have seen their incomes quadruple, while those of the poor and middle class have flatlined. The more this inequality grows, the sicker and more punitive our country becomes. The epidemiologists Richard Wilkinson and Kate Pickett have recently shown that every single societal problem, *with no exception*, can be tied directly to income inequality. As a result, the United States has higher levels of mental illness, infant mortality, divorce, obesity, violence, incarceration, and substance abuse than all other countries north of the equator. "In more unequal societies," they wrote, "people are five times as likely to be imprisoned, six times as likely to be clinically obese, and murder rates may be many times higher." Consider these two statistics: the United States makes up 5 percent of the world's population, but we consume 25 percent of its resources and we incarcerate 25 percent of its population. I don't believe those numbers are a coincidence. Almost all the wealth from extracting those resources, those fossil fuels, goes to the very richest, and the very poorest end up in jail because either they can't get by or they find illicit ways to get by or simply cope. Money that might go into education or even food stamps goes instead into the penal system. Money that might fund badly needed American infrastructure instead funds 761 military bases all over the world. Money that might be loaned by a community bank is placed as a Wall Street bet that a bond will default. Money that might reward real work circulates instead inside that same echo chamber of less and less tangible securities. Wealth becomes less accessible to most Americans, while the wealthy themselves use their power to ensure that politicians do their bidding, mostly in the form of lowering their tax rates and deregulating the industries they control. Large corporations shell out $6 billion annually to employ thirty-five thousand D.C. lobbyists to protect their wealth. Such game rigging has bred cynicism and pessimism among the body politic, and as a result, we have the lowest voter turnout of the world's forty industrial democracies. The more we retreat from, or are pushed from, the public sphere of influence, the more we lose trust in our public institutions and in one another. According to the National Opinion Research Center, levels of trust in the United States have fallen from 60 percent in 1960 to less than 40 percent in 2004. Into that vacuum, the imperious One Percent pours more money and accrues more power. That decline in trust has paralleled a widening income gap in the United States—currently the largest of any country in the Northern Hemisphere and the largest in this country's history, according to the 2009 census. When trust weakens and economic inequality widens, an epidemic of social maladies follows. What it all adds up to, said the Supreme Court justice Louis Brandeis, is this: "We may have democracy, or we may have wealth concentrated in the hands of the few, but we can't have both."

We obviously have the latter in this country, and I've come to believe that things will only get worse if we *don't* engage in some serious utopian thinking. Fighting for something like campaign finance reform is laudable, but that isn't what I consider utopian thinking because it is an effort to fix a plutocratic system that doesn't *deserve* to be salvaged. It isn't enough. Utopian thinking, by contrast and by definition, works *outside* the system, in a bottom-up fashion, to create a new paradigm and thus create a true form of democracy that is worthy of its name. In my view, such thinking must begin by addressing this country's most intractable problems, namely, our gross disparity in wealth and a fossil fuel–based economy that is completely unsustainable in the face of climate change, resource depletion, and the degradation of our ecosystems.

Because of those two realities, we live in a seriously *dystopic* country, one where both the political and the economic systems are failing us in very fundamental ways. Right beneath the surface of the utopia of consumerism lurks an ugliness and a darkness we are doing our best to ignore. According to a recent Gallup study, of all 436 congressional districts, the most dystopic place of all is the Third District of West Virginia, the one I drove through ten days ago. It is the poorest place in the country, and it is the sickest, in terms of both mental and physical health. There along the Coal River, strip mine operators have amassed incredible wealth while externalizing the true costs of coal mining onto the land and the people in the form of poisoned streams, toxic air, flash floods, shaky ground, and a deadly workplace. In other words, they have shared, or externalized, the illth while internalizing all the wealth. Recent studies published by the Institute for Health Policy Research at the University of West Virginia show that men and women living in heavy coal mining areas are far more likely to die prematurely of heart, respiratory, and kidney disease, and that birth defects occur in communities near strip mines at a rate 42 percent higher than in places without strip mining. That's what a dystopia looks like in the United States.

What would the utopian alternative look like? After those twenty-nine Upper Big Branch miners were killed in West Virginia in 2010, I drove up to Cleveland, Ohio, to find out. In the hard-worn neighborhood of Glenville, I found just the opposite of a shareholder-owned coal mine: a worker-owned business that installs solar panels throughout the city. Started in 2009, Ohio Cooperative Solar employs twenty-one men and women, mostly from Cleveland's lower-income neighborhoods. But Ohio Cooperative Solar isn't a welfare experiment; it's a business, one that was turning a profit five months after launching.

Actually, Ohio Cooperative Solar is part of a larger network of worker-owned businesses in Cleveland called the Evergreen Cooperative. It began five years ago when the new CEOs of Cleveland Clinic, Case Western Reserve University, and University Hospitals—all located within a one-mile radius of what's known as Greater University Circle—started giving some serious thought to the eight square miles of shuttered businesses and derelict homes in the neighborhoods that surround their institutions. At the peak of the manufacturing boom in the 1950s, Cleveland was the fifth-largest city in the country; today it is the fifth-poorest, and those well-paying manufacturing jobs are long gone. So the CEOs formulated a new strategy: if their individual "anchor institutions" purchased $3 billion worth of goods and services a year, why not redirect some of that purchasing toward a local economy that would employ men and women from the surrounding neighborhoods? If only 10 percent of that $3 billion was redirected locally, that would inject $300 million into an area with over 25 percent unemployment.

The philanthropic Cleveland Foundation ponied up $3 million in seed money, the institutions each added $250,000, and the Evergreen Cooperative was born. The primary goal was to create good, environmentally sustainable jobs that would not be outsourced. Since the Cleveland Clinic and University Hospitals weren't going anywhere, and since hospitals generate a lot of dirty sheets and towels, the Evergreen Laundry set up shop in October 2009 as the pilot business. Today the laundry, which uses energy-efficient washers and dryers, is housed in a modest one-story LEED-certified building beside Ohio Cooperative Solar. There are three frescoes painted on the side of the building that faces the street; at the top of each painting are the words PEOPLE PLANET PROFITS. That is the succinct philosophy of the Evergreen Cooperative, and it suggests how this new model breaks down the usual socialist-capitalist antipathy. The laundry employs fifty men and women who clean twelve million pounds of linens a year and who will eventually own 100 percent of the company. So are they socialists who own the means of production or capitalists who own their own company? The answer, I suppose, is that they represent a new economic model that can't easily be squeezed into such narrow dichotomies. They have solid jobs and are accumulating wealth, and they are doing so in a way that harkens back to Robert Owen's original vision of a unity village where labor was the only true measure of wealth.

The basic economic logic of any Evergreen Cooperative is to say to the anchor institutions, "What can we put together that you will buy?" The answer tends to fall along three lines: waste streams, food streams, and energy streams—goods and services that cannot be easily outsourced. So Ohio Cooperative Solar formed soon after the laundry with the goal of providing thirty installations of 100 kilowatt solar panels for hospitals, schools, and municipal buildings across Cleveland. In 2009 the Ohio legislature mandated that, by 2012, 60 megawatts of the state's energy use be solar-generated. But because most of these anchor institutions are nonprofits, they cannot benefit from the federal government's 30 percent kickback to businesses that invest in alternative energy. So, instead, Ohio Cooperative Solar recently installed a 100 kilowatt unit on the roof of the Cleveland Clinic, which will "rent" the panels and pay twelve cents per kilowatt hour for the energy they generate—comparable to the rate it pays for electricity from the grid. The co-op plans thirty more 100 kilowatt installations over the next three years—which is to say, the employees could soon find themselves the owners of the largest solar energy company in the Midwest.

When I pulled up behind the company's four-story warehouse, the office manager, Loretta Bey, met me at the loading dock and offered to show me around while I waited for the CEO, Steve Kiel. We wandered among stacks of shipping pallets loaded with solar panels, and Bey explained the basic operation of a large wet-spray unit used to blow insulation into leaky walls. (When Cleveland's inclement weather prevents installing solar panels, Ohio Cooperative Solar performs a variety of weatherization services to homes and schools.) We stopped at Bey's small, unair-conditioned office, filled with photos of her family. I asked what she thought of the company.

"This is the best job I've ever had, by far," she said. "I feel like I'm part of this company versus just working for it."

While about eleven thousand companies in the United States offer some form of employee stock ownership, many of these don't involve real decision making on the part of employees. But when making decisions for the company, Ohio Cooperative Solar operates on a one-worker, one-vote model for everyone, from the CEO to the newest hire. They all gather at 7:30 on Monday mornings to discuss company business.

"It's like we're part of the board," Bey told me. "We don't look at Steve [Kiel] as a superior. He's equivalent to us." And compared with your typical American CEO, he's paid accordingly. The company's bylaws stipulate that the difference between the highest- and lowest-paid member of the cooperative can never exceed a ratio of five to one. (The average American CEO makes three hundred times more than the average employee.) If a new employee is making $10 an hour and $21,000 a year, the CEO cannot make more than $100,000.

After a six-month apprenticeship period, Ohio Cooperative Solar employees can apply to join the broader Evergreen Cooperative. If voted in, they receive a two-dollar raise and begin buying into the company through a payroll deduction of $0.50 an hour. Over three years, this adds up to $3,000, an ownership stake that, based on the co-op's projections, should be worth $65,000 in nine years. (Median household income in the neighborhood is $18,000.) Still, Bey told me, "Being an owner is nice, but it isn't the most important thing. We're a team, and for a team to win, it has to be profitable. So everybody has to do the best they can to help the team. That's what makes it work."

Later I spoke with one of the crew leaders, Mike McKenzie, who echoed Bey's sentiments. "You feel like it's part of your own," he said of the cooperative, "so you take it a lot more seriously. People work better together because of the common goal of being more efficient and making the company more profitable. You share in the profits and you have some say in the direction of the company."

If that sounds like too much syndicalist thinking for most Americans to handle, rest assured that when the company CEO, Steve Kiel, showed up in basic businessman attire, he looked like the last person ready to lead a revolution. Kiel talked with Bey about some invoices that needed her attention, and then he and I walked up to his office, on the top floor of the warehouse. I told him about the twenty-nine dead miners in West Virginia and asked if he thought the Evergreen Cooperative model could be applied to coal mining.

He responded by bringing up another mountainous region, one in the Basque area of Spain, and a town called Mondragón. Like Appalachia, the Basque region is set off from the rest of the country both by geographical boundaries and by a distinct cultural identity that, in some ways, grew out of that isolation. During the Spanish Civil War, the Basques sided with the Republic, which promised them regional autonomy. In 1937, Franco rained down retribution on their capital, Guernica, and took as prisoner a young Catholic priest named Don José María Arizmendiarrieta. After the war, Don José María was appointed the parish priest of Mondragón, where he preached a social gospel of collective responsibility rather than individual salvation. Inspired by Don José María, five Mondragón men established Spain's first worker-owned company, called Ulgor, in 1955. Like Ohio Cooperative Solar, Ulgor started with just a handful of workers. Its original constitution and bylaws stated that there would be no outside shareholders; all business decisions would be made by the workers, with equal voting rights; and all profits were shared equally and placed into each worker's capital account. While Don José María never developed any systematic or ideological framework for the Mondragón cooperatives, he said this of his spiritual and social vision: "Cooperativism seeks to create a new state of conscience, of culture in a word, through the humanization of power through democracy in economic affairs, and through solidarity, which impedes the formation of privileged classes." Today, Mondragón is home to 120 cooperatives that employ 100,000 worker-owners. Its largest co-op, Fagor, earns $14 billion annually making electrical equipment and appliances.

Kiel has traveled to Mondragón twice with other members of the Evergreen Cooperative, and they are leaning hard on that model for guidance and inspiration. Echoing Don José María, who said, "The economic renewal will be moral or it will not exist," Kiel believes that "if you can collectively and cooperatively enter into an industry that is run for profit but practices some morals in that—community-based morals—you don't have to take everything and put it in the pocket of the highest producer." Instead, those concentrations of wealth are distributed more fairly to the men and women who, after all, earned it.

As CEO of Massey, Don Blankenship did not dig an ounce of coal—nor did most of his shareholders—but in his last year at the company Blankenship walked away with $17.8 million and a deferred compensation package valued at $27.2 million. According to Kiel, Ohio Cooperative Solar's approach is a little different: "What we're looking to say is, let's create an approach to economic development that is based on worker ownership of the means of production. And let's reward the workers, not shareholders in New Jersey, but people who work right here; let's reward the fruit of their labor." To that end, Ohio Cooperative Solar has developed a profit-distribution model that breaks down into thirds: one-third is based on a worker's wages, one-third on total hours worked in a year, and one-third on overall tenure with the company. It's a formula that seeks to reward commitment to the co-op and to the community.

"The deal we make with employees is that this is not an overnight ATM machine," Kiel said. "You're going to have to work here eight to ten years before you see the benefits of ownership. What we get in return as a community is people living in these neighborhoods for long periods of time with long-term job security, and that leads to the entire community stabilization we're looking for." What's more, when the workers are the stakeholders, long-term thinking about what's best for the company replaces the short-term, profit-driven motives of today's average shareholder.

When I spoke with him, Kiel was working on a dozen or so ideas for new cooperatives. He was running projections to see how many people each potential co-op could hire. "Most capitalists have a return-on-investment threshold," Kiel said. "Typically a venture capitalist firm is going to put up a million dollars up front and will look to get an annual return of seventy percent. We don't have that capitalist on board, so we have a different measure, which is how many people can we hire." So Ohio Cooperative Solar has a different kind of bottom line with a different definition of wealth. Under this model, wealth means good pay, health benefits, a democratic workplace, an equity stake for every worker, and jobs that don't get outsourced but do reduce the country's carbon footprint.

That is to say that this small company offers a model for solving, or at least beginning to solve, the problems of income inequality and unsustainability. One can easily imagine translating the Cleveland model to Boone County, West Virginia, where, as in Cleveland, there is high unemployment and a lot of poor people. And, as in Cleveland, there are anchor institutions (hospitals, community colleges, government centers, even prisons) that could shift their service needs to local, worker-owned businesses. The Cleveland model is obviously just one example of what I would call the serious utopian thinking, the radical reimagining, that we need to truly recalibrate the dystopic direction of this country, to begin pushing in the direction of solidarity and reconstruction. Yet by combining just two ideas from this book, the ideas of worker ownership and a local currency, one can begin to get an image (however sketchy a horizon image) of what a modern *eutopia* (a good place, a better place) would look like. Every successful American utopia from Pleasant Hill to Twin Oaks was a decentralized experiment where a very self-reliant community provided for as much of its own sustenance as possible. Any market economy *has to be* small and locally focused to avoid the abuses of the shareholder logic that says the only real value is profit. By producing first the things it needs, and importing after that only what it cannot produce, a community retains much longer the wealth it generates. In doing so, it also better defends against predatory corporations that feel no responsibility to the community, or to protecting its land, air, and water. Such an economy would subvert and decentralize the power of large corporate polluters such as Massey and Duke Energy while it shortens supply lines and therefore both produces and consumes less fossil fuel.

The American economist Kenneth Boulding once remarked, "Anyone who believes that exponential growth can go on forever is either a madman or an economist." To move away from the idea of exponential growth will obviously mean moving away from a manufacturing economy. (The United States has lost five million manufacturing jobs since 2000 anyway, and there's little sign of their returning.) More than that, though, it will mean finding new ways to define growth. That supposedly inviolable economic concept will have to be decoupled, as economists say, from the production of an endless supply of goods to mean, instead, rewarding human *activity* that doesn't rely on fossil fuels. The manufacturing that does remain will have to shift from resource-intensive industries to those that will both profit from and support a sustainable economy—industries built around public transportation, redesigned and retrofitted cities and buildings, and the production and delivery of renewable energy. Beyond that, our utopian past suggests that we should replace our current culture of accumulation with a needs-and-services economy that actually delivers on the promise of well-being instead of hocking flimsy substitutes made in China and Bangladesh. Our consumption of material goods tends to happen in isolation and tends to reinforce the competitive sense that what I have is better than what you have. Such a psychology and such an economy create an endless negative feedback loop in which we keep consuming to the detriment of the natural world, and toward no enduring sense of real satisfaction with ourselves or others. Studies have shown that though we consume twice as much as we did in the 1970s, our sense of happiness hasn't moved up an inch. Add to that Wilkinson and Pickett's research, which shows that weak community life is linked to increased consumption and, conversely, that greater equality lessens our pressure to consume. This country's gross domestic product, the sole measure of our economic success, has risen 80 percent since then, yet psychologists and sociologists can find little evidence that we are any more content than we were four decades ago. In fact, since 1970, the United States' Index of Social Health, a seventeen-indicator measurement that combines data on suicide rates, income inequality, and life expectancy, has fallen 45 percent. A graph that measures these two trends, GDP and social health, looks like a ski slope, with social health measured on the downhill run, while GDP rises like a chairlift. If GDP *were* a reliable indicator of well-being, we would be in a world of hurt, given that Americans consume five times more resources than the planet can sustain. Yet a mounting body of research has begun to show how the economy that destroys the natural world is really not the economy we truly desire, and for one reason: it doesn't deliver on what Aristotle called *eudaemonia*, or "well-being." Instead, well-being derives from what the political psychologist Robert Lane calls "warm interpersonal relations," "easy-to-reach neighbors," "encircling, inclusive memberships," and "solid family life."

An economy based on more authentic needs and services (good local food, good restaurants, good schools, good health care, good live entertainment, sustainable design, and clean energy) would, I believe, speak to a truer sense of well-being while simultaneously making our communities much less dependent on resource extraction. What's more, an economy based on human capital (labor, talent, conscientiousness) instead of natural capital (fossil fuels) and financial capital (debt) would go a long way toward increasing a sense of trust and conviviality within communities. Social capital would circulate alongside a local currency, and the local currency would help maintain the circulation of local goods and services. Thus a positive feedback loop would replace the negative loop I've just mentioned. And here's another positive feedback loop: the more we trust others, the more of the hormone oxytocin we produce in the brain; and the more oxytocin we produce, the more we trust others. In short, an economy of pleasure and purpose would replace an economy of accumulation and waste.

How can we place an actual scaffolding beneath such airy castles? I'm certainly not advocating a return to the isolationist utopian communes of the nineteenth century. I am, however, advocating for a new kind of economy that adopts or adapts many of their principles in the name of stronger communities and a stable environment in which those communities can exist. Because in this country what we need to do and what we're willing to do politically are such vastly different things, we *need* utopian thinking that can mine those gaps and offer a model for another way forward. One of the more inspiring aspects of such thinking is that we don't have to wait for quiescent politicians to act or for corporations to find a moral compass. We can work between the cracks of these vastly compromised institutions until the cracks grow so large that the institutions crumble out of irrelevance. Given that Wall Street banks have pretty much abandoned the traditional role of banking (making loans that benefit individuals and communities), why not create local, no-interest loan programs like the one Susan Witt spoke of back in the Berkshires? Why not create some version of a local currency? Why not start a Local Exchange Trading System where members of a community, often lower-income or no-income members, withdraw services they need (from home health care to tutoring) and deposit in exchange the talents and services they themselves can provide? Why not create larger credit-clearing exchanges that, if taken to their logical extreme, would eliminate the most destructive elements of modern banking? Speaking of a credit commons, why not work to take back the other commons (seeds, forests, rivers, alternative energy, public spaces, the broadcast spectrum, the atmosphere) through trusts that carefully manage resources and distribute any income from those resources through dividends paid to every stakeholder involved, not just stockholders of some distant corporation? Why not return wealth instead of illth to the commons? Why not establish land trusts that would prevent such speculative disasters as real estate bubbles and that would allow egalitarian access to the natural riches that human beings, after all, did not create and therefore should not enclose? Why not fight the problems of unemployment and climate change by setting up worker-owned businesses that service the anchor institutions of every city in the country? Why not reject the damages of oil-based agriculture and join the Community Supported Agriculture movement, in which subscribers buy directly, and eat seasonally, from a local farm?

That's by no means a comprehensive list of questions, but imagine how different this country would look if even a fraction of Americans took such questions seriously and acted on them. Of course all these ideas sound—I'll say it one last time—utopian. Yet the only thing that prevents us from acting upon any of them is our own lassitude, our prevailing sense that nothing important can be done to change the current state of things. That, of course, is exactly what the very few who buy and wield power in this country want us to believe. To succumb to that lassitude is to admit defeat and await the rising floodwaters. The only force that can overcome such lethargy is the engine of the imagination. Nothing fires the individual and collective spirit like the possibility of a more welcoming collective future and a more authentic personal present. We can head out today toward the utopia of reconstruction. We can build the road as we travel.

Notes
Acknowledgments

Notes

GENERAL SOURCES

George B. Lockwood, *The New Harmony Movement* (New York: D. Appleton, 1905); Donald E. Pitzer, ed., *America's Communal Utopias* (Chapel Hill: University of North Carolina Press, 1997); Daniel Walker Howe, *What Hath God Wrought: The Transformation of America, 1815–1848* (New York: Oxford University Press, 2007); John Humphrey Noyes, *History of American Socialisms* (New York: Hillary House, 1961); Ian Tod and Michael Wheeler, *Utopia* (London: Orbis, 1978); Lewis Mumford, *The Story of Utopias* (New York: Boni and Liveright, 1922); Eunice Minette Schuster, *Native American Anarchism: A Study of Left-Wing American Individualism*, Smith College Studies in History (Northampton, MA: Smith College Studies in History, 1912); Charles Nordhoff, *American Utopias*, American Classics Series (Great Barrington, MA: Berkshire House, 1993); Ernst Bloch, tr. Jack Zipes and Frank Mecklenburg, *The Utopian Function of Art and Literature: Selected Essays* (Cambridge, MA: MIT, 1988).

THE NEW CREATION

Thomas D. Clark and F. Gerald Ham, *Pleasant Hill and Its Shakers* (Pleasant Hill, KY: Pleasant Hill Press, 1968); Michael Leccese and Kathleen McCormick, eds., *Charter of the New Urbanism* (New York: McGraw-Hill, 2000); Theodore E. Johnson, *Life in the Christ Spirit: Observations on Shaker Theology* (Sabbathday Lake, ME: United Society, 1969); Robley Edward Whitson, ed., *The Shakers: Two Centuries of Spiritual Reflection* (Mahwah, NJ: Paulist Press, 1983); Thomas D. Clark, *Pleasant Hill in the Civil War* (Pleasant Hill, KY: Pleasant Hill Press, 1972);

William S. Byrd, *Letters from a Young Shaker: William S. Byrd at Pleasant Hill* (Lexington: University Press of Kentucky, 1985); Edward Deming Andrews, *The People Called Shakers* (Oxford, UK: Oxford University Press, 1963); Edward Deming Andrews, *The Gift to Be Simple: Songs, Dances, and Rituals of the American Shakers* (Locust Valley, NY: J. J. Augustin, 1940); Stephen J. Stein, *The Shaker Experience in America* (New Haven, CT: Yale University Press, 1992); Clay Lancaster, *Pleasant Hill: Shaker Canaan in Kentucky, an Architectural and Social Study* (Warwick, UK: Warwick Publications, 2001).

MONK'S POND
Thomas Merton, *Conjectures of a Guilty Bystander* (New York: Doubleday, 1965); Thomas Merton, *Zen and the Birds of Appetite* (New York: New Directions, 1968); Brother Patrick Hart and Jonathan Montaldo, eds., *The Intimate Merton: His Life from His Journals* (New York: HarperSanFrancisco, 1999); Michael Mott, *The Seven Mountains of Thomas Merton* (Boston, MA: Houghton Mifflin, 1985); Guy Davenport, *The Hunter Gracchus and Other Papers on Literature and Art* (Berkeley, CA: Counterpoint, 1996).

A BEAUTIFUL FAILURE
Robert Owen, *A New View of Society and Other Writings* (New York: Penguin, 1991); Leonard Warren, *Maclure of New Harmony: Scientist, Progressive Educator, Radical Philanthropist* (Bloomington: Indiana University Press, 2009); Frank Podmore, *Robert Owen: A Biography* (Honolulu, HI: University Press of the Pacific, 2004); George B. Lockwood, *The New Harmony Movement* (New York: D. Appleton, 1905); Celia Morris Eckhardt, *Fanny Wright: Rebel in America* (Champaign: University of Illinois, 1992); Leonard Warren, *Constantine Samuel Rafinesque: A Voice in the American Wilderness* (Lexington: University Press of Kentucky, 2004); Richard Rhodes, *John James Audubon: The Making of an American* (New York: Alfred A. Knopf, 2004); Arthur Bestor, *Backwoods Utopias: The Sectarian Origins and the Owenite Phase of Communitarian Socialism in America, 1663–1829* (Washington, DC: American Historical Association, 1950); F. Forrester Church, ed., *The Essential Tillich: An Anthology of the Writings of Paul Tillich* (Chicago, IL: University of Chicago Press, 1987); Charles Jencks, *Modern Movements in Architecture* (New York: Doubleday, 1973).

A SIMPLE ACT OF MORAL COMMERCE
Crispin Sartwell, ed., *The Practical Anarchist: Writings of Josiah Warren* (New York: Fordham University Press, 2011); Roger Wunderlich, *Low Living and High Thinking at Modern Times, New York* (Syracuse, NY: Syracuse University Press, 1992); Carl J. Guarneri, *The Utopian Alternative: Fourierism in Nineteenth-Century America* (Ithaca, NY: Cornell University Press, 1991); James J. Martin, *Men Against the State* (Colorado Springs: Adrian Allen, 1953); Octavio Paz, *Convergences: Essays on Art and Literature* (New York: Harcourt Brace Jovanovich, 1987); Andrew Kimbrell, ed., *The Fatal Harvest Reader: The Tragedy of Industrial Agriculture*

(Washington, DC: Island Press, 2002); Alexander Bryan Johnson, *A Treatise on Language* (Berkeley: University of California Press, 1947); Jonathan Beecher and Richard Bienvenu, eds., *The Utopian Vision of Charles Fourier* (Boston, MA: Beacon Press, 1971); Jonathan Beecher, *Charles Fourier: The Visionary and His World* (Berkeley: University of California Press, 1986).

HOW SHOULD PEOPLE LIVE?

Kat Kinkade, *Is This Utopia Yet?: An Insider's View of the Twin Oaks Community in Its 26th Year* (Louisa, VA: Twin Oaks Publishing, 1994); Paul Shepard, *Coming Home to the Pleistocene* (Washington, DC: Island Press, 1998).

A CLEARINGHOUSE FOR DREAMS

Fairfield Porter, *Art in Its Own Terms: Selected Criticism, 1935–1975* (Cambridge, MA: Taplinger, 1979); Charles Simic, *Dime-Store Alchemy: The Art of Joseph Cornell* (New York: Ecco, 1992); Deborah Solomon, *Utopia Parkway: The Life and Work of Joseph Cornell* (New York: Farrar, Straus and Giroux, 1997); Brian O'Doherty, *American Masters: The Voice and the Myth* (New York: Universe Books, 1988); Lindsay Blair, *Joseph Cornell's Vision of Spiritual Order* (London: Reaktion Books, 1998); Kynaston McShine, ed., *Joseph Cornell* (New York: Museum of Modern Art, 1980); Dore Ashton, *A Joseph Cornell Album* (New York: Viking, 1974); Peter Barnes, *Capitalism 3.0: A Guide to Reclaiming the Commons* (Oakland, CA: Berrett-Koehler, 2006); Peter Barnes, *Capitalism, the Commons and Divine Right*, E. F. Schumacher Lectures (Great Barrington, MA: Schumacher Center for a New Economics, 2003).

THE PINE BARRENS ANARCHISTS

Anthony Flint, *Wrestling with Moses: How Jane Jacobs Took on New York's Master Builder and Transformed the American City* (New York: Random House, 2009); Thomas H. Greco, Jr., *The End of Money and the Future of Civilization* (White River Junction, VT: Chelsea Green Publishing, 2009); Ellen Hodgson Brown, *The Web of Debt: The Shocking Truth About Our Money System and How We Can Break Free* (Lowden Hill, UK: Third Millennium Press, 2007); Robert A. Caro, *The Power Broker* (New York: Random House, 1974); Robert Swann and Susan Witt, *Local Currencies: Catalysts for Sustainable Regional Economies* (Great Barrington, MA: E. F. Schumacher Society, 1988); Madeleine B. Stern, *The Pantarch: A Biography of Stephen Pearl Andrews* (Austin: University of Texas Press, 1968); Robert Axelrod, *The Evolution of Cooperation* (New York: Basic Books, 1984).

HUNGER NOT TO HAVE BUT TO BE

Carl Bode, ed., *The Portable Thoreau* (New York: Viking, 1947); Harlan Hubbard, *Payne Hollow: Life on the Fringe of Society* (Frankfort, KY: Gnomon, 1974); Harlan Hubbard, *Shantyboat: A River Way of Life* (Lexington: University Press of Kentucky, 1977); Walter Harding, *The Days of Henry Thoreau: A Biography* (New York: Alfred A. Knopf, 1965); Odell Shepard, ed., *The Heart of Thoreau's Journals* (New

York: Houghton Mifflin, 1927); Robert D. Richardson, Jr., *Henry Thoreau: A Life of the Mind* (Berkeley: University of California Press, 1986); Sterling F. Delano, *Brook Farm: The Dark Side of Utopia* (Cambridge, MA: Belknap Press/Harvard University Press, 2004); Robert Sullivan, *The Thoreau You Don't Know: What the Prophet of Materialism Really Meant* (New York: HarperCollins, 2009).

SOME HEARTBREAK, MUCH HAPPINESS
George Wallingford Noyes, ed., *Religious Experiences of John Humphrey Noyes* (New York: Macmillan, 1923); Spencer Klaw, *Without Sin: The Life and Death of the Oneida Community* (New York: Penguin, 1993); Pierrepont B. Noyes, *My Father's House: An Oneida Boyhood* (New York: Holt, Rinehart and Winston, 1937); Maren Lockwood Carden, *Oneida: Utopian Community to Modern Corporation* (Syracuse, NY: Syracuse University Press, 1998); Jessie Catherine Kinsley, *A Lasting Spring: Jessie Catherine Kinsley, Daughter of the Oneida Community* (Syracuse, NY: Syracuse University Press, 1983); John Humphrey Noyes, *Bible Communism* (Putney, VT: Putney, 1849); Constance Noyes Robertson, ed., *Oneida Community: An Autobiography, 1851–1876* (Syracuse, NY: Syracuse University Press, 1970).

WHAT IF?
William Foote Whyte and Kathleen King Whyte, *Making Mondragón: The Growth and Dynamics of the Worker Cooperative Complex* (London: IRL Press, 1988); Ginger Strand, *Inventing Niagara: Beauty, Power, and Lies* (New York: Simon and Schuster, 2008); Tim Jackson, *Prosperity Without Growth: Economics for a Finite Planet* (Sterling, VA: Earthscan, 2009). Mark Anielski, *The Economics of Happiness: Building Genuine Wealth* (Gabriela Island, BC: New Society, 2007); Richard Wilkinson and Kate Pickett, *The Spirit Level: Why Greater Equality Makes Societies Stronger* (London: Bloomsbury, 2009).

Acknowledgments

I want to thank Jin Auh at the Wylie Agency, who believed in this project even before I did.

Thanks to Sean McDonald at FSG for reining in my inner curmudgeon and releasing more light into this book.

Thanks to the University of Kentucky's English department and College of Arts and Sciences for financial support of these travels.